AF572767

Heide Hatry
Heads and Tales

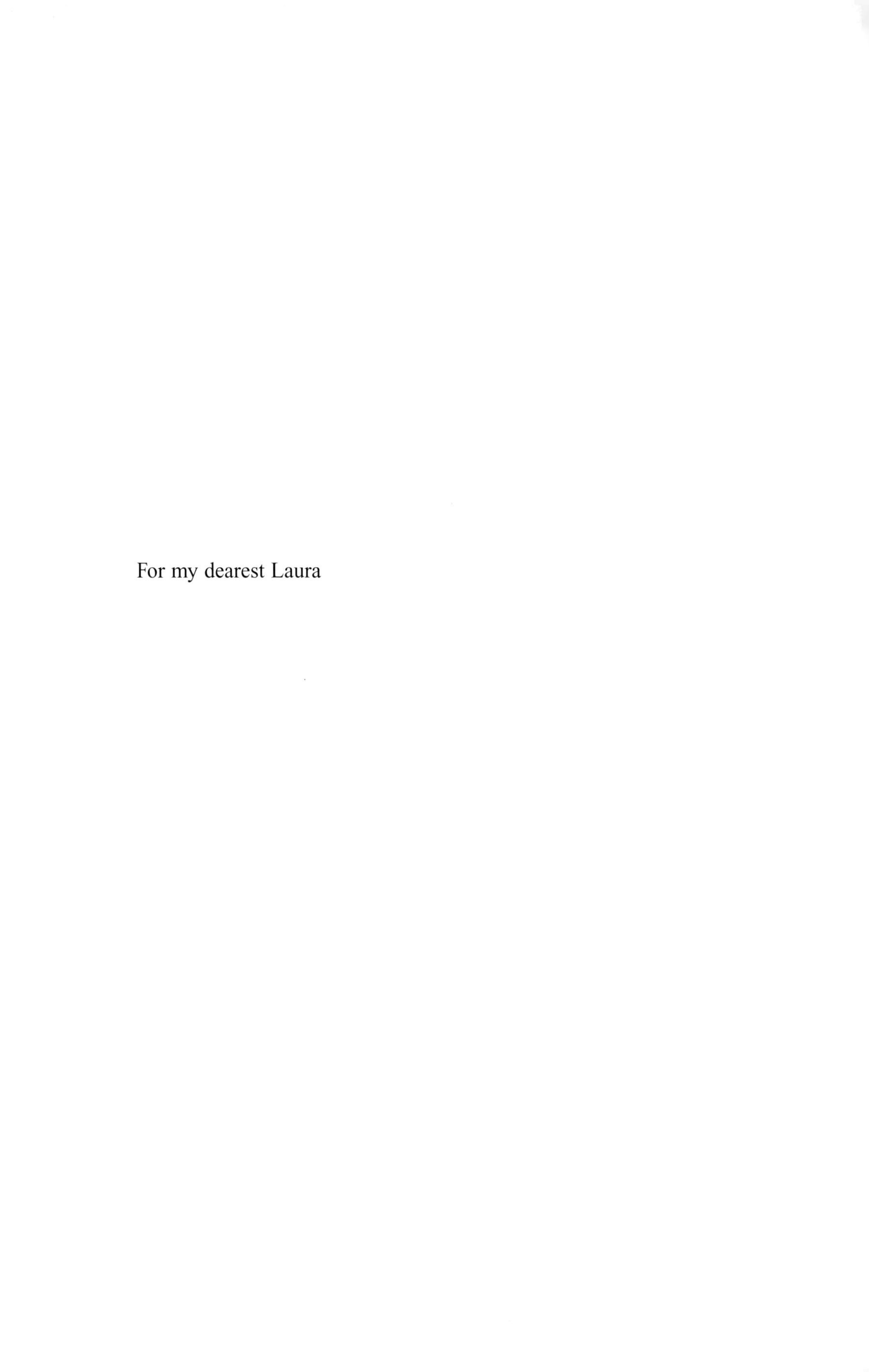

For my dearest Laura

Heide Hatry
Heads and Tales

Twenty-Seven Stories
and Twenty-Seven Portraits

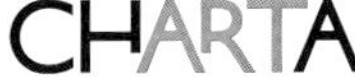
CHARTA

Contents

Catharine A. MacKinnon

Introduction - Giving Her Life

Asked to imagine another woman's life – *this* woman from her shoulders up – women here imagine banal horror, despair, hopelessness. Sluggish, dazed, cold, familiar, she "can't get the point of herself straight" (Carol Novack, *Crazy Broad*), like a stubbed-out cigarette on broken pavement. She is alone to a depth philosophers of alienation have never plumbed. When other women reach out to her, their solidarity tends to be a gesture to little end beyond itself. Nothing helps really. Rarely overcoming, she gives birth to someone else, a baby we are allowed to imagine will have a life that is not like hers (Rosanna Yamagiwa Alfaro, *Big With Child*). Or she protects a bird she killed, keeping watch over its suffering-to-death, preventing loutish men from desecrating its already violated corpse (Lydia Millet, *Sexing the Pheasant*). This she can do. Her own semi-sleepwalking life is seen with clarity only in retrospect, when it is too late. "What's done is done. It's about the horror beginning to be assimilated."* Newborn babies, killed pheasants: over these she has momentary power. Over those, and her own fatal knowledge, her own suicide. Never over living her own life – safe, joyful, triumphant.

Look into another woman's eyes given image in pig flesh. What other women see is year after year of being acted upon. Sexual abuse that never goes away, leaving tracks in the body as well as the mind. Much rape called anything but. Relationships predictably, but unpredicted, gone askew and awry, as she daily lays down her life for those around her. Endless trips to doctors who do not help. She is acted upon as a body but the scars that are left are spiritual: silent, aching, almost without even memory of hope lost. But her despair is not grandly existential; it is circumstantial. If things did not go as they did – with men, primarily – they would not be as they are, feel as they do. Her passion spurts to the surface on occasion, rarely to salutary effect, often as a last-stand valedictory. The possibility that this life of misery, tedium, terror could be different for her, carry her own meanings, is always there just around the corner, which makes the fact that it seldom turns that corner utterly heartbreaking.

Each woman here has her own style, but Heide Hatry's portraits also convey everywoman, nearly all the same woman and feeling tone underneath the skin. What the style says of the self is complex. Each one's particular life story is learned from the smallest details of dress and demeanor – which, as it happens, is how women learn to look at one another. Who is she from that wrinkle, that fur collar? Where did that hair wake up this morning? What family history is hidden behind that cut of those eyes? Embodying this woman's way of looking at women, these portraits are not a series of examples of generic women or abstract woman. If amalgamated from what seem initially to be laden clichés, even stereotypes, each is definitely someone in particular, first imagined visually by the visual artist, then given a certain specific life verbally by the verbal artist. Neither monumental nor metaphorical, the portraits hardly resist meaning. If anything, their meaning is too familiar, overdetermined. The life context each portrait embodies is so quotidian as to be almost virtual. Every detail is something we have already seen, its meaning pre-coded. We read the life from the face and its close material surround from decollete up, filling in the rest of the body down – the cross of the legs, the slouch or tautness of the stomach or stockings – imagining we know the rest of her from there. As the writers imagine it, her world is mostly one in which everything is over for her. Other than these nearly postmortem sketches, no one is keeping track. She twists in the wind.

Even as each nightmare belongs to her alone, these portraits and stories as art create and inhabit a particular social world. The looking and writing in this volume are connected not as art and criticism, but as art and art. The referent of the stories is the world, not the world reproduced simply but the world imagined by the visual artist, who seems to be copying but is instead, almost god-like, creating life by distilling a commentary on it in deceptively literal form, who then has writers give her images back a fuller world, filling in the background, coloring the foreground, casting her in a moving picture short subject of her life. The words are under the spell of the images, which is where they belong. Hatry's portraits thus inhabit a life visually even when made from a dead pig and the characters, as they often are, are given a verbal death. Although tangible, providing the credibility of the real, they are not real, but embody an idea of their reality, and so are also "exercises in an emancipation from the tyranny of matter."** Thus does an uncompromising message of dead-ended hopelessness, in facing up to it squarely, offer up a deeply buried hope.

The resulting book – not a catalogue or comment on the exhibit but the exhibit itself – is accordingly not a trapped hall of mirrors but a layered murmuring dialogue between image and word, book and world, artists and audience, in a conversation that comes close to theater. The politics of this spectacle within two covers is markedly democratic and participatory in its invitation. You can give these women a life.

* T.J. Clark, *The Sight of Death* (New Haven: Yale University Press, 2006), 81.
** Leon Wieseltier, *Spirit in the Sky*, in *Constable's Skies*, ed. Frederic Bancroft (New York: Salander-O'Reilly Galleries, 2004), 61.

Rosanna Yamagiwa Alfaro

Big With Child

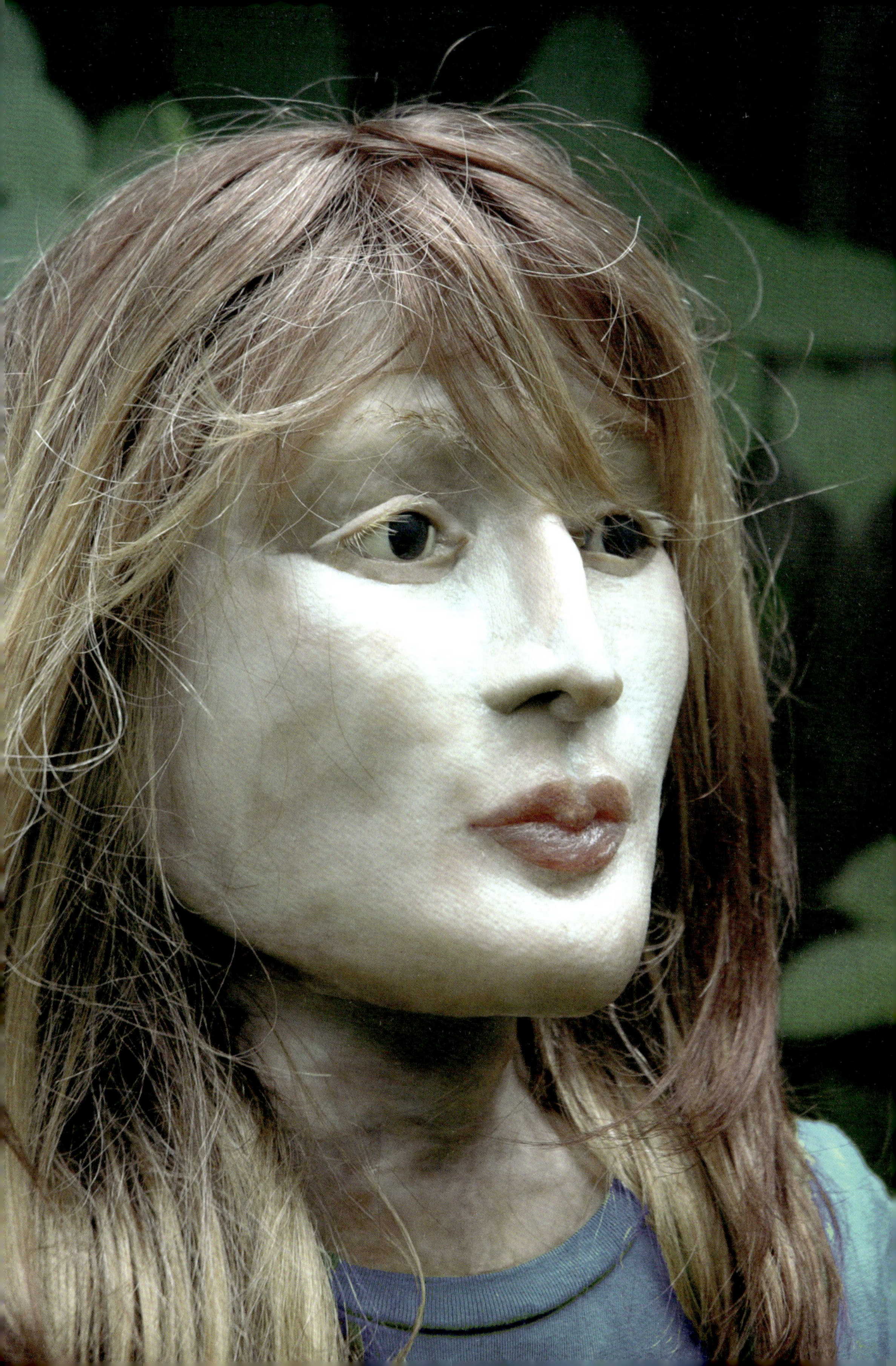

CHARACTERS	PLACE
Steve, 34, an assistant professor	Hamlin, Maine
Jill, 26, an employee at Bed and Board	TIME
Kenzo, 28, an assistant professor	1969

JILL and KENZO together. STEVE in his own space.

JILL
I can feel it. (pressing the left side of her belly) Right here. It's like a little knot.

STEVE
(to audience) She asks me to feel it ten times a day.

JILL
Let me show you. Put your hand right here. (putting his hand on her stomach)

KENZO
(awestruck) I think it's hiccuping.

JILL moves into STEVE's space.

STEVE
So, did you find out how much it costs for an abortion?

JILL
(to STEVE) $200, $600 depending. The nurse said my feelings are much more important than yours. A woman's likely to get severely depressed after one of these operations.

STEVE
It's not really an operation.

JILL
Clinically depressed. Especially after giving birth to a dead two-month-old fetus that already looks like the kid she's always wanted.

STEVE
$200 is a lot of money.

JILL moves into KENZO's space.

JILL
That's when I made up my mind definitely to have the baby.

KENZO
Serves him right.

JILL
Kenzo, you're the only one I'd tell this to, but having a baby's such a sensual kick. I mean my breasts are bursting at the seams. And the two small hands inside there are always squeezing my ovaries. (suddenly standing up) When they're not squeezing my bladder.

She makes a quick exit as KENZO joins STEVE.

STEVE
She's hell-bent on destroying her husband and her marriage all for the sake of something that's not human. Legally they're not human. I never dreamt I was going to marry someone even more primitive than the laws of the land. Civilized babies come into the world by mutual consent. I thought Jill was an educated woman, interested in ideas, in books, in being a person. After ten years of marriage she suddenly reveals her true colors.

KENZO
I guess you're right that she's changed. She has, but not really. I've always felt closer to her than to you – no offense – so I personally find these new developments, well, quite stirring.

STEVE
All these years I've given her a pretty decent life – a movie a week, three trips to Europe in ten years of marriage.

KENZO
It's not that she hasn't been working her butt off, selling towels at Bed and Board.

STEVE
You notice her perfect sense of timing. It's her way of saying, "If my husband gets booted out of the English department I'm not lifting a little finger to help him. In a couple of months I'm taking myself out of the job market and, what's more, giving him an extra little mouth to feed." Well, she can't blame me if I desert her or send her back home to her mother. If I don't get tenure, it's her funeral. It's her baby.

KENZO
You're heartless.

STEVE
We had this agreement we'd never even talk about babies until I got tenure. So she goes ahead and …

KENZO
… has this immaculate conception?

STEVE
Exactly. She doesn't understand I'm out here at the university doing my high-wire act. That there's this incredibly thin line between having a respectable job for life and …

KENZO
Look, I understand.

STEVE
If we had just ourselves to worry about I wouldn't be half so upset about this whole tenure business. I could have taken a year off – we could have survived on her earnings.

KENZO
You might even have written that novel you keep talking about.

STEVE
Why not? But now, overnight, she's cut all our options. She's doomed the two of us to a life of mediocrity.

KENZO joins JILL in her space.

JILL
Please. (patting her stomach) I want you to tell me what you hear.

KENZO rests his head on her stomach.

KENZO
(beat) It's scurrying inside there like a mouse.

JILL
Watch out that he doesn't kick you. He sometimes digs his knee into my kidney.

KENZO
You're so lucky, having a baby.

JILL
What you hear are all my womanly mechanisms switched on and humming. There

isn't a thing Steve can do about it.

KENZO
I'd give my little finger …

JILL
Kenzo, I haven't told Steve yet, but I quit my job today.

STEVE joins JILL in the kitchen.

STEVE
You what?

JILL
The nurse says I have to take it easy. My blood pressure's up fifteen points. There's too much sugar in my urine and not enough iron in my blood.

STEVE
Shit! I've spent the last three months worrying myself sick over you and the baby. I haven't been able to spend one minute on the damn book.

JILL
You haven't worked on the book for as long as we both can remember. You said you no longer believed in the Pre-Raphaelites. That was three or four years ago, way before the tenure case, way before the baby was a glint in your eye.

STEVE
The baby was never a glint in my eye.

JILL
You said the Pre-Raphaelites were completely irrelevant.

STEVE
Of course, they're irrelevant in the grand scheme of things. What isn't? But if you had any imagination at all you'd realize that a book on the Pre-Raphaelites might have lead to tenure and a full professorship, which might, in turn, keep us from starving. In that way the Pre-Raphaelites are very relevant. It's criminal to get pregnant in the midst of this job market. (opening the refrigerator) Now, if they don't give me tenure I'll be forced to sell myself short and take the first menial position that comes up. There's absolutely nothing left in the fridge.

JILL
I saw Kenzo today. He was at some anti-war demonstration in the morning. Then he spent the afternoon with me watching the kids at the playground.

STEVE

Well, he has time for such things, doesn't he? He's got six more years before he comes up for tenure. (staring at her) Jesus, you're blowing up like a balloon. The less we eat, the bigger you get.

They both move to their own spaces. STEVE watches JILL as she removes her sweater.

STEVE

(to audience as JILL stands in front of the mirror admiring herself) Have you ever noticed the morphology of pregnant women, the way they're too fat and too thin at the same time? Everything's left the limbs and converged dead center. The bones stand out in her wrists and ankles, but in the middle she's huge – like a melon on toothpicks. She bumps into things since she can't gauge the distance between them and her stomach. She falls down the stairs because she can't see her feet.

JILL and KENZO at the playground.

JILL

The only time he takes me out these days is midweek to the movies under the protective cover of darkness. Tell me truthfully, am I freakish looking?

KENZO

Just call me any time you want to parade about in your new state. You're the most beautiful pregnant woman I've ever seen.

JILL

You should be writing. Aren't you giving a paper at the Yeats Society tomorrow?

KENZO

I've never put literature over life. (patting her stomach) Yesterday I came to the playground without you.

JILL

Why?

KENZO

I was out scouting. And I picked up some interesting bits of information for you. For instance, one woman said most babies crawl backwards before they crawl forwards. And that blueberries came out whole in her baby's stool looking exactly the way they did when they went in. She said, yes, her baby had his new incisors, but he hadn't nipped her once while nursing. Then she asked me what I was doing Saturday night.

STEVE
(to audience) She douses herself in oil, but that hasn't kept the stretch marks from spreading across her breasts and the lower half of her belly. I saw them one afternoon when I came home early from work and surprised her admiring herself – as she often does – in front of the full-length mirror.
She had taken off her smock and stood there naked in her slippers. Frankly I hadn't wanted a thing to do with her for weeks, but that night I surprised myself with the extent of my passion, if that's what it was. I wanted to let the air out of her balloon.

KENZO and JILL join STEVE.

STEVE
The universities of Oslo, Kuwait, Kyoto, and the West Indies, I've applied to them all. If I'm denied tenure my only chance for next year is if someone dies.

JILL
Or gets pregnant.

STEVE
I had a dream last night.

KENZO
I was having a pleasant dream last night too, but Rufus caught a mouse and decided to share it with me.

STEVE
I was in Stockholm and they were giving me the Nobel Prize …

JILL
For your novel.

STEVE
Right. Maybe. Anyway there was this thunderous applause as I went up to the podium and collected my Oscar, but the funny thing was I wasn't happy at all. I went back to my seat with the audience still on its feet clapping, and I whispered to Jill, "Does this mean I get tenure?"

KENZO
Poor Steve. This fucking tenure business.

JILL
It's turning him into a monster. Every time I throw a tiny stone in his direction, I get this avalanche back. Really, I feel like the Vietcong.

KENZO
I got really worried when you bolted out of the faculty meeting today.

STEVE
I couldn't breathe. My temples were throbbing.

JILL
And yesterday at the movies he trampled over everyone's feet and ran up the aisle.

STEVE moves into his own space.

STEVE
(to audience) I don't know what to do. I mean, Jill's done this crazy thing. She's gone completely nuts, and I'm the one who'll be committed. I can't get down on my hands and knees to play donkey at my age. I'm not toting someone around on my back. Five years ago I might have had the energy to take on a baby. Now I can barely look after myself. (beat) We can't go on like this. I haven't had a good night's sleep in eight months. At night she wakes up screaming with knots in her calves the size of golf balls. She's spectacularly huge. Her belly button's risen almost level with her stomach. When she breathes the stomach remains motionless. Only the belly button goes up and down.

JILL lying on her side on the sofa. KENZO comes in with a stuffed animal.

JILL
Oh, Kenzo. Not another one.

KENZO
We want him to grow into a sensitive, caring child, the opposite of his dad.

JILL moans a little.

KENZO
(sitting down beside her) Are you all right?

JILL
I'm fine.

KENZO
Are you sure?

JILL
It's just that sometimes I feel so sluggish I wonder if the baby's suffocating. Or becoming dull-witted. I was up all night worrying about it. Sometimes he's so still. I haven't felt him stir since this morning.

KENZO
I think I should call the doctor.

JILL
I'm sure everything's all right.

KENZO
I think you should follow Steve's advice and go straight home to your mother. I'll come with you.

JILL
Of course not, Kenzo. Don't be silly. (feeling her stomach) Wait. Wait. I think I just felt a thump.

KENZO
Are you sure?

JILL
There's another.

KENZO
(putting his hand on her stomach) You're right. You're right. I'm feeling the kicking of little feet up here.

JILL
And I'm feeling the flutter of little hands between me and the bed.

KENZO
It's turning now. It's turning.

JILL
I'll flip up my smock so we can watch it move.

STEVE enters. KENZO exits.

STEVE
(kicking a stuffed animal from one end of the floor to the other and waking her up) So what are you doing with your time these days?
I called you three times from the office yesterday to check about the mail, and you weren't in. Where were you anyway? At the hairdressers, making yourself beautiful?

JILL
Don't be mean.

STEVE
(kicking something else) I hope you're doing something very important because this house is going to hell in a handbasket.

JILL
Isn't it.

STEVE
Are you waiting for me to come home from a hard day's work to wash last night's dishes? The house is beginning to smell. Is it the garbage or what?

JILL
At least it's not me. I took two baths today. (pulling clothes out of a paper bag) Look at what one of the women gave me today at the playground – baby clothes. (pulling them out) Aren't they sweet?

STEVE
Please, Jill.

JILL
I'm showing you something important. Otherwise you won't be prepared a month from now when the baby arrives.

STEVE
I can't stand this. (stuffing the baby clothes back into the paper bag)

JILL
You should know what's going to happen when the baby comes. You should let me tell you …

STEVE
What? Tell me what?

JILL
Things I've learned from the women on the playground.

STEVE
What things? For Christ's sake.

JILL
Well, what to expect when the baby nurses, for instance. Evidently you hold a baby like this and his little head bobs up and down or whips from side to side in its anxiety to get a good grasp on the nipple. Finally it snatches the breast in its little fist and brings the nipple to its mouth.

STEVE
I think I've learned enough.

JILL
When he's finished they say he'll pat my breast with the palm of his hand, or he'll delicately finger the nipple between his thumb and forefinger. He'll go cross-eyed with interest.

STEVE
Wonderful.

JILL
One woman said whenever her baby suckled at one breast the other squirted halfway across the room. And it's funny – at the playground, without looking too closely at her I can actually tell which breast the baby has yet to empty because that one's bigger, rounder, and standing maybe two inches higher than the other.

STEVE
How long has this vase of wilted flowers been sitting on the kitchen table?

JILL
Please.

STEVE
What's this circle of burnt crumbs doing around the toaster?

JILL
Please.

STEVE
We're living in a pigsty.

JILL puts her hands over her stomach.

STEVE
Don't do that.

JILL
I think …

STEVE
(violently pulling her hands from her stomach) You think what, bitch?

JILL
Bastard!

STEVE shakes her violently.

JILL
Stop it! (breaking away) Stop it!

STEVE
(lifting up both hands) Imagine picking a fight in your condition. You should really be more careful if you want that baby. Well, I don't have time for this kind of bickering. I have important things to do.

JILL
Important things? What important things?

STEVE
I've got to go. The tenure committee's meeting today.

JILL
Today? How long have you known this? Why didn't you tell me?

STEVE
Because I can't talk to you anymore, haven't you noticed? I'm going to the office now so they'll have to tell me the bad news straight to my face, those cretins. And if they've decided not to give me tenure, then you're leaving tonight. It's your fault if I didn't have the peace of mind these last nine months to finish up my book. When the chips are down it's your own wife who stabs you in the back.

STEVE exits. JILL holds her stomach and screams. KENZO comes running in.

KENZO
(to audience) I drove her to the hospital. There was no time for slipping her out of her clothes and into a hospital gown. It was too late for enemas or local anesthetics.

JILL
It was like indigestion at first. Ahhh!

KENZO
Hold on to my hand as tight as you can.

JILL
As if I'd eaten a green apple for breakfast. Then I felt the muscles tightening in my lower back. Ahhh! Why hasn't he called, Kenzo? The tenure committee met two hours ago. He must have heard by now. (she lies down) Ahhh! Ahhhh! Ahhhhh!

KENZO
(to audience) I pretended I was Steve and followed Jill into the operating room. The lights were so bright I fainted. Only for a moment. But in that moment I saw the trunk of Jill's body become a vacuum cleaner set in reverse, spewing objects out. Pop. Pop. Pop. The long lost articles hidden between the sofa cushions, her turtle that thirty years ago had climbed out of its plastic dish with its palm tree island, also the stream of abuse she had absorbed these nine months, the dust that lined the walls of the hallway and gathered in the corners behind the doors where an adventurous baby might crawl and then put its fingers and toes in its mouth. Pop. Pop.

JILL lets out her last and loudest scream. She sits up.

JILL
(to audience) When I gave the last push my breasts felt full to bursting. It was as if the electric nozzles were attached to the teats of a Guernsey cow, and the milk began to flow, at first drop by drop, and then as if the dam had burst open. I felt it spilling out of me, gallons and gallons of it, light and sweet like coconut milk but streaked with the richest cream, enough to nurse all the starving children in Biafra.

STEVE bursts into the empty house.

STEVE
(ecstatic, holding a bottle of champagne in his hand) I did it! I did it! The stupid idiots gave me tenure and a $2,000 raise. Jill, are you here? Anybody home? (searching through the house) Where the hell is she anyway?

KENZO
(to audience) It was twins. Twins. They emerged, their little arms and legs flailing. The doctor swung up their glistening bodies, one after the other. The nurse wrapped one up and put it in my arms to hold.

Roberta Allen

Fear

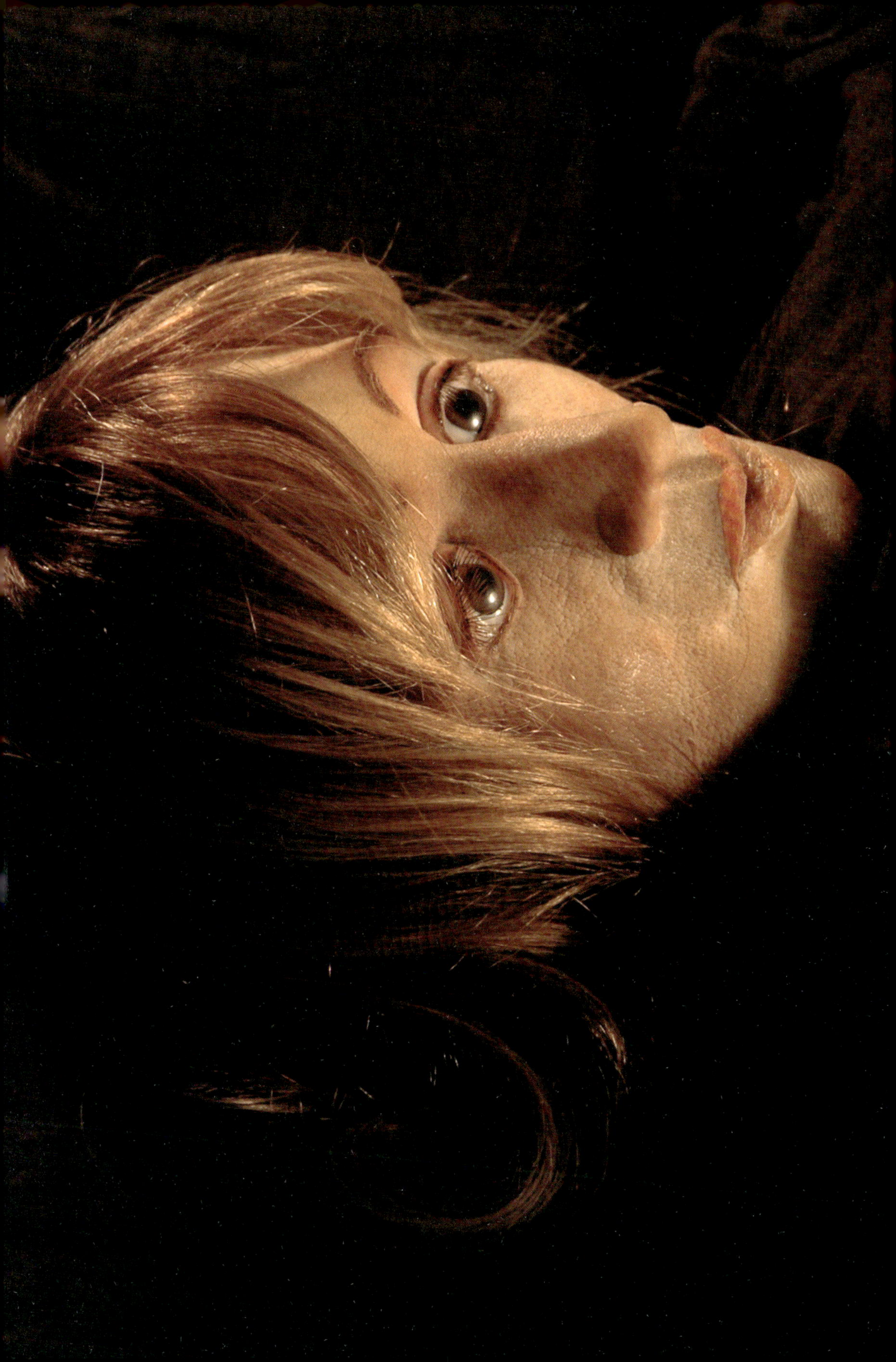

After the young woman was raped in New York, it took several months for her to work up the courage to go by herself to Saint Martin. She thought that surrounding herself with black people on a small island would help her overcome her fear of black men. Soon after the rape, she sold the meager fixtures in her downtown loft and moved into an apartment a friend dubbed "the subway car" that smelled of leaking gas from the basement boiler. But then she met Tommy, an artist like herself. Tommy had a quirky sense of humor. Once he did a painting of Van Gogh's severed ear that looked as though Van Gogh had painted it. Tommy was a big handsome guy with a gruff voice and a face that said to the world: Don't mess with me. Though the woman found Tommy exciting, she wasn't sure she wanted to live with him even after she moved in. When they were alone, he could be soft, even gentle, but he collected Nazi memorabilia and when he drank, he was capable of almost anything.

Before they met, he had split open his friend Arnie's hand with a knife. Though she never felt she was in danger, she was often afraid of what he might do to somebody else. This particular fear she forgot on Saint Martin. In Phillipsburg, the little Dutch capital, she rented a bungalow on the beach, away from the traffic and tourists on Front Street. Though the bungalow was costly, she could see the ocean through the window without raising her head from the pillow. But when she dozed off with the light on, which made her feel safe, she was startled out of sleep by a man tapping on the window. He turned out to be a hotel employee – much to her relief – sent to warn her that it was dangerous to keep the light on at night.

The next day on Back Street, near the edge of town, which was quiet, she rented a cheap room at a guesthouse where blacks from other islands stayed.

On a walk to the French sector, the woman, horrified, found herself in front of a high chain-link fence. Behind it, dozens of tourists, with sunglasses and globs of white lotion on their noses, lay as though dead on chaise longues while black waiters in white uniforms served tropical drinks. Her eyes followed the chain-link fence out into the ocean where it ended by a pile of rocks, too steep and slippery to climb. She felt more in sympathy with the poor blacks than she did with the white tourists though she was afraid at night walking back after dinner to the guesthouse.

When she was afraid in Saint Martin, she turned inward. Like the turtle she saw one night by the road, she hid inside a shell. The shell protected her, or so she tried to believe. She wanted to feel safe inside it, the way others feel safe inside a church. It was the place where she lived, away from home. God must live here too, she thought. But even though she tried to believe this shell was God's invention to keep her safe, she would be suddenly seized by fear on long solitary walks out of town and had to force herself to turn around to make sure she wasn't being followed. She also worried about the men she passed every day on the nearly empty beach where she swam, but the only one who ever spoke to her, as she came out of the water, pointed to little crabs disappearing down holes in the sand.

The middle-aged mulatto who owned the guesthouse on Back Street invited her every evening to drink rum on his terrace, three flights up. With him, she came out of her shell. She breathed freely as they looked at the stars, flung by invisible hands through the sky.

They laughed together, happy to have each other's company. One night they didn't see any stars. A hurricane was brewing, and down below a herd of frightened cattle knocked down fences and trampled vegetable gardens. While they watched, cows scrambled in all directions, their cries muted by the wind which sent leaves and branches flying. Trees snapped or trembled and swayed. As they sat on the terrace, the woman and the mulatto drank more rum than usual. When the rains came, they watched the street flood instead of going inside.

Awakening in her room next morning, hung-over, the woman missed Tommy. She missed his loft with the big double bed and the pin-stripped sheets his mother had given him, though she didn't miss the Nazi weapons displayed in glass cases and the charred remains of Arnie's motorcycle standing in the doorway – the motorcycle Tommy had set fire to the night he stabbed Arnie's hand.

When she returned from Saint Martin, the motorcycle was still in the doorway. The loft looked the same but, a few days later Tommy surprised her by suddenly blasting Nazi marching music on his stereo early in the morning. Still drunk from a party the night before, half-naked, and hallucinating, he hurled the stereo, a large butcher knife, and a huge rubber plant out the window, barely missing the Con Ed men drilling on the street, three floors below. Within seconds it seemed to her, six screeching police cars pulled up, lights flashing. Tommy, mumbling incoherently, his body bathed in sweat, bore no resemblance to the Tommy she knew, but his madness was vaguely familiar as cops cuffed him, ready to take him to the psycho ward at Bellevue – where her father had been sent twice – until she persuaded them that Tommy, a "respected" artist, was drunk, not mad. Being a woman who looked sane and trustworthy, they believed her and delivered him to the detox tank, but she never went back to Tommy's loft, preferring the "subway car" apartment she had lived in before she and Tommy became lovers, and she thought for a while she'd be safe.

Rebecca Brown

What Happened to Her

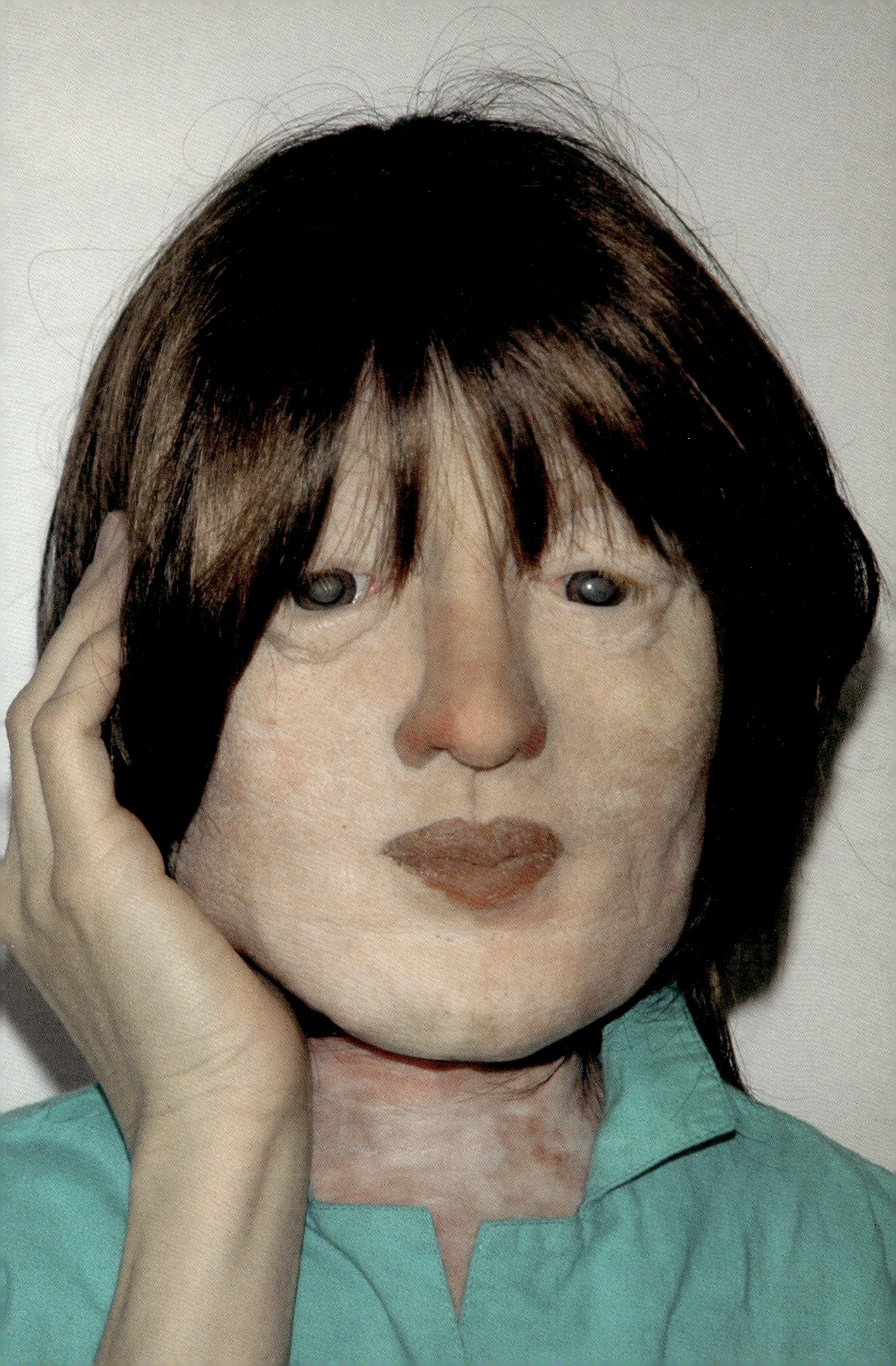

It was as if it had been written on her skin. Like whatever was going to happen to her just would, it couldn't not, it was already in her cells, her genes, marked on her throat, her neck.

But she didn't know that yet. She thought things could be different. She didn't understand that there were different kinds of lives and different kinds of people, and that however you were was the way you were and it wouldn't ever change and you couldn't change it. There were people who had good things and got more good things and there were people who did not have good things and got bad things, then worse.

For a while, when she was young, she had this idea, because everyone said it that if she did the right things, was quiet when they told her to be and always nice and waited her turn and didn't cut in line someday she would get the things she wanted.

She tried to be nice and actually was, not faking it, and tried to say the right things and do the right things but the right things didn't happen to her, the wrong things did.

That's what happened to her.

She tried very hard and waited hard, was patient, hopeful, if that is not too strong a word, because she believed someday her ship would come in. It could someday. It would! Maybe someday soon! Maybe the meek and the miserable, the losers, the girls with stringy hair and splotchy skin, the girls who couldn't even make the chorus line, the fat girls and the girls with lisps, with hair lips, girls who'd looked like sluts from the day they were born, the earnest girls with hearts of gold who someone should have seen beyond the surface of but never did, who should have gotten a break but never did, would inherit the earth someday. Or even just a part of it.

Meanwhile, the other people had everything, even, especially, things they appeared to not even notice, things they and their kind had always had and always would have, things that were such a part of them, as if they had a right to them, those riches others less than them did not deserve, and therefore, would never get. For if they did, it would be a waste because they wouldn't know how to appreciate those fine things because they were so … uh … uh … so … uh – coarse. So in a way, the ones who had those things kept them both literally and/or as if under lock and key, though they pretended not to, from coarse people like Debbie as if they could grab them away which was a crock of shit. Debbie would never get any of those things. Those people would never spread those things around. Even if you pried them out of their cold dead hands, because they had kids and the kids would inherit them! So no one, that is no one who was not already one of them, no one, that is, like Debbie, ever had a fucking chance.

Which is partly why those people could seem, though this may not be exactly the right word, gracious. As if they were above the low, foul, filthy, wanting of this world. As if above all want entirely! Although if somehow someday someone did manage to take away a little of what they had, they'd want all right. They'd be screaming and kicking and calling out their dogs and lawyers on you, want, wanting back what was theirs, by god, that someone coarse and low and filthy had tried to steal from them! Especially if it was some loser slut like Debbie.

The way the world was, was that those people would always have what they always had and never lose it.

They never would be beaten down or knocked around or grabbed by the throat and throttled until she got it through her thick fucking idiot head that she deserved it, that she and all her loser kind had brought their misery on themselves, even secretly liked their misery, the knocks in the teeth, the grabbings by the throat, the yellings, the calling her things, the making her do things then when they were finished, the tossing her out, the bruises on her skin and arms and neck.

Debbie forgot she had ever been different, or young, or had ever, if this is not too strong a word, hoped.

Though even when she was a kid she'd seen old women like that, women who weren't actually all that old, just looked it with their pitted, splotchy skin, their busted fingernails, their hands stained orange with nicotine and wrinkles around their eyes and mouths and bruises and red places on her neck that looked like someone had tried to strangle her or rope burns. That look in her eyes like nobody's home, like all the lights are out.

Debbie used to wonder, when she was young, where women like that came from.

Then she learned.

Debbie tried for a while to be philosophical about it. Debbie tried to put her best foot forward and look – not in the mirror, no never there – but on the bright side, for a bright side, to have faith in the future that someday, etc., and keep her heart in the right place and her eyes on the prize, her eye on the ball, her back to the …? her heart on … her sleeve? in her throat? her heart in her – neck, on her neck, on the line – her neck – in – a rope –

Chin up, Debbie! Chin up! Chin up!

Oh, how very, very hard she tried.

Debbie had a friend, another girl, Anji, who also had it bad, who actually had it worse than Debbie. This gave Debbie – what – hope? That someone else, someone she loved, had it worse off than she? That wasn't hope. It was something terrible to feel glad you weren't as bad off as someone you loved and Debbie did feel bad for Anji, she pitied her.

Should Debbie have done more than pity her?

Should Debbie have tried to take on what Anji had? Should she have been willing to change places with Anji? Should she have tried to? Or was it enough that Debbie talked with Anji about better things like how someday they'd get out of here and go down to Mexico or Montana or Utah and open up a little shop and

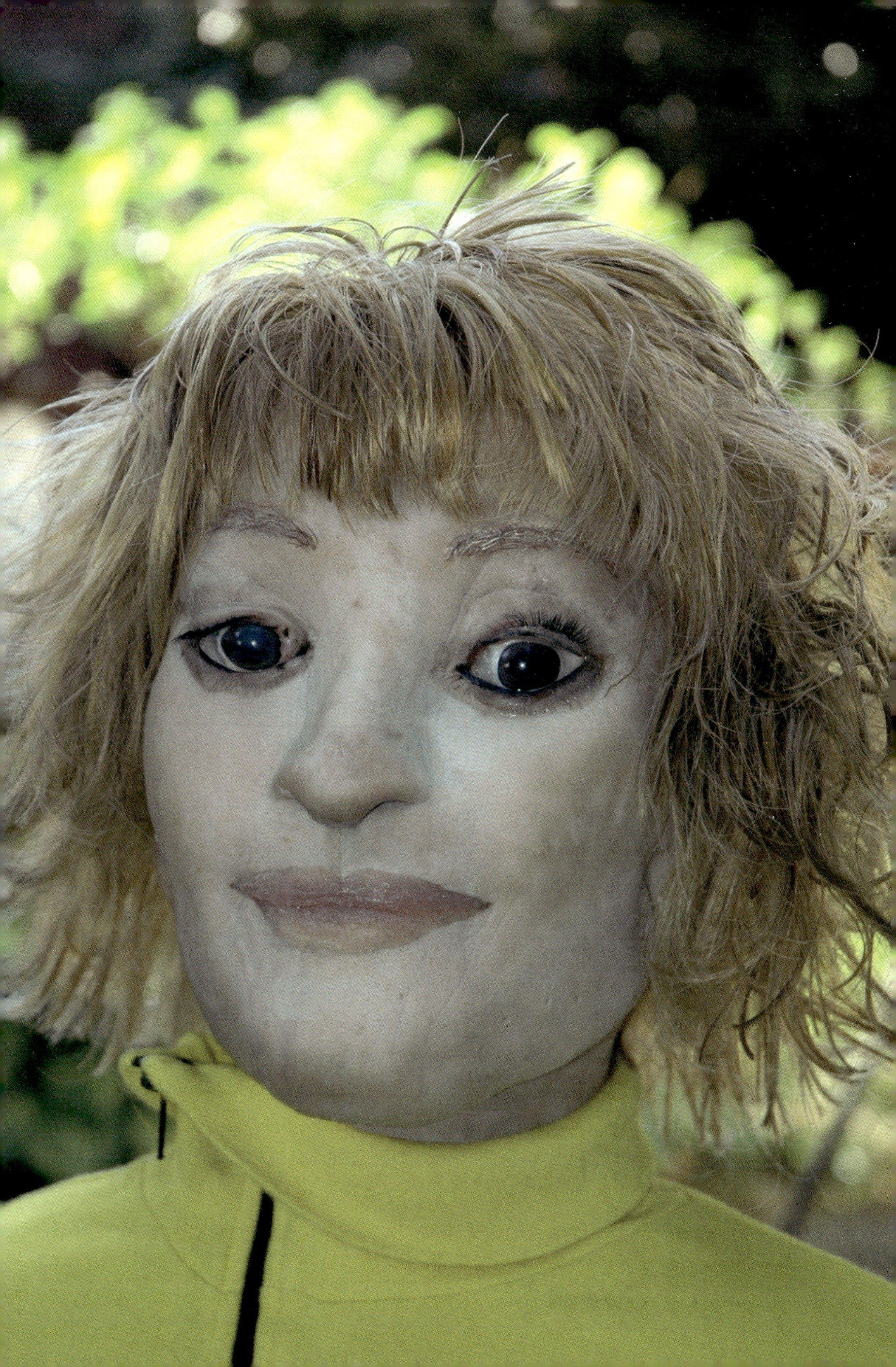

have their own little business and be their own bosses and the men they would meet would be nice. Mormons were supposed to be nice. They didn't drink and they liked being married. Or even New York where they could make a lot of money fast, and then be able to quit. They wanted to quit. Was it enough to talk like that or was there something else Debbie should have done for Anji? Debbie wanted to be good.

But no one could ever change places with someone else. There were different kinds of lives and different kinds of people and however you were was the way you were and you couldn't change it. There were people who had good things and got more good things and there were people who did not have good things and got bad things then worse and Debbie was one of the latter and so was Anji and there wasn't anything either of them could do about it.

Though Anji tried. Anji became a "blonde" because life was supposed to be better as a blonde. "If I only have one life to live, let me live it as a blonde!" they said on TV. Blondes were supposed to have more "fun." A lot of actresses were blonde, both on TV and in the movies and, so they heard, on stage, beautiful ones that everyone loved. But Anji's life did not get better. It got worse. Because when certain people saw her fake hair they could tell even sooner that she wasn't what she was trying to be and was asking for it. As in, did she think she was fooling anyone?

There was also something wrong – even before she became a blonde – with one of Anji's eyes. It was smaller than the other one and had this look like it was coated with something. Not cataracts, she was too young for them, but something. Like maybe it wasn't seeing or like the lights were out and nobody's home which when you think about who could blame her.

Or maybe it was seeing, only not seeing what everyone else was. Maybe it was seeing when things got better someday.

Then one day Anji stopped being around. Debbie looked for Anji but nobody'd seen her. The cops came around and asked about this "blonde" girl and somebody said they'd seen her getting into someone's beige or somebody else said gray truck or somebody else said van. Somebody said she'd been talking about heading out of town and that she had a cousin somewhere or maybe a brother. With a ranch? In Montana? Mexico? Or that she'd met a guy from New York who was going to get her on the stage then in the movies.

Had Anji gotten away but not told Debbie? To somewhere good and not invited her? Was she, finally, as selfish as anyone? Should Debbie look for her or follow her? Or was there only room for one wherever she had gone?

Debbie tried to imagine Anji in Mexico with someone rich. Or on a big ranch in Montana or with a nice guy with a job or on stage.

For there is always room for someone else.

Lights up on an empty stage.

A light bar with no lights has been lowered from above and rests about 12 feet above the stage floor. It's dark so we can't see a thing. The back of the stage is a bare brick wall. Alongside the back wall, on the floor, lie coiled ropes, thick bristly ones. The floor is scuffed from years of everything. A couple stacks of folding chairs, cigarette butts. Dust bunnies. A lipstick that's been stepped on. Little pieces of paper rolled up or folded a million times with stuff written on them that no one will ever read. Matchbooks without phone numbers in them. Things no one should have said to her. Things no one should have done to her. Ways people were to her. Ways she was. Stuff she couldn't stop thinking about. Stuff she kept going over and over in her head because even though it was useless to think about she just couldn't stop unless she really truly stopped. Pencils with erasers rubbed down and the paint chewed where you could see the teeth marks except you can't see anything because it's completely dark for all the lights are already out.

Is anybody home?

The sound of a chair being dragged across the floor. The sound of a rope being knotted.

The sound of a rope being thrown up over a bar. A few attempts go wrong but she keeps trying. The sounds of a woman sighing, a huff. Another throw, the sound of the rope going over the bar, the sound of a woman mumbling something to herself. The sound of a woman standing on a chair. The sound of a noose being tied. The sound of a sigh, as if relief, the sound of a chair being kicked, a chair falling over, a thunk, a sway. The sound of something swaying. The sound of swaying and swaying until she stops.

Mary Caponegro

Ill-Timed

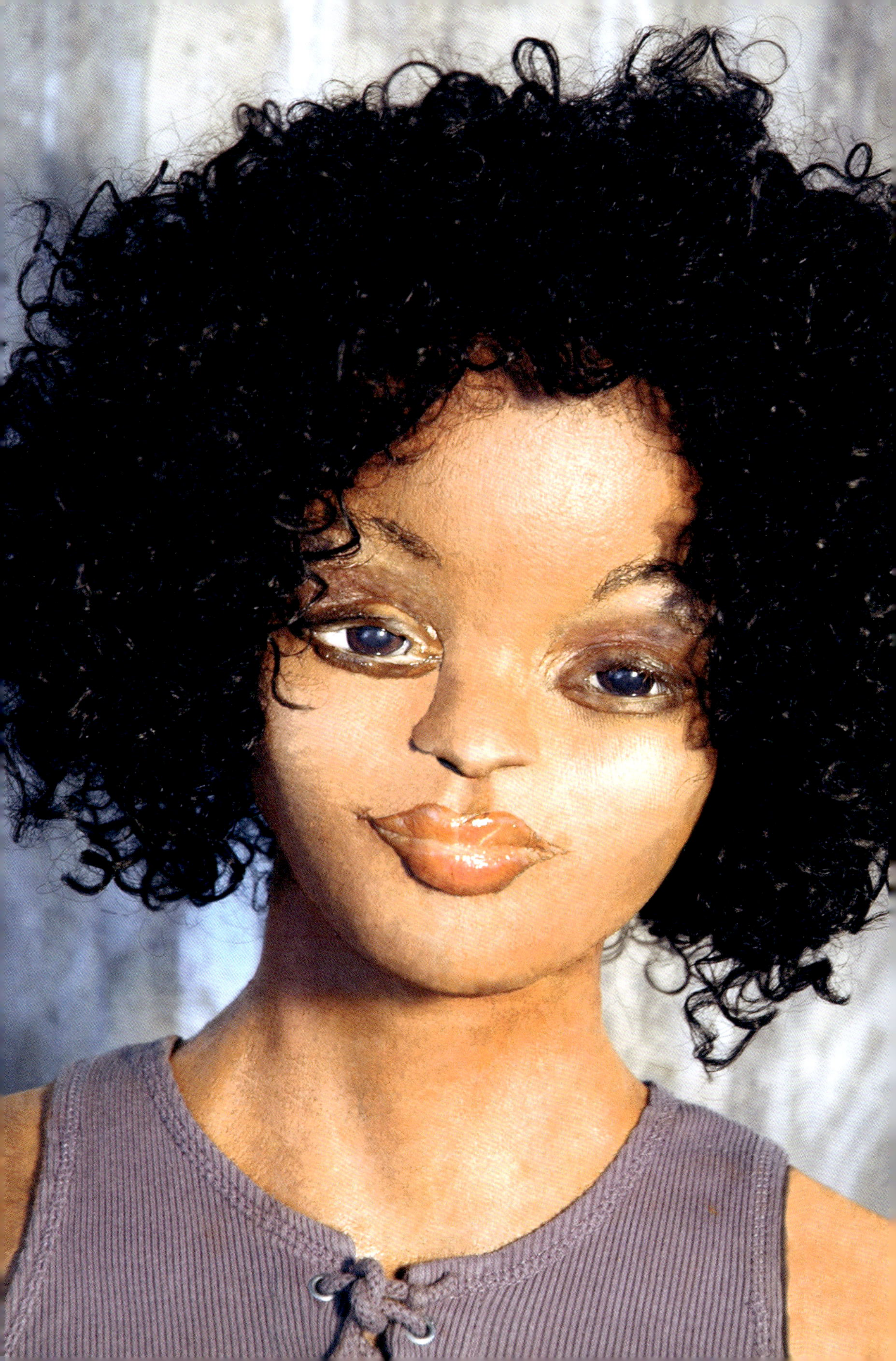

Paula deems the waiting room sad. It lacks charm. It lacks character. It lacks tchotchkes. How can one have confidence in a doctor whose office seems the professional equivalent of a commuter apartment? Judging from the lack of amenities, the guy could barely swing the rent.

Who could be inspired to heal between these dingy, barely decorated walls? The only source of color is the tower of magazine spines radiating, even to Paula's weak eyes, that unmistakable *National Geographic* gold.

Like a zombie, Paula finds herself drawn to the tower of yellow, as if it truly were gold, infused with magic; a segmented spire housing Frodo's magic ring. (Just imagine, she thinks: I could be the world's first albino hobbit!) She enjoys a private session of mirth within the cheerless ambience; she wants to burst into the doctor/patient inner sanctum to report her joke to Alex, who would also laugh, who would say, hey, that's a good one, P. At least the old Alex would laugh, perhaps laugh and then scold, as she habitually did at even the faintest whiff of Paula's self-deprecation. The new Alex seldom had the impulse or the energy – and was most likely too preoccupied – to laugh.

Inside a skinny man with graying hair and wire-rimmed glasses scrutinizes his new patient from across the room, squinting and pacing like a painter sizing up a model for the most auspicious vantage. His gaze could only be called penetrating; it is certainly intimidating. His eyes bear down on her skin, bore into her body, exhibiting a different male gaze than Alex is used to – an investment in her body entirely clinical. She finds herself surprisingly defenseless before this man who wants a diagnosis, not a fuck. Silent for over five minutes, he then presents a barrage of questions: from trivial to profound with seemingly no hierarchy, questions which she answers as if her life depended on it. And in her mind, it essentially does, for no conventional diagnostic tool has yet managed to yield an answer. So bore away, she speaks through her own warm, deep brown eyes to his impenetrable steely ones; bore in, bear down and bear fruit, as no breed of X-ray has yet done.

Paula, in the waiting room, surveys the stack of *National Geographics*, plucks issues more or less at random, browses. One proves far more relevant than she could have imagined, its "centerfold" a staggering shot of rock climbers' makeshift accommodations. Even as recently as several months ago, in a relationship now just shy of its first anniversary, Paula would have earmarked that photo for one of her daily valentines to Alex: intrepid rock-climbers, with elaborate dangling appendages and miles of rope, inching their way up a vertiginous cliff face. And depicted on the opposite page were the gravity-defying temporary dwellings in which they apparently spent the night, their tents pitched into the side of the mountain, sleeping vertically, with literally no ground beneath their feet, sleeping, as it were, on air. Yes, even six months ago she'd have said to her then still new lover, look, that's *your* clan, or drawn a little diagram in ink over the photo with an arrow leading from Alex's name (lovingly scribbled by Paula) to the most precarious tent, then drawn a large outline of a heart encircling it. *My heroine. My Superwoman.* She would have done the uncharacteristically *un*citizen-like gesture of tearing the page out of the magazine, depriving future browsing waiting-room patients of the awe of that image, just to surprise her lover with that cute little thinking-of-you gesture, hidden under a pillow or taped to the bathroom mirror – a spontaneous valentine. But today she only stares at it bemused, as one might view an image connected to an ancestral past. Besides, it practically gives her vertigo to look at it, since street level, in Boulder – all five thousand feet of it – is plenty high for Paula, whose myopia etcetera transforms *every* object to a distant mountain.

"So what did he say?"

"In God's time not your time."

"Come again."

"In God's time, not your time."

"What does my time have to do …?"

"No, *my* time, he said to *me*, quote, in God's time, not your time, end quote."

"For 200-something dollars, that's the prescription! You're kidding me, right?"

"No, I'm serious. Can you calm down?"

"What is this, fundamentalist homeopathy? Two species of hokum fused? Is that *all* he said?"

"No of course not, he said lots of things, but that was more or less the … conclusion."

"So there's no medicine to take or anything?"

"Well yes, these." Alex holds out a tiny manila envelope seemingly sized for a doll, and Paula pinches its sides to peer in.

"These are … these are some kind of candy, for heaven's sake."

"No, it's not candy. Sugar is what's on the outside, what you see, but apparently there's something else in there you *can't* see that will help me … over time."

"Over God's time, you mean?"

"Yes, I suppose. Can you call that cab now, I'm really tired."

"You're always tired."

The original philosophy behind the nightly video shows was to help Alex regain the strength and confidence that the filmed image of herself displayed – to reconnect with the B.C.F. of physical achievement. But to Paula's consternation, instead of galvanizing Alex, they exacerbate despair, take her further from any prospect of robust reality. In fact, from Alex's perspective, it seems a dream, that she could ever have been weightless, or adventurous. Was it truly she who floated through a porous sky, active enough to embrace passivity, relinquishing the right to lead as she danced with gravity? What could be more expansive than the air's embrace? What greater surrender was there than the bold act of freefalling, feeling one's muscles instinctively tensing to compensate for limitlessness? What greater exhilaration? – especially if Paula could be clinging to her as they floated.

For Alex, one of the more subjective aspects of skydiving's allure was the symbolism inherent in the stages of its training: At first the novice is virtually soldered to the instructor, as dependent as a baby kangaroo inside its mother's pouch – the necessary prerequisite to autonomy. When through this apprenticeship-slash-symbiosis, one achieves a skill level adequate for solo falling, she becomes independent, and finally certified to be the mother of another baby kangaroo, whom she of course had designated Paula. And in these fantasies of Alex's, mother was transformed to lover when the clinging was no longer mentoring or craven desperation but a compound exhilaration. She and Paula would be sexually coupled, their tongues commingled as they plunged, kissing deeply in the endless vulva of the sky – thus the sensation of controlled surrender to both lover and a mythic mother: time stopped by eros. This was the clichéd fantasy of making love while flying taken to its most extreme instantiation. For Paula, on the other hand, being up above the clouds seemed not only physically but emotionally precarious. She thinks of recent tabloid headlines: U.S. astronauts in parking lots with mace, Austrian balloonists in a jealous rage. Sky plus love made woman pathologically light-headed.

Alex puts her head on the desk and gauges five, *just five minutes*, then I'll surface, fortified and rested; but when she lifts her sluggish head the inch or so required to glimpse the watch strapped to her wrist, its face now as close to her gazing eye as a monocle would be, she sees that five has dilated to ten, fifteen – could it be twenty-five whole minutes since she succumbed, once again, to inertia. Dozens of sleek, dark braids cascade, like delicate woven strands; these weavings mask the slender but unbending semaphores that lie upon the small, white face whose perimeter is festooned with numerals.

Where is the crane, she silently asks the window, to help lift this boulder? After such high-powered education, would it were knowledge that made for such a heavy head.

Alex's head: inert like some oversized paperweight plopped haphazardly on a desk, heavy as bronze or brass but in fact comprised of stubborn bone and whatever useless jelly housed therein that strains to fashion thought and will of increasingly feeble signals. Although maybe it's a tad more elegant than that, maybe a Brancusi-sculpted paperweight, a beautifully shaped if currently useless skull; in fact, perhaps a regal one. Didn't a former love declare her head to be as elegant as Nefertiti's: royalty? He'd been her longest love because he'd noticed something other than the portions of her body most conspicuously female; the "hey, you got great tits, great ass, great tummy, calves – and unlike most chicks, – abs!" had become predictable, even undesirable: men and their stock perceptions, stock articulations. No doubt that was why when Leroy said, not you *give*, but you've *got* great head, well, she was startled to attention – five years worth of it. In fact she scarcely gave another man a glance; her glances thereafter tending to be reserved for women. Those five years went by without blinking, it seemed, but now five minutes possess the elasticity, or perhaps stagnancy, of eternity – some entity, in any case, irrelevant to ticking time.

Time in Alexandra's mind has formed itself as gray-brown sludge and she is trying to step free of it; meanwhile, the uncharitable watch hands are not reaching forth to pull her to safety, but rather covering their face in an indifferent see-no-evil stance, while tacitly instructing her to do the same – to hide her shame each time a passing acquaintance, stewing in a braised nostalgia, croons, "my, how you've changed; how could such a gorgeous, vivacious … do tell me, now, Alexandra, how did you manage to let yourself … go?" Oh the shame of it, the shock of it, that she who previously could leave no minute unfilled, who seemed to set a record every second, could tackle twenty tasks before breakfast, was now reduced to mopey mantras like, "I'll gather my strength," or "five minutes rest and then I'll be up to the task." But by that time, who could remember which task it was anyway.

So many tasks: so little strength, Alex has posted on her door, or rather Paula has posted on Alex's door.

"OK, Paula, I believe you that this sign was meant to cheer me up, but it actually reinforces everything I need *not* to think about, OK?"

"Would you rather have something completely humorless? How about a cryptic, optimistic fortune-cookie slogan? Or better still, something generically upbeat in a new-age kind of way, off the back of one of your zillion herbal tea boxes? In fact, we can raid Celestial Seasoning's stash, since they're virtually next door."

"Yeah, something upbeat like *'abandon hope, all ye who enter here'*?"

"Ask them if they'll change their name to Infernal Seasonings – when we take that free tour of their plant."

Rising from her chair seems to take as much preparation as parachuting, perhaps more, given that Alex has always had the tendency to act instinctively, the riskier the better, the more challenging the less procrastination. A much different sort of risk than those of recent vintage, such as pricing, behind Paula's back, a number of remote-control La-Z Boy chairs. (She had once dubbed them the cushy equivalent of an ejector seat.) Alex has investigated this not only online but in person at the Flatiron Mall, on a surreptitious expedition – which cost her a great deal in energy. She watched attentively as several salesmen demonstrated the salient features that made this chair unique in all the world, and concluded that their product lived up to the clever brand-name that transformed derogatory into commodity. (Her mother would undoubtedly endorse the notion of a Lazy-girl chair custom made for Alex.) Nonetheless, the daughter who much of her life had scorned automobiles and elevators and escalators now found herself enchanted by the remote control back and seat-tilting mechanism, never having imagined that she of all people would come to intersect a demographic of sedentary middle-class senior citizens.

Alex, in a life both recent and yet irretrievably past, has often fallen voluntarily from heaven through glorious blue and cumulus, now only to find herself parachuting through viscid, grayish-brown hell, each Dantean circle thereof. The plunge contained none of skydiving's exhilaration, but all of the tedium; it was the equivalent of driving to the airfield and suiting up on the off chance that the weather would be suitable, frequently only to have to start from scratch again the next time, driving, suiting, gearing-up, then huddling in the plane. What this new falling lacked was the thrill of the grand finale: the grabbing on and actually jumping out and down into open sky, and the pièce de résistance moment of truth, opening the chute.

"George Bush Senior did it at seventy-five, for God's sake," she'd goaded Paula. She'd made her come along for Alex's thirtieth birthday, yes, practically coerced her with her zealousness – for which she feels a touch of remorse now. "Is that your idea of an inducement? – that Bush's father did it?" was Paula's initial response, but eventually Alex changed tactics and lured her with the sensual dimension of the experience. That birthday wasn't all that long ago, and yet she is a different body now. It's all she can manage to rise from a chair or to lift up her head from her desk. Every hard-won millimeter is like fifty meters of Olympic pool with an exhausting Australian crawl or ten miles of uphill mountain biking or three consecutive running marathons. Oh, why bother to make comparisons? Suffering is not a metaphor.

Now if life were a Tour-de-France bike race, and she the cancer-ridden champion, Alex feels she could have something formidable and white-whalish huge to conquer, something tangibly tragic – like a mountain insisting you vanish or vanquish it. She could pace herself heroically against a universal, validated, A.M.A.-approved enemy.

Paula, meanwhile, inverse of athletic, is perplexed by sporting's capricious specificity, contentious with the sequence of activities that constitute an Ironman triathlon, for instance. Why, she asks, should there be 112 miles of cycling, 26.3 miles of running, 2.4 miles of swimming?

"Who comes up with that? They seem such arbitrary measures."

"Who comes up with anything?"

"Gee, that's informative. Glad to have an expert in the family! Come on, you know, like water boils at 112 degrees; light travels at 186,000 miles per second. Is there some science behind these equivalences? Calibrated energy expenditures for different activities or some such?"

"Suddenly you're Little Miss Statistic! And anyway, it's not like there aren't modified versions of those measures. For less ambitious athletes. Or beginners. Whatever."

The other still refuses to indulge her lover; she will not be sympathetic to Alex's asinine coveting of cancer. Thus she turns crabby, sarcastic.

"Go for it," Paula goads. "You always wanted to compete on a man's terms. I bet if you try hard enough to get testicular cancer, you'll set a precedent. Declare it unconstitutional that women are left out of the running."

"Correction: not Little Miss Statistic, Little Miss Sarcastic."

"And don't forget you can exploit all of these doping scandals. You might even end up champion by default. If all the steroid-driven athletes end up disqualified, you'll be the only one left who didn't cheat, because you were too weak even to compete! You said homeopathic remedies are undetectable in the bloodstream, right?"

"That's correct."

"Perfect then. Can't you hear the broadcast now? Those silly athletes tried to enhance performance with testosterone, and Alexandra Davis showed them their mistake; she did it all with sugar pills. The tortoise, ladies and gentlemen, wins the race!"

"Paula's Paradox, is that it?"

Better then, to dwell within the realm of sensation. Today, Alex will concentrate on skydiving; if she can't bring her body to the sky, she'll instead bring the sky to her mind. She'll describe the exhilaration in every possible permutation, to whomever will listen, i.e. Paula. "In freefall, you surrender to gravity until the parachute offers resistance, which is a form of assistance; it's like a condom that slows you down so you don't have cosmic premature ejaculation."

"You mean premature annihilation," Paula says, when Alex offers this – to her absurd – analogy, feeling in this moment that her lover lacks appropriate perspective – needs a corrective to this romanticized interpretation. "You're ignoring that statistical minority of parachutes that don't open! The broken condom, if you will. And those are just the obvious predictable perils. Don't forget that Austrian or German woman who knocked off her lover's lover!" The argument was futile anyway. The sport of skydiving, in Paula's eyes (granted not as sharply focused as her lover's) is essentially the celestial equivalent of a kid holding his nose and springing off a diving board into a massive wad of blue. She says as much. But this is not a useful metaphor for Alex, because from her point of view she has become precisely that kid, she has plunged in and never surfaced, as if in diving she acquired a ball and chain around her ankle; as if, in fact, her leaden head and dangling body, once nearly weightless in space, had itself become a ball and rattling chain.

Even so, water is life-giving, nurturing, healing. Therefore Alex enfolds herself within the warm, now-filled tub, letting it envelop her as if she were a baby in amnio, unable yet to survive on her own. She feels as if she could stay forever in this warmth. A full nine months, at least. Every so often she reaches forward to rotate the hot water tap until perfect temperature is reestablished. She begins to feel as if she were a tea bag and the tub a cup, the tap a boiling kettle's spout, and only after no more heat is forthcoming does she remember that Paula was about to do the dishes when she started.

It is unlike Alex to be inefficient. For example, she was once exclusively a shower person. But everything she now is is unlike her: at least unlike the her she once was. (This is the most mystifying aspect of it all, Alex finds, that she has, in spite of herself, gradually become her own unlikeness: a fully inverted person.)

Therefore it seems philosophically untenable to acknowledge boundaries, to move from one activity to the next, for how can one discern or fashion closure if experience itself is utterly unstable?

Alex has thus found ideological support for her failure to eject herself from this eventually only lukewarm womb, soon to grow uninvitingly cold. Not until her toffee skin is puckered and saturated does she emerge to wrap herself lethargically in a towel. The step that once communicated morning briskness now is mournful, listless.

"You were in there for almost an hour. And you didn't even wash your hair. What were you doing? Did you hear me?"

Alex is not about to tell Paula that she was doing healing visualizations: picturing a parachute, mentally opening it as if it were a jasmine pearl in hot water, or a rose from the Tea House garden where she had drunk the very tea the jasmine pearl produced, or a dandelion blooming in space; then when it reverted to a dandelion again, she would concentrate on the delicate filaments, each fragile one, steeling them against the wind, fortifying them with her determination such that no one could blow, that no one could blow ...

If she were to share this with Paula, she knows the response will be, "How big a check did you write to get that exercise?" – along with the coda, if she were in a particularly snippy mood, "Or did they teach you that at Harvard?"

"Did you hear me?"

"Yes, I heard, Paula. I don't know why I stayed in so long. I'm waiting for change, I suppose."

"What, did you put a dollar bill in the soap dish? I don't want to miss it when the faucet spews out four quarters."

"You're a scream."

"Hit the jackpot and didn't even have to go to Vegas. So much for *filthy* lucre!"

"Are you finished?"

"Am *I* finished? Is the hot-water finished?"

"Look, I'm sorry for hogging the hot water, but apparently you're not for being a prick."

"I can't be a prick, I'm a clit, remember? And a lesbian-in-training to boot."

"Your training wheels should have come off six months ago. And I'm trying to explain something I don't quite get myself. It's not easy."

"So what *has* been easy lately? Name one thing."

"Pissing you off."

"Touché."

At first the sensation of being with a woman was strange for Paula. Lesbian acquaintances had described an experience predicated upon familiarity. They had said it was like touching yourself, untutored, natural, and yet this is not a useful reference, because Alex for Paula, is anything but familiar; she is exotic beyond assimilation, her difference the quintessential attracted opposite. Alex equals Cinderella after transformation, and Paula is her ash-blonde, soot-smeared precursor.

(But then, almost anyone, appearance-wise, cannot help but be other to Paula.) Alex was not alone in waiting for change, for after processing the attentions of several lovers of less than flattering motivation: Out-of-charity Matt, and on-a-dare Trevor, and out-of-curiosity Jason, Paula had become increasingly adept at touching herself!

In their initial weeks together, she felt transformed by mere proximity, as if vicariously through their connected breath, Paula could endow herself with Alex-energy, Alex-competence, Alex-beauty. Yes, that was the original formula: Paula of hermetic beauty fused with Alex of ineluctable beauty. But somehow without warning, it reconstituted itself as Paula, witness to the precipitous, inexplicable decline of the seemingly super-endowed Alex, who on sculpted legs could once run like a gazelle, a match for any mountain lion. Why, just the sight of those calves, those thighs, those gluteal lobes could make men hard as they jogged in her dust at Chautauqua, and made Paula herself, precisely eleven months ago, experience an internal sensation markedly contrastive to the sauna's dry heat as she, seated below, perused their creamy curvature before her eyes. What more perfect vantage could there be for the myopic, astigmatic captive audience, as the voluptuous mouth high above those sculpted calves uttered playfully the equally creamy invitation, "would you like to be on top?"

And that was how it started.

Neither could believe their love had logged nearly a year.

In Alex and Paula's private universe, time was not measured against the prelude to and aftermath of Christian resurrection. For them, B.C. – supplemented by a third letter – became the acronym for "before chronic fatigue" and those initials were capacious enough to accommodate an infinite storehouse of nostalgia. And from that line forward, infinite regret.

Two women: one statuesque, svelte and shapely, stunning really; the other also tall, but less developed of figure, somehow even more commanding. This second woman's stunningness is almost literal, her skin much lighter than the first one's flawless café-au-lait complexion. She is almost preternaturally light.

She suggests a Nordic blizzard sky compared to the other's burnished aura.

For Alex one might offer the following descriptors: tawny, toffee, golden honey, mocha. Paula thinks and speaks of her in just such terms. But for her own self, Paula claims that nouns are more forthcoming – wite-out, laser printer paper, desert sand.

"I love the color of your skin, it's warm and tawny, glowy."

"And I love *yours*, O land of the midnight sun."

"More like midnight florescent bulb!"

"Oh, cut it out already. Bask in your uniqueness. In fact, I have an idea: Let's take a little excursion that will help you get a new perspective."

Two women, mesmerizing to the naked eye of bystanders, strolling arm in arm in downtown Boulder, saunter through the elegant arcaded streets, placing synchronized feet over red brick, passing under green awnings, peering into the windows of antique shops, bookstores, cafes, boutiques. An emporium of vintage clothing and accessories lures them in, or rather Alex sees it and lures Paula in. Then both succumb.

"One of the best things about a lesbian lifestyle is you always have someone to shop with, don't you think, P?"

"Isn't that a tad superficial for an Ivy League thinker? Aren't you reinforcing every gender stereotype?"

"Well of course silly, I don't mean *best* in any substantive respect. But if we're racking up the day-to-day fringe benefits, I certainly prefer an enthusiastic partner-in-crime to some … macho martyr humoring me, pacing back and forth looking at his watch while clearly feeling awkward and bored. As if some sexy garment in the bedroom could materialize out of thin air, without a shopping process."

"Alexandra Davis, raising shopping consciousness around the globe."

At that point, such sarcastic comments were considered playful, and intended so, and always tempered by a compliment: "You know that looking at his watch was just to count the minutes until he could get you back home into bed and have you to himself."

And then some coded shorthand reference, such as "strictly missionary," which would make them both dissolve in laughter, regardless of who might be watching.

"Far be it from me, my sweet, to denigrate the sport of shopping: the only one a klutz like me has a prayer of participating in, and besides, it's only when we're window shopping that you remember to adjust your pace to a mere mortal's. On non-shop-walking expeditions, I can barely keep up with you."

"I'm working on that, P. It's hard for me to keep my energy in check."

They load their arms with long satin evening gowns and feather boas, urging each other to try this or that item, fingering fabric, vintage everything, fake-fur stoles and elbow-length gloves, pill-box hats with netted brims and tear-shaped, pearl-headed pins, not to mention velvet capes and satin slips. The boutique's name? Couldn't you guess? "The Whole Nine Yards." And the two take up the giddy spirit of compulsiveness. They find themselves the sole occupants of the large communal dressing room. Conveniently, no sales-girl sits dispensing numbered plastic chits to keep a tally of the items taken in. Thus they have the liberty to use it as a private theater, strutting, preening, observing every gesture of each other in the mirror. "I think this silky peach material is so sensual, I could come just putting it on." "That's too tight," Paula says to Alex as she sucks in her breath while enduring the fastening of a corset. "It's supposed to be tight, that's the nature of a corset," Alex scolds playfully, as she continues to pull the unfileted satin fabric taut across the other's bust, spanning from burgeoning cleavage to navel, guiding each tiny hook into its respective metal eye. "But it's uncomfortable." "Think of it as a pair of strong hands cupping your breasts." "There's a difference between cupping and strangling." "It makes your nipples erect." "It will probably give me a rash … or a stroke." "I'll do the stroking," Alex says, and transfers her fastening hands down below the other's waist "Alex, we're in a public place." "Public makes it even hotter. Let that get you even wetter." "I guess I should have known better than to take my black pearl onto perilous, decadent Pearl Street, where so many sensual, bourgeois distractions reside."

And so on and so forth, as the clock ticks toward dusk, when in homage to surfeit, and further – i.e. deferred – foreplay, they put some articles on hold, and go out for tea with the intention of returning, invigorated, for a second round. There is apparently no limit to how many items can be held, or for how long, despite store policy. No salesgirl ever failed to fall for Alexandra's charms. To see her in their wares was worth extending hours, worth bending rules.

"Tell Oprah next time she goes purse shopping in London to bring you along. You're good as open sesame!"

The two skip down the street, arms linked, the mountain ever at their side, rejecting numerous closer opportunities for refreshment so as to press on toward Fourteenth Street and Alex's beloved Dushanbe Tea House.

"Fine by me; I've never been to London – though my parents seem to think I should have played Wimbledon a few times by now. In fact given that I'm all of thirty, they'd expect at least a Serena Williams Australian Open comeback on the resume by now."

"I know what you mean. Sometimes parents can go overboard with confidence."

"Not exactly confidence in this case, more like arrogance. Do it best or don't bother – that kind of attitude."

"But that works out fine, since everything you do you do the best."

"Thanks, sweets, but first of all you're biased, and secondly, it's a bit more complicated than that."

"Well, I'm still listening. Or would you rather wait until we're at the Tea House?"

"No, I can walk and talk no problem: one of the fringe benefits of training!"

"So talk then!"

"OK, I'm formulating here, give me a second!" Alex takes a deep breath. "I think that since it was assumed I could win Wimbledon if I bothered, it therefore followed that winning a Widowmaker was a pretty asinine goal. The only thing that ever made a sport legitimate in their eyes was to do it world-class and competitive. And televised."

"Well, rest assured, I don't need you to win at Wimbledon. But don't make me the widow either, OK?"

"You have my word."

"It's kind of surreal having this fancy shopping mall right at the border of a mountain park. A little Disneyesque."

"No more surreal than a mall off some highway between industrial sites, à la your home state."

"Excuse me. *Our* home state. You can take the girl out of Jersey, but you can't take …"

"OK then, our home state. But you'll get used to those juxtapositions, believe me. In fact, why don't we take a five-mile hike right now instead of getting tea before we make our purchases. Twilight is magical up there."

"Number one: You know I couldn't possibly keep up with you. Number two: I'm nervous about those mountain lions, especially after you told me about that poor boy who got killed by one. Number three: I'd trip in the dark coming down; you'd have to carry me into the dressing room."

"That could be romantic: carrying the bride over the threshold."

"Let's plan a more sedate excursion instead. How about tomorrow we take that free tour of Celestial Seasonings."

"How can I take that tour, sweet P? It's like a New Yorker going to the Empire State Building or the Statue of Liberty. It's something tourists do."

"You told me secretly you always wanted to. Besides which, tea as local symbol doesn't quite hold up to 'huddled masses yearning to breathe free.' Furthermore, as we established a few moments ago, you're not exactly a native yourself."

"True enough. Just a transplant like the rest of Boulder."

"You're not kidding. Every one around here seems to come from somewhere else. That little knickknack shop right there, in fact; the owner told me she was from the east coast."

"I see you've been collecting data."

"And I need to collect a little more right now. Sit with me on this bench a minute; you walk so fast!" Alex reluctantly complies after her lover physically restrains her, one's hands cupping the other's hips, maneuvering her toward the nearest bench. "Time for a little southwest yuppie people-watching."

"They look the same as any other day. More likely they'll be checking us out."

"But really, Alex, aren't you ever bothered by the lack of diversity? It seems awfully white here."

"I thought you said that you were awfully white, P."

"Touché, A."

"I just can't win, it seems. Most of my life I get told I look too white, I talk too white. My siblings all resented me because I was the lightest of the litter. Then on a whim I move out west and presto change-o, I'm the blackest chick in Boulder!"

"Whereas *my* siblings were just relieved that it was me instead of them that drew the gene-pool joker from the deck."

"In my case, love, it was the ace, as far as they perceived it. And aces make envy. And envy is nasty. And that's why it's nice to go west young woman, far from home, and leave the roots to rot."

"That's some strong image. Rotting roots. I better make sure to repot you carefully." She pats her lover's bottom tenderly as if it were a mound of fertile soil, unfazed by ogling passersby. "Hey, look at that amazing bedroom. What a fancy furniture store! Can I repot you in that king-sized bed?"

"If you repot yourself right next to me."

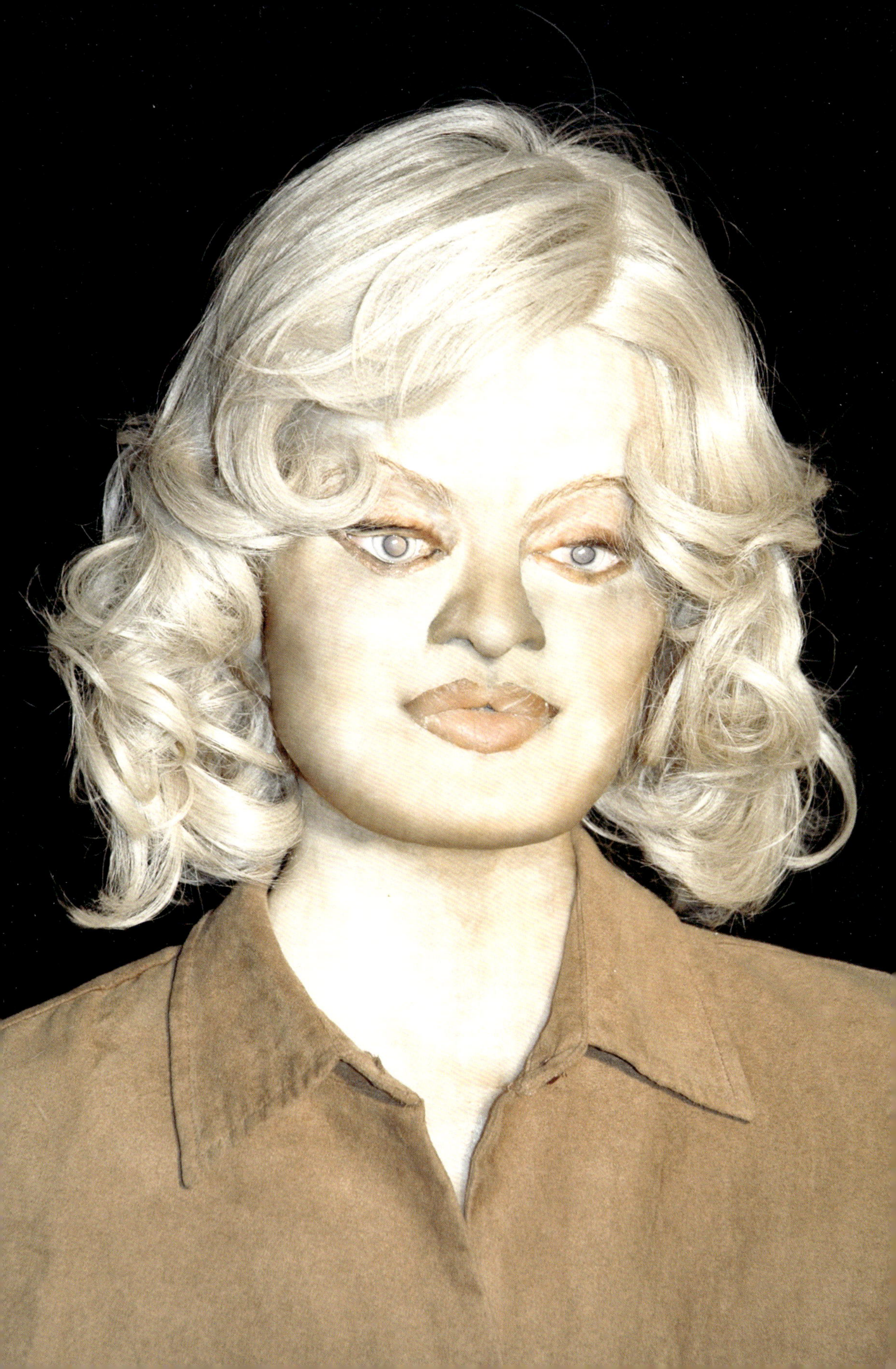

"Deal! So your parents never visited you since you moved here?"
"Not so far, no, and probably best to keep it that way."
"Maybe they could come for Thanksgiving though; I could meet them."
"Thanksgiving of 2020 maybe."
"Or we could fly to Jersey for whatchamacallit, Kwanzaa."
"You go for Kwanzaa. I'll stay here. And it's a bit more dignified without the whatchamacallit prefix, OK?"
"No need to be defensive."
"I won't if you don't trivialize."
"We're not about to have our first fight, are we?"
"I hope not, because I had some sexy plans for our return to The Whole Nine Yards. So let's get off this bench and to the whatchamacallit *Choihona* – or for the layman – Tea House."
"Yes, ma'am!"

"Who has the Jade Spring?" Alex points to herself with an eager, slender finger, nearly intoxicated by the aroma of her very favorite green tea. The waiter sets down one pot from his tray and deftly pours into an elegant glass cup.
"The Boulder Tangerine's for me; I'm feeling fruity."
"Now behave, Paula," Alex threatens, behind a sly smile.
"I think they should bring out the samovar from the glass case just for you."
"And the Tajik crown and wedding dress while they're at it."
"But if we had a wedding, you'd have to tell your folks."
"That's incentive for a rain check!"
"The thing I still don't get, Alex, is why the champion risk-taker never even tried to tell her parents she prefers women. You went to a high-powered, elite college, proved yourself, were obviously exposed to all kinds of sophisticated new ideas; you'd think they might be open to discussing different views. Broadening their own horizons. I'm just worried that one of these days they'll get suspicious and then the shit will hit the fan."
"The fan's already shit-faced, I'm afraid, my dear. I've been in the dog-house ever since I betrayed my gilded B.A. and went with matter over mind."
"You mean with body?"
"Exactly."
"This delectable body? You hardly needed a degree to make a living. They're lucky you're not modeling or doing porn flicks, for heaven's sake. Sports are pretty wholesome in comparison, I'd say. What's their problem?"
"Their problem – which in their view is *my* problem – is that they both slaved so that I could have choices, and then I made the one they never imagined – I chose not to use my intellectual advantage for … intellectual … exclusively intellectual … purposes!"
"How is the tea today?"
"Sublime, as always."
"Care for anything else then, ladies?"

"Just the check, thanks. Anyway, where was I? Their idea of options consisted of politics, law, academia, medicine, finance, possibly social work. Maybe think-tanks, NGO's. But decidedly not freelance promiscuous athleticism."

"But you're so multifaceted; there's no athletic activity you don't excel at. Or haven't taught. You even led that blind guy on a mountain-climbing expedition. Obviously destiny: preparation for me!"

"You're nowhere near legally blind, my dear, and even if you were, it wouldn't have to be an obstacle. Look at Sabriye Tenberken, for instance – she's trekked across the globe despite the fact that she's been blind since she was twelve."

"No doubt even to Tajikastan, is that what you're about to tell me? Why not invite her here for tea and inspiration? She'll hop right over. Maybe she can fly too!"

"She's in Tibet right now, teaching blind kids."

"Geez, all this heroism, altruism; where do people get the energy?"

"There's some truth to that old saying, right? The more you do … "

"I know I know – I'm lazy though. I think I'll just keep following my fearless, gorgeous leader. That blind man had no idea what he was missing; mountain vistas were the least of it!"

"Thanks, P. Believe me, his eyes didn't turn that exquisite mauve."

"Thanks, A. You're very sweet. Back to your parents though, my point is you've had plenty of responsibilities."

"Irrelevant from their perspective. A career in *recreation* is an insult to an Ivy League education, they said. Emulating the worst of the Wasps. Conspicuous indolence."

"Kind of like languishing away the day trying on vintage clothing?" Paula is thoroughly smitten and smiling, leg more exposed here at the bar than if it were under one of the wrought iron tables, nevertheless shamelessly rubbing her lover's, surrounded by Edenic vegetal arabesques and in sight of seven mythic ethnic women cast in bronze, all gracefully bearing water vessels atop their heads.

"I call that conspicuous romance, not indolence!"

"The more conspicuous the better, knowing my gorgeous exhibitionist – which I presume in your folks' eyes would be an even more egregious sin? Dare not speak its name etc.?"

"So you're beginning to see why I didn't push the lesbian disclosure. After I took so much flak getting into the kayak, how could I risk coming out of the closet?"

"I see, I see, the blind girl said – no really, Alex, I do. I hear you. But as long as you're stuck in the closet anyway, you might as well fill it with clothes, right? And if we don't get back before she closes up, you'll be getting some more flak – this time from that adoring salesgirl at The Whole Nine Yards. Even your charms might turn into a pumpkin by midnight."

So back they go: Paula and her Alexandra, or Alexandra and her Paula, invigorated with sufficient antioxidants, just as they had planned, for their second round.

"Are we allowed to take all this in here?"
"No one's coming after us, are they?"
"I could never wear something like this in public."
"Sure you could."
"You mean *you* could. Only a gorgeous, tall, svelte, stacked …"
"Wo wo, let's get some perspective here. Your body's got its own charisma."
"Yeah, ironing board charisma?!!! – I'm so steamy!"
"That would be the iron, not the board, I believe."
"See, told ya!"
"Did you notice that beauty was supposed to be diverse in the twenty-first century, including unconventional notions thereof? Remember all that hoopla over Chloe Sevigny in her first flick?"
"Easy for you to say, since meanwhile, conventional beauty never goes out of style."
"Black beauty in this culture has not exactly been a convention except in the form of a little white girl's horse."
"Who needs to get with the twenty-first century? Don't cry bigotry to me; there's not a single man or woman on the planet who would find you less than gorgeous."
"And so I'm set for life, is that it? Being designated beauty queen, ripe for objectifying, provides perfect fulfillment?"
"Well, is it so farfetched, for someone who just told me only hours ago that she bases sexual preference on the better shopping partner?"
"You're a stitch … speaking of which, check out the stitching on this little number."
Through their banter, they keep gazing at themselves and each other in the mirror, zipping, buttoning, adjusting the other's straps and hems and shimmying into tight skirts and diaphanous silk dresses cut on the bias. Paula, to the naked eye – because her own eyes require extreme proximity to the object being viewed – at times appears a child who wondrously assumes her own reflection is another self.
"Being cut on the bias does nothing for me, it's biased toward curves, it makes the most of curves!"
"For God-sakes, you're not a eunuch! Stop trying to tone down your difference, play it up, be outrageous. Go for broke; you're gorgeous! You have breasts, you have buttocks; your curves are just … subtle." She takes the cigarette holder from the counter between two fingers, purses lips to make an ersatz blow, and Paula mimics her pucker for pucker and closes in for a playful, barely-making-contact kiss.
"Don't blow smoke in my face."
"Then how about we trade smoke in your face for tongue in your mouth?" Alex insinuates boldly the aforementioned organ. Upon retracting it, she says in husky Dietrichesque voice, "A little artificial respiration to repair that nasty, corset-induced …" – a tongue-induced caesura is inserted for suspense; the sentence then resumed – "cardiac infarction." From this point on, imaginary smoke rings

repeatedly morph into tongue.

"I could *get* a heart attack this way, since your kisses take my breath away."

"I'd call that big-time progress, Miss official lesbian-in-training."

"And a big-time heart attack too, once we add the anxiety of the sales girl coming in to check up on us."

Then with the ceremony of a groom lifting his beloved's bridal veil for the sanctioned kiss, she raises Paula's voluminous taffeta skirt, kneels at her feet, presses her lips reverently against her satin crotch, and exhales warm moist breath.

With long inhalations between phrases, Paula voices breathily her last concern: "Given that most stores don't allow returns of bathing suits and underwear … I'd say we're closing in … on a 'you broke it you bought it' scenario here."

"Or you blowed it you bought it!"

"You came in it, you go in it?"

"Nice one, P."

"Are you sure this is OK?"

"Does it feel OK?"

"It feels" – and Paula lies back, at last relaxes so as to prepare for an exalted tension – "exquisite."

Paula remembers now the giddy fervor of that intimacy, materialist frivolity turned steamy sensuality. That was the beginning. That was month number one. Or was it two? But it seems a thousand years ago. Some past life securely, irretrievably, in the B.C.F. archival zone. An archive laden with long walks and protracted kisses, constant motion and surprises, unexpected but exciting gestures, every minute an adventure.

In contrast, now, excursions are not frivolous, no levity is forthcoming. The remote control feels like a block of stone in Alex's hand; feels as if it must be made, just like her sculpted head, of lead; how great an effort is required to reach and lift and press, then press again – almost as great, it seems, as the effort of rising, and then raising hand to change the channel manually. And even so, she will not bother Paula to come to the doctor's office with her tomorrow. She will take the bus, she will be independent. Somehow she will find the energy, and save Paula's assistance for the out-of-town, more challenging appointments. She will not let this relationship become a live-in care arrangement. Once in a while when Paula least expects it, she will – although in ways less thrilling than before – surprise her lover. Even surprise herself – for she returns from her next appointment winded but intact.

"So what did he say? Jesus, you're practically hyperventilating. Lie down."

Alex reclines, stretches herself the full length of the couch, still breathing irregularly.

"Well …" She pauses until her breathing is controlled. "He said it could be stress, it could be Rocky Mountain spotted fever, it could be fibromyalgia … "

"Do you want some Evian?" Paula races to the kitchen and returns to Alex, who nods, extends her arm, receives the bottle, sips. Paula sees the Evian as some distended version of a baby's bottle, around which Paula would do well to maintain her grip – its neck a kind of nipple that stood in for Paula's own. She should be holding Alex to her breast, Alex who needed mothering and more. And yet, she was no mother, Paula. She barely managed lover. She forced herself to concentrate on Alex's breathless report.

"It could be lupus, it could be some other nebulous autoimmune condition, it could be psychosomia, it could be none of the above."

"Wait a minute. This is the internist? That's what the real doctor told you?"

"... fraid so."

"So that's it? Total ambiguity? Nothing more that can be done?"

"Well, something can. Tests can be done, for what it's worth. Lots of tests. Blood work. And I have to see a neurologist."

"Didn't I always tell you should have your head examined?"

That evening, Alex gathers – in imagination – all her idle climbing equipment: ropes and harnesses, locking caribiners, superclip and daisy chains, extended range cams, and uses them – not to belay and rappel on rock – but simply to scale the mountainous stairs, placing each slippered foot onto each wooden platform as if it were snow-covered rock, or as if the glossy wood veneer were actually a coating of ice. She must keep thrusting her Cryro ice-ax, with what little strength she can muster, to gain purchase, one riser at a time – she who had never for a minute feared a Pamela-Pack-like forearm injury or the prospect of Tod Skinner's fatal tragedy, she who had wished to follow in the footsteps of Kit DeLauriers, freeskiing champion who climbed and skied six thousand feet – and in a mere three weeks – from seven summits of the Himalayas. The banister is beside the point, since Alex is practically crawling – thus skiing back down would be out of the question – but if she can just make it up the stairs, she'll surely reach the summit – not in this case the exotic Hilary Step or Lhotse Face or even the familiar Flagstaff Mountain, but her very own blissfully horizontal bed! The default goal of her activities has mutated from being vertical at any cost – the higher up the better – to being horizontal as consistently as possible. She has adopted Kit's mountaineering mantra: "like your life depends on it" and adapted it to her own absurdly mundane circumstances. The expression "to climb into bed" has never been taken quite so literally.

Paula tries to steer clear of Alex's household adventures, for both their sakes, unless she's needed. Whenever Alex mounts the stairs, she goes into another room to seek distraction, but her mind does not stray far. She wonders if her recent tendency to see wheelchairs everywhere is some kind of psychosomatic visual phenomenon – the way when Alex almost bought a Subaru – in the B.C.F. time zone of course – it seemed that every other vehicle on the highway was an Outback or a Forrester. Heightened attention making epidemics out of moderate statistics. Of course, what use is that comparison, given neither woman now is of any use behind a wheel, the first because of lethargy and inability to focus, the second because of vision that defies the correction of corrective lenses.

While Alex naps, Paula catches herself gazing in the mirror, finding little favor with the image of herself, an image that in the old days was consistently enhanced by Alexandra's verbal, tactile hermeneutics. Her pale unstable eyes, her hair, her lips, her ears, her nose, the disappearing color of her skin, none can stand up to Paula's self-directed disapproval. Without her consultant behind her to transform the image, she is nakedly critical, mournful. The beauty that Alex had over time persuaded her she possessed reverts feature by feature to unattractiveness. She asks this homely-at-best visage in the mirror what had become of the glory days; the heady, carefree, early love days. I'll tell you what happened, says Paula theatrically, to the twinned recipient of her own rhetorical question: Those lust-driven, luck-laden, head-over-heels days have dwindled, dried up and possibly died. Then she hears Alex calling her: is there a visitor, who in the world is she talking to now?

More and more often, Alex feels a kinship with Joe Simpson, the abandoned mountain-climber of *Into the Void*: broken and hobbled; slouching toward base camp, making his miraculous return down the mountain only to find an ignorant, well-intentioned, highly unskilled helpmeet, i.e. Paula. Once severed from the symbiotic Simon Yates, Joe Simpson had been stunningly resourceful. Surviving against all odds, he had employed counting and singing to keep himself breathing, to keep from surrendering sanity. Alex yearns to be that creative, in service of her considerably less majesterial mission. The mountain is her mind. Or is it body? Her conflated body/mind. Early on, during the glory days, Alex had rented the documentary from Blockbuster to initiate Paula into the excitement of the climb, but these months later, it continues to provide a reference she had not intended. They have often asked each other, on the worst days, "would you cut the rope" – each understanding that they have to answer honestly, completely honestly, to this high-stakes hypothetical question, which has in turn spawned ancillary questions, such as "who would you prefer to be: the dangler or the danglee?" The verbal back and forth at best is philosophical, at worst, claims Alex, tautological, the latter evidenced in Paula's latest answer "that depends if *you* would cut the rope."

One man's tautology is another man's common sense, says she who often stubbornly insists on having the last word.

Paula favors creativity as well. She prefers it to order. For example, she would rather institute eccentric decorating schemes than organize or do the housecleaning. But once in a great while, she gets a spurt of energy, and tries to be responsible: sorts through the mail, tidies things up, does dishes, even vacuums. Last night, she spent several hours assigning Alex's myriad equipment into designated Rubbermaid bins that she had purchased on sale and brought back via bus, two at a time – bins labeled for climbing vs. hiking vs. skiing vs. cycling vs. camping etc.

She'd seen the scheme in *Outside* magazine and got inspired, then made an executive decision that each sport be consigned to long-term storage, given Alex's situation. The one that had been labeled BEER in *Outside*, she eliminated, then substituted, with the label TEA, assuming it could accommodate the overflow from the burgeoning kitchen cabinets. She is proud of her handiwork, decidedly more practical than her usual artistic ventures, but prouder still that she will carry on in honor of this surrogate adrenaline, and finally address the bills and such that are piled high on the living room table, amidst abundant information about various charity triathlon events. Alex, as usual, is supine on the sofa with a blanket over her.

"Hey, I wasn't sure if you wanted to renew your subscription to *Rock Climber*."

"What do you think?"

"Maybe reading about climbing might be a good substitute until you can actually do it again."

"Nah. Just let it expire."

"That obviously goes for *Rock and Ice* then too. *Adventure*?"

"Ditto."

"*Harpers*?"

"Let me sleep on it."

"*Outside*?"

"Maybe we should keep that one for you, since you were so inspired by it to organize, even though you never asked me if it was OK."

"Ask if it was OK to keep living in total chaos? – right. How about *Ebony* then? I'm on a roll here."

"Let me think about it."

"What, too upbeat?"

"Something like that."

"Maybe soon you can subscribe to just plain *Bony*?"

"Good one, P."

"Someone should start a magazine for albino women."

"And call it what? *Bino*? *Biny*?"

"How about … *Alabaster*?"

"That's great, actually. That's quite clever. Why don't you do that? Really, P. It's a good idea."

"Think I've got my hands full right now."

"Deep down, you don't think you or your compatriots deserve a magazine, that's the problem."

"Never too tired to play the shrink, eh?"

"I deserve a turn occasionally, don't I? And isn't there a grain of truth in what I'm saying?"

"I guess. There might be, but the whole idea is ludicrous."

"Why is that?"

"Because it would just end up stigmatizing albino people even more, and all the non-albino normal people would be repulsed by it."

"Why do you assume that?"

"Because I've lived on the planet thirty years in my skin, that's why. Oh and by the way, as long as I'm disposing of these subscription renewal notices, why don't we decide how to handle that bill from the homeopath. Apparently *Blue Cross* won't cover it, since he's not an M.D."

"It'll just have to wait until next month, when I can pay it. I doubt he can afford a collection agency."

"Or would you like me to write on the back of the bill that we'll pay up in God's time?"

"Touché, P."

In general, the décor of Alex's apartment is considerably more homespun in the nearly a year that Paula has cohabited with her. The elegant austere black and white photographs, the breathtaking landscapes, the paintings and wall hangings, the posters from the Contemporary Art Museum and the Harvard diploma (framed by Alex's parents) have been almost occluded by the brightly colored daily valentines and ancillary homemade artifacts, some of which in recent months have veered from sentimental to sententious. Most recently, for instance, Paula has hung from Alex's door a homemade calendar sheet consisting of repeating rows of newly christened weekdays: a substitution for the *Women of Climbing* calendar that had hung there before. At first the columns read like gibberish, inelegant and cryptic; they do not bear the dignity of a Julian or Mayan or Gregorian equivalent. Across the top edge of the poster board reads Acuday, Chiroday, Homeoday, Neuroday, Reikiday, Shiatsuday. Pronouncing softly to herself, Alex finally catches on but does not laugh. Then Paula appears behind her.

"Do you like it? It's the official New-Age Body Calendar?"

"Well, you cheated, putting in neurology, if the premise is avoiding the conventional."

"Poetic license. Tokenism. Whatever. You know, these body-workers really have it made. They cop a feel and you get charged for it."

"You are *really* paranoid. Paula Ann Paranoid!"

"I'm working on the illustrations too – Acuday sports a different kind of pin-up girl, you might say. You'll be the model for her, naturally. We can patent it and market it and pay off the medical bills."

"Did you realize you left out the seventh day?"

"Yeah, that was deliberate too. The seventh day is cranial-sacred – just for rest. aka God's private time."

"But tomorrow is cranial-secular, remember? You promised to go with me to the neurologist."

"Fear not, dark damsel in distress. I've already set the alarm. But for the rest of the evening, I'm going back to cleaning this place up before I lose my motivation."

Paula finds this waiting room comparatively – in fact surprisingly – upbeat. If not downright jolly.

Having left her bioptics at home and thus hindered in reading, she is relieved to have distraction in the waiting room – lest she be tempted to do something reckless, heartless, such as abandoning her lover in favor of the shuttle to the Denver International Airport, though of course she would be courteous enough to leave this information with the receptionist, so that Alex wouldn't be completely stumped as well as shocked when she emerged from her appointment with the neurologist.

A white female caretaker is in the process of occupying her black male charge by placing a starched white handkerchief atop his head; letting it dangle daintily in front of his face, then, in an exaggerated gesture, snatching it away, repeatedly, just as one might do to amuse a child. How genuine seemed her and the other woman's amusement as they did so; how jolly they all seemed. But how uncomfortable Paula felt in the jolly ward, in fact, jolly jealous of the fun they appeared to be having – despite the disability that rendered the man simple and chair-bound. What in the end was the difference, Paula asked herself, between a mental and a physical impairment, if a wheelchair was the vehicle for each? Whatever was wrong with this gentleman, he at least wasn't too tired to smile, to laugh. Thank you for smiling, she wanted to tell him – I don't get enough of that at home. And it was nice to have someone else be the spectacle for a change! She wanted to thank him for that too. For once *she* didn't steal the show.

Paula amuses herself by imagining the hanky as a renegade item from a magician's bag of tricks. The kind that is placed over a ball and then lifted, the ball having meanwhile inexplicably disappeared. What if the jolly ladies found that suddenly under the hanky there was no more head: the most delicate decapitation ever, not by blade but by veil – a convenient way to solve a neurological problem!

See no evil. Hear no evil. Speak no evil. Think no evil. Off with his defective head!

Meanwhile, inside the inner sanctum, the neurologist is unimpressed with Alex's explanation – "feeling fuzzy" does not facilitate a diagnosis – he suggests she furnish him with greater specificity. How can she convey the way her head feels filled with outer space? Or is it more like Styrofoam peanuts? The doctor does not understand the term "spacey." Could she be more concrete? "You know, *spacey*" (realizing she is only repeating louder, at best re-inflecting, as if trying to communicate an English word to a non-native speaker): not focused, not locked-in, like an wobbly office chair with the casters loose, like a lamp with its bulb not completely screwed in, dizzy, a little off-kilter. "Ditzy," she suspects the neurologist wishes to substitute: not dizzy, but ditzy. Alex strains to come up with a better metaphor. It's as if thinking were hearing through water, or seeing through scrim – but not impressionistic, pretty-picture beauty, doctor, something murky, muddy, far from lovely: something bog-like. A body immured in a bog, doctor, surely you've heard of a bog?

He seems to take notes skeptically, proclaims her situation unremarkable, but nonetheless prescribes an MRI. Just to be sure, to rule out tumor. Rule out several diagnoses, in fact. If she insists, they'll even do a spinal tap. Alex will not insist. She does not care to be tapped; she feels thoroughly tapped out, in fact.

While the pricey specialist is proving useless, Paula continues to watch the ludicrous yet somehow charming, inexplicably endearing game between the private nurse and her docile charge, the white cloth draped over the man's brown cheek, then snatched away by the agile white hand, the third woman seeming to provide moral support and additional mirth. So thoroughly distracted is Paula in fact that she doesn't notice Alex has come back out to the waiting room and stands beside her.

"Paula, it's over, I'm done. We can go."

"I'm deeply spectating this game of hanky-head," she stands and whispers into Alex's ear.

"What are you talking about now?"

Paula rises reluctantly and they walk side by side to the elevator.

"Never mind; guess it's a you-had-to-be-there kind of thing. So what did he say?"

"He said lots of things that don't add up to much, but the conclusion is I ought to have an MRI."

"Didn't I always tell you you should have your head examined?"

"You already used that joke. About my coming here to the neurologist. Don't you remember? Maybe *you* should have your head examined!"

"Touché, madame, touché. Why don't we do them side-by-side?"

Paula hasn't any idea how relevant her flippant comment is. Nor how potent for her lover, who is currently preoccupied with specialized concerns regarding camaraderie: that skydiving, skating and flying can transpire in tandem, but most medical technology cannot accommodate the embodiment of moral support. This is the failure of feminist – no, humanist – gestures in medicine, Alex decides: that you can be accompanied into the examining room by a same-sex pal at pap-smear time, or give birth surrounded by a roomful of invited guests, or have the local hospital host a colonoscopy party, and yet an MRI is explicitly *not* designed as a bicycle built for two. (No doubt useful – albeit inadvertent – preparation, she supposes, for entering the vacuum known as death.) The radiologist will read the lineaments of Alex's brain, but she herself, unmentored, can decipher her suddenly transparent psyche. She hadn't bargained for the buy-one-get-one-free fringe benefit of medical technology – for how perfectly the 3/4 hour claustrophobic aloneness would rhyme with the emotional texture of her thus-far inscrutable illness. Experience – who would have guessed? – was just the vestibule to metaphor.

These are the perks of illness, aren't they? Growing pains that leave you maimed, excruciating revelations, ninety mile-an-hour psychic crashes euphemistically referred to as epiphanies. She prefers regressing into memory, into the vestibule of Whole Foods, where side-by-side, she and her love would find themselves as pumped up with adrenaline as when they were about to climb or parachute or ski. (At least for Alex, athletic metaphors worked best to characterize that excitement.) Paula, she recalled, was charmed by the design of the environmentally resourceful cart: a hand held basket that could mutate into a wheeled cart with one maneuver. She'd always opt for wheels while Alex, muscle-woman, favored carrying. In either case, they'd roam the amply stocked aisles, overwhelmed with options, giddy with health, bringing erotic charge to every aspect of this mundane process: looking, smelling, touching, choosing, whether vegetable or animal or mineral. For instance, in prepared foods, they'd request a taste and feed it to each other, as if ice cream on a spoon. And if it happened to be cranberry walnut bread day at the bakery, they would grab several of the warm loaves fresh from the oven, hoarding uninhibitedly, breathing in the yeasty sweetness, noses right up against the crust, and gorge, side by side, high on the surfeit of opulent salubriousness – yes, a veritable orgy of salubriousness. Claiming the corner booth in the dining area, they'd tear off chunks with their hands in a new-age Neanderthal fashion and commence feeding it to each other like wedding cake, unabashedly making a scene.

"This could be someone's wedding cake, right?"

"Well … carrot cake was big back in the nineties, but cranberry-walnut wedding bread is still ahead of the curve, I'd say. A custom whose time is not yet come."

"If you keep feeding me these warm sweet morsels, my time might be yet come – so to speak."

"Hmmmm. Keep feeding me incentive and I'll keep feeding you from my hand. Besides, our wedding cake has to be chocolate and vanilla, right? Don't you remember? Blatant symbolism? Our racial statement instigating global harmony and freaking out your mother!"

But as Alex, solo, present tense, lies rigid in her metal tube, the absence of eros is palpable. Assaulted by an unanticipated cacophony – thus unable to meditate – Alex's consciousness constructs a surround-sound, magnetic resonance waking-dream. Every conceivable version of game is stationed around her, representing in miniature everything at which she once excelled, now turned on her, dangerously out of control. Acoustic chaos assaults her in the private cylindrical stadium. The repertoire is exhaustive: table tennis, hand-hockey, pinball, etc., but the tables and courts and such are stationed upside down as well as right-side up, curving when necessary to conform to the specific contours of her confinement. The miniature balls: tennis, ping-pong, golf, pin, racquet, not to mention hockey pucks and such, are whizzing around at considerable speed, very vigorously, upside down, as she lies on her back, inert, with buzzers going off, nearly deafened by the din of collective thwacks from balls and flippers. In her "altered state," she cringes lest she be hit because she has no visor nor helmet, no elbow or shin-guards, no goggles, not any protection whatsoever. She's battered and buffeted, mentally, by the anticipation. It's like a model village of mini-games, a thriving metropolis of demi-activity hurtled at mega-decibels en masse against her lethargy. She feels as if she's been thrust into a racquet-ball court, not as a racquet-bearing player but a horizontal floater with neither projectile nor net as defense against the murderous, relentless thwack thwack. She wants to curl up, become fetal, to shield her body with her own embrace, not lie like a pole in a space capsule, in this metal body-condom, this alienating stationary elevator.

When later she tries to explain it to Paula, the latter jokes that Alex must have been the actress in *Fantastic Voyage*, but after seeing how disturbed her lover is, she changes tune, gets serious, invokes Freud's *The Interpretation of Dreams*: the famous illustration in which the urge to pee is progressively aggrandized into a puddle, a pool, a pond, a sea: a body vast enough to accommodate a sailing ship. According to Paula's analogy, Alex's anxiety somehow absorbed the magnet's aleatory music and transformed it into yet more threatening forms.

"But can it really be analogous since I wasn't asleep, and since peeing is something internal while the ping-ping MRI sounds were external?"

"You're awfully picky, after all my hard analysis. You must have gone to Harvard. Look A, what do you say we get something to eat? I'm starving. We can go to your beloved Dushanbe place. I read somewhere that westworld.com voted it most romantic restaurant in Colorado."

"Then maybe we should save it for our anniversary. Until all these medical expenses get sorted out, I think we shouldn't splurge on fancy food. But I could always use a cup of tea."

And so it is agreed that they will take the Supershuttle out of Denver and get off at the stop nearest downtown, to recuperate luxuriously amidst the decorative Tajik splendor of the Boulder Tea House. But after purchasing tickets and boarding the bus, amidst an altercation between the driver and a female passenger protesting the fact that seat belts seem to be installed for only every other seat, Paula, impatient, begins to question her exhausted lover.

"Do you feel up to answering questions?"

"I'll give it a try."

"So what exactly happens at a consultation with a homeopathist?"

"Homeopath." Alex hasn't the energy to mask her disappointment.

"Whatever."

"Look, I've just this moment come out of a nearly psychedelic technological out-of-body experience and you're asking me for a blow-by-blow account of something much less scintillating ..."

"Use any other term than blow, OK?"

"Sure, fine – a minute by minute account of an essentially tedious and now week-old clinical exchange ..."

"Look, no one I talked to before ever cited an MRI as a life-changing experience. And I thought we already discussed it."

Their argument is interrupted by the distressed passenger explaining yet again that she wishes to sit with her husband, directly next to her husband, so they can converse. "Is that so much to ask? Do you think that's too much to ask," she buttonholes Paula, who feels as always cursed by her conspicuousness. A University of Colorado student steps in to mediate, more the opportunist than the altruist, suspects Paula, who guesses he intends to impress Alex, sitting ever closer so as to imbibe the aura of her once robust, now fragile, somehow still magnetic beauty. Paula wants to tug his yellow ponytail and whisper in his ear, "young man, suppress your gallantry, your hard-on too, for things are not what they appear!"

"Do you care about my feelings? At all?"

"I guess if I didn't I wouldn't have been sitting in yet another waiting room for at least an hour, during the course of which I found myself trying to pass the time by trying to imagine exactly how a homeopath makes a diagnosis."

For minutes, many minutes, Alex tunes out Paula; she tries instead to focus on the mountain's lineaments, to let the Rockies be her meditation, her fixed point, a visualization that just happens to be actual. And what more logical fixed point could one have? At least one member of the range was there in the background wherever you went, both standing out and blending in, providing a painted backdrop for the charming awnings and tile sidewalks and come-hither-all-ye-southwest-yuppies shop windows. At times, from afar, it appeared so tantalizingly real, you could touch it from here, and then out of the blue it said simultaneously, you can't have me, come and get me, good luck, sucker, I'm your white whale, made of shale. A perverse combination of come hither and *noli me tangere*. Or in the vernacular, "you go, girl" plus "no way, Jose."

In her past life she had many times physically mastered the mountain; but now she had to climb *through* it with exclusively her mind, and would, she thinks, succeed, were not that scowl of Paula's formidable in much the same way. When they reach the Flatiron Mall, she finally surrenders.

"OK, we'll go through the process, step by step. What do you want to know?"

"Do you lie on an examining table with a paper gown and all that?"

"I didn't lie. I sat. On a chair."

"With your clothes off?"

"On."

"That's it? He didn't even examine you? All that time?"

"He examined ... verbally. Kind of like you are now ... cross-examining."

"I'm not cross-examining. I'm just curious. You said that if I stayed in Boulder, you'd be my new-age education mentor, remember? And I stayed! You owe me. Besides, I want to make sure you're not wasting your money and time."

"Don't be disingenuous. You're already sure that I am and you know it. And isn't it *your* time, not mine, that you're *really* concerned about?"

"Don't forget God's time. God forbid we waste that!!!! Look, who knows? Maybe I'll go to a homeopath someday. Help me prepare."

"You're full of shit." The student looks protective on Alex's behalf; Paula knows already he would not give her the benefit of a doubt, even if Alex hurled insults, or even blows, upon her.

"No really, is it basically like an interview?"

"All I can tell you is I answered questions. They required thought. The thought, as I recall, was rather tiring."

"Like whether-you-believe-in-God kind of questions?"

"No."

"In reincarnation?"

"No."

"What sort of questions?"

"Less grand, less existential. He wanted to know my preferences."

"OK, I'm starting to get the picture. The sixty-four million dollar question: Do you sleep with men or women? Two hundred bucks for a placebo with a come-on at no extra charge." The C.U. student is eavesdropping without any subterfuge now.

"Chill out already! One hundred percent *wrong*. He didn't even go there. They were much more mundane preferences he was asking about – billions of them."

"Could you give me an example?"

"What are you, the Gestapo? The only one that sticks in my mind is, Do you like chocolate better than cheese?"

"What has that got to do with anything? It seems completely arbitrary!"

"You'll really have to ask the doctor that question."

"The doctor! The doctor! The quackster, you mean. The guy never spent a day in medical school. Or divinity school for that matter. Next time we'll cut out the middleman and go straight to the preacher – it's cheaper! God's time, my ass. What if someone is indifferent, what if they like chocolate and cheese absolutely equally?"

"Maybe there's a type for that too: indifference or indecisiveness."

"So he asked billions of questions, and that's all you can recall."

"My short-term memory is pretty shaky lately, you, healthy one, may remember! It wasn't yesterday. And as I mentioned before, I'm tired, and you're tiring me more with every question you ask."

"You'll have to forgive the companion for craving a little diversion now and then."

"You know, I liked when you were stupid funny. That was one of the things I liked best about you – you were corny, silly, funny. But the brittle edge is not becoming. Lose the edge, OK?"

"Why should I let you control my personality? I've got my wish list too, you know."

"Because you've gone from corny to crabby."

"And you've from horny to snappy!"

"Touché already. OK. I stand corrected. Let's try to curb our irritation, shall we? Back to practical matters for a minute. What do you want for dinner tonight?"

"How about corn on the crab?"

"How about we go out to the Tea House?"

"We're already going to the Tea House – she who needs her head examined!"

"I mean for dinner, not just tea."

"As reward for what? Since just a little while ago you said we couldn't afford eating there."

"For getting through the day."

"And what about our resolve to be frugal?"

"Oh, fuck it."

"What – going? Or being frugal?"

"The latter, the latter."

There is surely something otherworldly, or at least unearthly, about the interior design of the Dunshabe Teahouse, with its highly elaborated intricate mandala-like patterns and rich turquoise hues, letting Alex lose herself in imagery of sky or ocean. She tilts back her head as if on a marionette string to better take in the sumptuously designed coffered ceiling with which no cloud formation could compete, an ornately sculpted sky held up with cedar columns.

"I just love that Tajik wedding dress."

"The crown is even better; I can see it on your regal head."

"A crown of thorns might be more apropos at this point. We'd need two anyway, two crowns, two gowns."

"But there's just one in the display case, and it's only logical that it goes to the beauty queen."

"You still think I'm a candidate for the eighth beauty, eh, after all this?"

"It's perfect; as a statue you wouldn't have to expend any energy."

"Yeah, I would. They draw water, remember? That's what those dishes on the head are: water vessels."

"I'd hold your dish for you. And add a dish of plov to go."

"Could you be serious? I thought you hated plov."

"Well, it could never compare to this delicious chicken dish with pomegranate sauce with the name only you can pronounce. But listen, here's a news item; I take back my suspicion about that quackster coming on to you. It isn't logical."

"Will wonders never cease?"

"I figured out if homeopathy is based on that premise of like curing like, then same sex couples must be just what the doctor ordered, right?"

"Whatever you say, P."

"I guess I'm a homeo-sexual now. Dyke cures dyke."

"Homosexuality, perhaps you've noticed, is no longer considered a disease. Hence it needs no curing."

"Well, excuuuuuuse me!"

"But one more question, Alex, really truly, not a joke here, if homeopathy is based on everyone having a type, and if you're as different as you claim to be from what you were before, i.e. the you I met approximately a year ago, how can any homeopathic doctor know what type you truly are and thus what remedy to give you?"

Alex parts her lips presumably to form a response to Paula's utterly sincere question, but then closes them again, looking quite perplexed. Suddenly she starts to weep, her tears a complementary motif within the vast turquoise embrace, amidst repeating shapes of decorative vegetal arabesques, of medallions and lozenges, grapes and pomegranates, of butterflies and barley chains, partridges and peacocks, of mihrab trees of life and stylized roses.

"I came here in good faith, believing in the Tajik mayor's motto, '*When friends sit and talk in a teahouse, fatigue disappears*.' Why is it, Paula, that after a few minutes conversation with you, I always want to change it to '*abandon hope, all ye who enter here*'?"

"Brett, we'll take that check now, if you can."

Jessica Hagedorn

Toxicology, Or: Portrait of Mimi

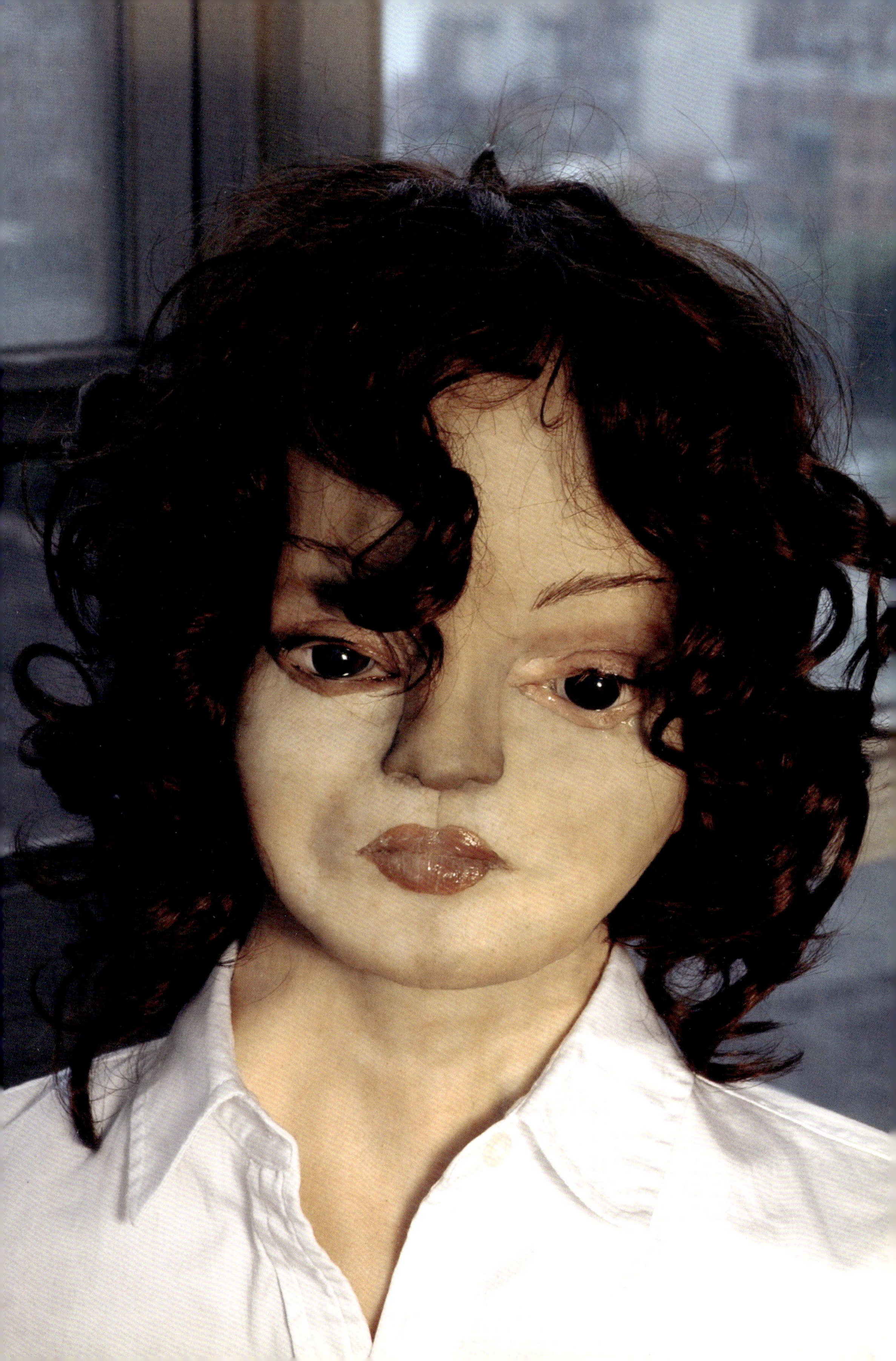

Mimi contemplates the word *fame* while pouring herself the second to last bit of precious fuel from her stash in the freezer. On the rocks, garnished with a twist, the premium-blend tastes dangerous and smooth. Mimi relishes each oily sip of her cocktail, fights the urge to guzzle it down. Cost of gas rising, prices highest they've ever been on the day the gorgeous young actor decides to kill himself, the same day Mimi filches the shipping box from Mrs. Schnabel's recycling bin and makes a bed for the dying animal. The dead actor is famous. The dying animal in Mimi's overheated apartment is not.

There is no product to be found in all of Manhattan or Brooklyn, or any other borough, for that matter. One shimmering drop left in the humming fridge. Mimi licks her lips, fights the urge to swoon. She flips open her cell, rereads last week's text message from Bobby:

Bitch b cool
Cuzn of mines 2 fuckin bad.
Bad bad not good bad.
Fnd nu srs. Dnt panic

Then he sent one more, seconds later, before disappearing for good:

I wl mis u

The days fly by. So much work and nothing to do.

Mimi lights up one of those small Cuban girlie cigars, a cherished souvenir from Bobby's many clandestine trips to Bobby-wouldn't-say-where. Even after all these months, the cigar tastes fresh. She stares out the window at the shell of a high-rise luxury loft condo being built across the street. Each floor starting at six point six. Rooftop gym, spa, pool, garage, natch. Doorman, valet service, 24-hour concierge, no brainer. The architect's famous and Dutch.

Mimi's view of the river's now blocked, but so what? Mimi's always avoided looking at that river; the river reminds her too much of the greasy oceans beyond. Mimi chides herself for getting morose. One shimmering drop left in the humming fridge; take it slow and easy, Mimi. And speaking of fame, just like that most famous of famous Lorca poems about death – Mimi glances at the clock and cheers up. Five in the afternoon. *At five in the afternoon, exactly five in the afternoon …* Lorca's hypnotic lament conjures the image of a young matador being gored by a Lydian bull. Five in the afternoon. Mimi takes another hit off the dainty cigar and wonders why she can't remember any other lines from the poem.

Five in the afternoon. At exactly five in the afternoon! You're such a drama queen, Mimi. Mimi It's All About Me-Me! Why the tears? You don't know any matadors. You never knew that poor, dead actor.

Cost of gas rising. And rising.

The animal crawls out of the shipping box, huge glassy eyes fixed on Mimi. It howls. It stinks. It's time. It's really dying.

I can't help you, Mimi says.

She's the squeamish-type. Never mind the low-budget slasher films she concocts with such glee. You've seen the trailers. Supermodels trapped in desolate hostels in the Black Forest. Trembling jocks strapped down and eviscerated. Mimi's an auteur, so good at dreaming up genius scenarios. Next time you invite her to a dinner party? Watch the way she suddenly stops eating. Watch the way she flings her knife and fork, aiming straight for your face. The cutlery flung with such *élan*!

But when it comes to a suffering animal, the chick's a wuss.

Mimi stubs the cigar out in the sink. Restarts her computer. DISCUSS. SHARE YOUR THOUGHTS, urge the online bulletin boards. Sad. Tragic actor guy. So young! R.I.P. How could you? Oh, man. You were the source of our national pride.

LIKELY A SUICIDE OR ACCIDENTAL OVERDOSE. The headlines confuse and contradict just minutes and seconds after the famous actor's corpse is discovered by his tantric masseuse. Mimi turns the flatscreen TV on, turns up the volume to drown out the sounds of the dying animal. Apparently, the actor's body has not been removed from the building. Apparently, the Tantric masseuse had a key. Apparently, the Tantric masseuse, the one carrying an umbrella and a set of keys, slips out the side exit while no one is looking and hails the first available taxi.

Police barricades hold back the growing mob of grieving fans. Hundreds and thousands of them, patient and determined. I am here to bear witness, a woman announces for the cameras. A man dressed like an arctic explorer shakes his head and murmurs, Unreal. This is so unreal.

At five in the afternoon. At exactly five in the afternoon. Mimi's gaze wanders past the dying animal, the ticking clock, over to the ancient, humming fridge. That last, odorless, shimmering teardrop, waiting. Mimi must decide. And soon.

Jennifer Belle

Losing Sequins

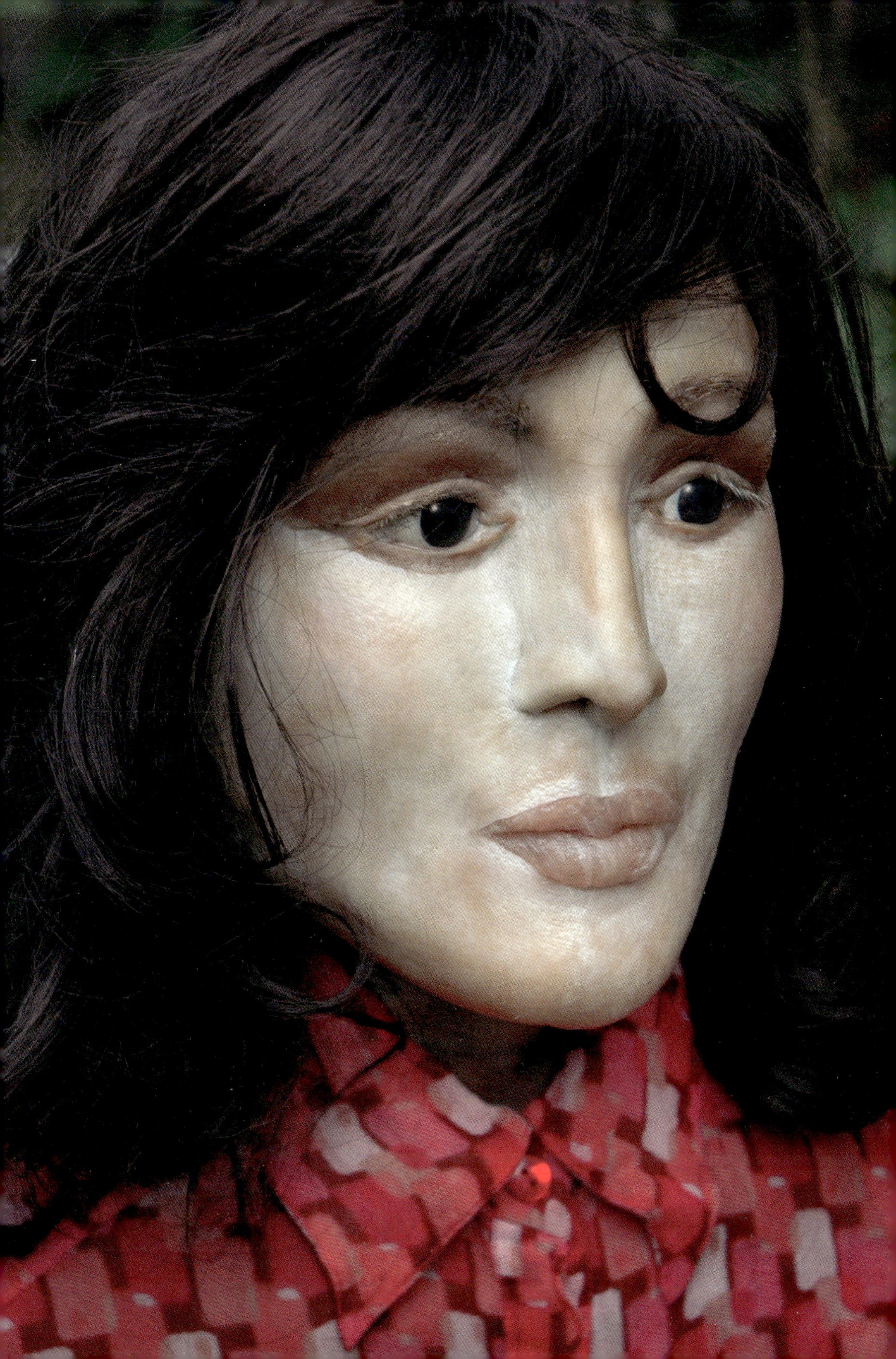

Before she came to take care of the baby there were several who hadn't worked out, mostly because they got on the nerves of the mother. They put the baby to sleep on his stomach, or they didn't clean at all, or they gave her constant mumbo jumbo advice about breast-feeding, or they spoke Spanish to the baby, or they were *too* religious.

She had liked the one named Juana. But Juana's son got in a car accident and there were constant MRI's to go to and she couldn't work Sundays because she had to go to church to thank God for saving her son's life. Which was understandable.

Then came Diahn, the cousin of a stranger she met in the playground, Viola from *The Irish Echo* who didn't show up, and Shawna who sat in the living room eating Doritos, even when people came to visit. When this one – Gita – came for the interview it was different. She liked the way she looked, they were wearing the same color, apple green, and they both had long hair.

When she had checked Gita's references, the nice mother she worked for now said Gita always put herself together very well. They wanted to keep her two days a week, which was perfect because she only wanted her part-time; she'd had a baby for a reason, to be with him. And there was usually something suspicious about the ones who only wanted to work part-time. They either had some sort of screw loose or they left as soon as they found a full-time better position.

The mother could tell, by the way she came all the way from the Bronx for the interview and arrived right on time, that she really needed money, which was a good thing in a nanny.

"How old are you," the mother asked. She felt strange asking a personal question like that, but that was the point of an interview.

"Forty," the nanny said. Her voice was a few octaves too high but still nice.

The mother was thirty-six, but a very young thirty-six, and the nanny seemed like a very young forty. The mother liked that she was forty, most of her friends were forty, she felt comfortable with forty, but she was embarrassed that she had asked.

"Do you have any children?" the mother asked. She waited for their names and ages and who was taking care of them and why it wouldn't interfere with the job.

"Children, no," the nanny said.

The mother looked up, surprised. This was wonderful news. There would be no earaches to rush home to in the middle of the day and the mother wouldn't have to spend time wondering how the nanny could enjoy the job if she had abandoned her own children in some far off land. She had spent so much time wondering about that and trying not to be judgmental.

"Have you ever taken care of a ten-week-old before?"

"Yes, I have fourteen nieces and nephews."

"So you wouldn't be scared to give the baby a bath?"

The nanny laughed. "I have plenty of experience. I just told you I have fourteen nieces and nephews. I took care of all of them."

"Because I was nervous the first time I gave him a bath," the mother said, in her usual self-deprecating manner. Maybe that was why they were constantly giving her advice. That, and the fact that it was her first baby, and her house was always such a mess. Her power slipped away with every clump of toothpaste in the bathroom sink and pizza box in the living room. There was great power in being neat. When they showed up at noon and she was still unshowered but wrapped in a towel, holding the baby with a clump of her long hair grasped in his tiny fist, walking from room to room looking for his pacifier in the piles of clutter, they must have known she was not in control.

The mother showed her around the apartment, avoiding her messy bedroom where the baby was asleep in his bassinet at the foot of their bed, telling her what the job entailed, her own definition of light cleaning. "I love these curtains," the nanny said in the baby's room, touching the beautiful gold fabric.

"They're made from saris, from India!" the mother said. She loved them too. They were covered in gold embroidery with rings of tiny pearls, gold beads, and gold sequins. At night, with the lights out, they sparkled like stars. "Are you from India or Pakistan?" the mother asked.

"I'm from Guyana, but I'm of Indian descent. You know Guyana? It's near Brazil," the nanny said.

The mother wanted to hire her. She spoke absolutely perfect English, with just a slight Indian whine. "Are you available to start right away?" she asked.

"Yes. But can I ask you some questions?"

The mother watched while she pulled a tiny Post-it out of her pocket and read from it. "Do I get paid if I'm sick?"

"I'm not sure," the mother said. She felt defensive. "It's only a part-time job. Twenty hours a week. I'll have to see. Next question?"

"Okay," the nanny said, softly. "Do I have federal holidays off?"

"Federal holidays?" the mother repeated.

She paused, taken aback by the sweetness of the question. By the way it had been carefully written on a Post-it. By this girl, just four years older than her who seemed so much younger, who lived here illegally and was concerned with Federal holidays. The mother didn't even know which ones were federal holidays and which ones weren't. It showed in an instant how much she took for granted every day, with federal holidays up the yingyang, so many she didn't even have to cherish them. None of the other nannies had brought a Post-it with a question on it. "Yes, of course you can have those days off, just let me know when they are," she said.

"And what will I be paid?" the nanny said.

"Oh, I'm sorry," the mother said. She suddenly felt terrible. "It's twelve dollars an hour." She said it in her same confident way, confident in knowing that was the going rate in the neighborhood, twelve to fifteen, although she had paid Juana fourteen, but she suddenly felt terrible about it. "Is that okay?"

"Yes, it's okay," the nanny said.

"Great!" the mother said. "And you have to take care of your own lunch. If there's ever anything in the house you're welcome to eat it but you can't count on us having anything but cold pizza." The mother felt terrible again.

Before she left, the nanny asked to see the baby. "Of course," the mother said, laughing nervously, wondering why she hadn't thought of that. The nanny stood over the bassinet and looked down at him. "I've been hoping for a little one to take care of for a long time," she said.

"I wonder why she doesn't have children," the mother said to her husband in bed that night. "She's forty, you know." In her mind she could see the number forty on the birth defects chart in the pregnancy book. She could see the number 35 and the statistics next to it, and the statistics getting significantly worse as the age increased, 36, 37, 38, 39, and then – and this number was printed in an alarming red – 40. One in three. Or maybe it was one in thirty. Either way it wasn't good.

In the morning the mother greeted her at the door wearing nothing but a towel and handed her the baby before she had even taken off her boots.

"We're really glad you're here," the mother said. Maybe that was the mistake she'd made with some of the others, seeming too grateful.

"So are you married?" the mother blurted out, as the nanny happily took the baby.

"Married, yes. For four years."

"But you don't want children?"

"Yes, I want children very badly. But I've been trying for four years and nothing has happened."

"Have you seen a doctor?" the mother asked.

"No," the nanny said. "It costs too much money."

"No insurance?"

The mother felt like an idiot. Of course she didn't have insurance. Going to someone like Dr. Heiffowitz would cost two or three weeks' salary just for the initial exam. A sonogram, day three bloodwork, progesterone series, a post-coital test to check the viability of her husband's sperm, would be out of the question.

The mother saw the birth defects age chart in her mind again. She felt terrible. "I should get in the shower," she said, self-conscious to be having this conversation in her towel. She went into her bedroom for awhile and lay on her bed wondering why someone like this nanny couldn't get pregnant and she could with Dr. Heiffowitz's help. After she showered and finally dressed she nursed the baby one last time and was about to leave the house when she stopped for a moment to watch him in the nanny's arms. Somehow in the nanny's arms, she could fully appreciate him. Those pears for cheeks! She could barely force herself to walk out the door.

"Do you know how to tell when you're most likely to get pregnant?" the mother asked. Her heart started pounding although she wasn't sure why. No reason to feel uncomfortable talking about this. She was practically an expert. "You know there's only about forty-eight hours a month, or maybe only twenty-four, when you're able to get pregnant. You know the …" She couldn't think of any possible word. "Mucous. That's in the vagina?"

"Yes?" the nanny said. She seemed interested and open to this.

"When a woman is ovulating the mucous is very thin like egg whites."

"Okay," the nanny said. She looked like she was concentrating.

"That's how you know you are able to become pregnant."

"I will try that," the nanny said, as if it were a recipe for an omelet.

"You should," the mother said.

The mother watched her run the vacuum. She was tall and tubular, slightly barrel shaped, but not fat. Her legs and arms were thin but she was thick in the middle, her midriff puffed out of her low-waisted jeans and high-waisted sequined shirt. The mother suspected the nanny might have fibroids, which she herself had been forced to have removed two years before she became pregnant. Three had grown back but hadn't interfered this time.

The mother was suddenly dying to know if it was fibroids that had kept her from getting pregnant. The nanny was running the vacuum cleaner hose over the couch and the mother had a violent urge to vacuum the fuckers right out of her.

She always felt a little bit guilty about the vacuum cleaner because she got it for free after the September 11th attacks on the World Trade Center. Everyone who lived within a certain radius of the towers got a free Eureka bagless. She felt she was benefiting unfairly from other people's tragedy.

"I'm going now. There's two bottles of breast milk in the fridge," the mother said. Pumping at night for the nanny to have milk the next day was like something from a Grimm's fairytale. A strange offering. It was like being there but not being there, more intimate than a nanny cam. Her milk was so valuable. The one thing that separated her from everyone else. She pumped in bed, the powerful suction making her nipples stretch and swell to look like penises. Nature was strangely imperfect. The precious milk filled the bottles drop by drop. Milk was why, she was sure, cows were worshipped in India. Actually, she really knew nothing about India or anything like that, but she would like to have known.

"The vacuum's broken," the nanny said, the next day. All the nannies had complained that it didn't work well.

The mother was almost relieved. "I'll throw it out," she said. "What kind do you like? I'll get the kind you like. Maybe the yellow one that English gay guy invented."

"Maybe your husband could fix it?"

"Fix it? No," the mother said. "You don't just buy a new one in Guyana, do you?" the mother said.

"No. In Guyana something so simple as a sack of flour costs twenty dollars," the nanny said. "And so is a bag of carrots."

"I guess you don't eat too many carrots," the mother said.

"Yes, we do. Sometimes, we get them." The mother was constantly scooping whole bags of things like carrots and onions out of the bins in the bottom of her refrigerator and throwing them away when they had rotted. She couldn't imagine ever having any need for a sack of flour. If she wanted anything with flour in it she would just buy it made, with the flour already in it. "You know, until I came here, I had never tasted coffee."

"Coffee? Really? That's incredible!" the mother said. The more she tried to quit this stupid tone she had found herself taking, the more exaggerated her reactions seemed to become.

Her husband brought up two coffees from Oren's every morning when he walked the dog. Coffee in bed, her one cup of the day because of the breastfeeding, was her greatest pleasure. Hot in the winter, iced in the summer with a Splenda. "Life in my country is a terrible struggle, you know. Three men in my family have been killed there, by the Africans. My father was killed, you know. My family owns a cambio so I worry about them all the time."

"That's terrible," the mother said. "Maybe *I* could take a look at the vacuum."

The nanny put it in the middle of the living room floor next to the Gymini. The mother crouched in front of it, turned it on, and saw there was no suction. There was a tumbleweed of black hair and sequins in the plastic canister. On the underside there was a sticker with a phone number on it. The mother called it and told a man with a southern accent that it wasn't working.

"Do you happen to remember when you got it?" the service man asked.

"September, 2001," the mother said, guiltily.

The man said it was probably something called the belt and told her to get the pointy kind of screwdriver. The nanny helped her remove the something or other and they discovered the broken piece of black rubber. All she had to do was buy a new one.

She said a long good-bye to the nanny and the baby and the dog and, knowing if she didn't do it right then she would never do it, went straight to the drugstore to try to buy the vacuum belt. On the way to vacuum parts, she passed the Pampers aisle, and just seeing them made her milk come in. She grabbed her breasts, not caring who in the drugstore happened to see her do it. She never thought she'd be buying Pampers and grabbing her breasts in public, her jacket pockets filled with pacifiers, a small wooden maraca, and a musical Elmo. She had thought she would be peeing on ovulation predictor sticks and pregnancy test sticks and sitting in Dr. Heiffowitz's waiting room for the rest of her life.

When she had been ready to give up trying to have a baby, Dr. Heiffowitz had said, "I see no reason why you shouldn't be able to." When he said it, in his quiet Israeli accent, she had to fight the urge to spread her legs right then and there and beg him to be the father. Why wait all the way until the end of the day when her husband would come home from work? "You have a beautiful follicle," he had said and showed it to her on the sonogram screen. "You should ovulate tonight or tomorrow." Then he showed her her husband's sperm on a slide under a microscope, going gangbusters. "Look," he said, his voice filled with almost childish wonder. "Excellent sperm. Highest level of motility! We rarely see this high quality. I see no reason why you couldn't get pregnant tonight." When he saw no reason, *she* suddenly saw no reason. It was like a lens cap had been covering her cervix and now it was being lifted. She could see the excellent motile sperm attach itself to her beautiful follicle. She could feel it.

Just thinking about his kind, blue Israeli eyes, she was moved to tears.

"Did you get the vacuum cleaner part?" the nanny asked her when she came home.

"What?" She had forgotten all about the vacuum. "No, I got something else," the mother said.

She handed her the CVS bag. "It's an ovulation predictor kit," the mother said. Actually it was five boxes of them, each one costing twice the nanny's hourly wage.

She took the bag back from the nanny, ripped open one of the boxes and unfolded the instructions. She read the instructions to the nanny even though she could have recited them by heart. "You hold the stick under your urine stream. When did you get your last period?" she asked.

"On the fourth."

The mother went to the kitchen and got the International adoption calendar some agency had sent her when she was looking into getting a baby girl from China and circled the first day of the nanny's period. She told the nanny to start testing, first thing in the morning, right away, even though the directions said to wait until day fourteen. "Everyone's always telling you to wait," the mother said. "Never wait. That's the first rule of in …" She was going to say *infertility* but luckily she stopped herself. "In getting pregnant."

"Pregnant," the nanny echoed, taking serious note of the first rule of getting pregnant.

The mother's heart raced with excitement.

"You didn't even say hello to your son," the nanny said, kissing the baby on the forehead and laughing.

That night she'd asked the nanny to stay late so that she and her husband could go to a fundraiser for a documentary film a friend of hers was editing about a homeless crazy woman who lived in Central Park.

She and her husband took seats in the auditorium and the director made a speech asking everyone to contribute money so that she could finish the film and get it into festivals. A portion of the proceeds would go to help out the woman who was the subject of the film.

"Did you bring your checkbook?" she whispered to her husband.

"How much should we give?" he whispered back.

She didn't know but she wondered how much it would take to get their names listed in the thank yous at the end. On the screen the homeless woman peeled off her filthy clothes in a kind woman's house. The kind woman was interviewed in her dining room with a big silver coffee set behind her. The mother felt terrible about the nanny. She regretted the ovulation kits. It wouldn't work and it would give the nanny false hope. It was all too much. The homeless woman, and the poor nanny peeing on those awful sticks, with no chance in hell of having a baby without Heiffowitz.

"Maybe I'll take her to Heiffowitz," the mother whispered. "But what if she gets pregnant? Would she be given Medicare or Medicaid, and if so, would it cover amniocentesis? Or what if she refused amnio out of fear or for religious purposes. She's forty. What if she has a Down's baby?"

The nanny had told her about one of her nephews having black fur as thick as a bear's coating his feet and legs. If you saw him wrapped in a towel it was terrifying. The mother had been wrapped in her towel when the nanny had told this to her.

"Where does it end?" her husband asked. "If it's a Downs baby would we pay for it to go to a special school?" They hadn't even started a college fund yet and barely paid off their own bills from Dr. Heiffowitz. "And even if she does get pregnant, and has the amnio and the baby is fine, what if something goes wrong with the pregnancy? What if she loses the baby?"

"Loses the baby?" the mother said. If it hadn't been for her high-risk obstetrician, their baby would have died due to her low amniotic fluid. She was put on bed rest and had expensive sonograms and non-stress tests twice a week. "But money! Money shouldn't stand in the way of having a baby. Dr. Heiffowitz can find out if she needs an antibiotics series, or progesterone, or thyroid medication. Or maybe it's fibroids or even a problem with her husband! Remember when he showed me your sperm!" She said it too loudly and the people in the seats in front of them turned to look.

"Or what if you put her through all that and she simply can't get pregnant. There's infertile women all over the world," her husband said.

"This isn't all over the world, this is New York." Lately when she tried to talk to him she often wished she hadn't bothered. But as she watched the homeless woman in the movie, she felt thankful for her baby and her husband and her nanny and her dog, and of course, for Dr. Heiffowitz.

That night she dreamt she was feeding the baby on the stoop of the building where she used to live. She was feeding him her milk from a teacup and when she turned away for a moment, a Siamese cat lifted her leg and pissed in it. She brought the cup to her nose to smell if the milk was still okay, but of course it was spoiled, putrid. She woke with a terrible, foreboding feeling.

"Did you do the ovulation test?" she asked the nanny.

"Yes, I got two lines!"

The mother, holding her yellow towel around her, beamed with excitement. "Did you have sex?" she asked, making her eyes very wide as if that would somehow help make this an acceptable question.

"Yes, we did do it," the nanny said.

"Good!" the mother said. "That's very good!"

She called Dr. Heiffowitz' office, on her walk to the gym, and spoke to his assistant, just for the hell of it. "I have a quick question," the mother said. "My nanny can't get pregnant. But she doesn't have any money and she's here illegally so I was wondering if …"

"Well, I don't know what we can do if she's here illegally. Has she filled out a patient questionnaire?"

The mother felt terrible. It was a mistake to mention her status, which now that she thought about it had nothing to do with it. It must, she realized, be possible to get pregnant without a social security number, people probably did it all the time. "I'd like to make an appointment for her," the mother said. "Send the patient questionnaire to my address."

When it came she sat on the couch with the nanny and went through the questions in a casual, upbeat tone, as if it were the most normal thing in the world.

"What was the date of the first day of your last period?" "Were you a DES baby?"

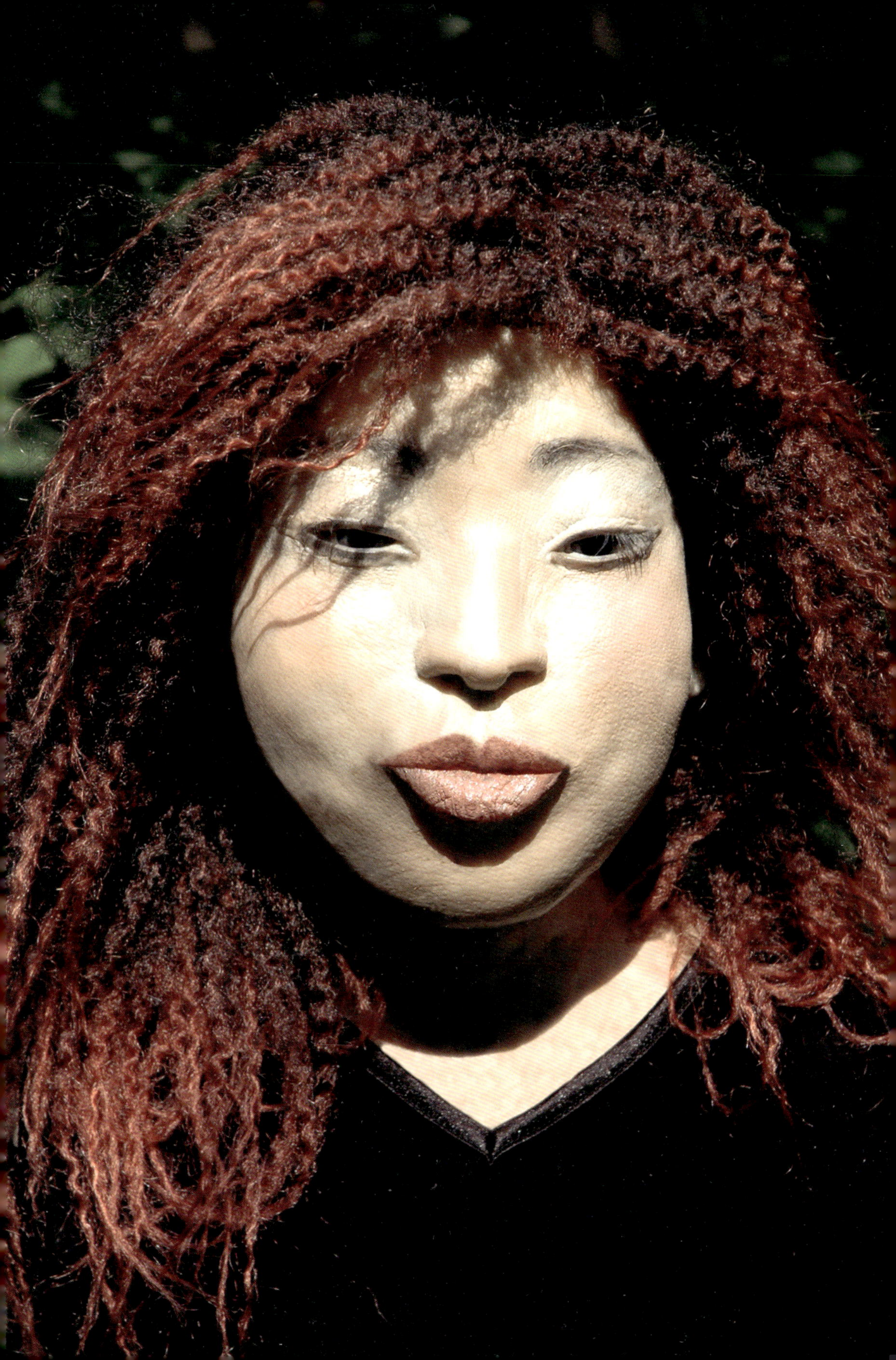

"Have you ever: had a hysterosalopinogram, traveled to another country, been implanted with an IUD?" The mother explained each question to the nanny. Now this was how to interview a nanny, the mother thought. Instead of *do you have references*, it should be, *have you ever been diagnosed with endometriosis?* And instead of *can you occasionally stay late if my husband and I have dinner plans or theater tickets*, it should be, *has your period ever been late or absent all together?*

"Number of births, number of abortions, number of miscarriages?" the mother read out loud.

She was about to write "none" when the nanny said, "I've had two abortions."

"Okay," the mother said, sportily.

"When I was in Guyana I had a boyfriend for many years and I got pregnant with him two times, you know. But my family is enemies with the man's family so they said I had to choose. They told me if I continued with that man no one in my family would ever speak to me again."

"So you didn't marry him?" the mother asked.

"No, I married the man my family had in mind for me. My family is very important to me, you know."

No, the mother didn't know. This was a tragic story with a terrible ending. It was like Romeo and Juliet without the happy relief of poison.

"Do you ever think of him?"

"Him, yes," the nanny said. "He is married now."

"So the problem could be your husband's sperm," the mother said, bitterly. "If you were able to get pregnant twice before."

"No, my husband has two big children in Guyana."

The mother felt crushed by this news. She lived with this man in the Bronx somewhere, his mother in the apartment upstairs. He did some sort of dangerous job clinging to the outside of office buildings like a fly. And the strange thing was she didn't seem at all unhappy; the whole family gathered to watch cricket matches from her country thanks to some sports cable package she had ordered. The mother had to almost admire the ability to enjoy something as stupid as cricket when she was forty and childless.

She tried to imagine her apartment, immaculately neat, the kitchen smelling of a fragrant, spicy fish stew. All the things the mother had sent home with her in shopping bags – un-used wedding presents, and birthday presents, a fifty-dollar candle from Barneys. For a moment the mother wondered if she was committing some kind of on-the-job sexual harassment, forcing the nanny to divulge her personal abortion stories like that. She tossed the questionnaire she had been holding onto a pile of papers trying to seem casual.

"Well, anyway we got this taken care of so we can just send it in and then decide what we want to do next." She scooped up the baby to say goodbye and was startled to see a mark on his forehead between his eyes. But it was just one of the nanny's sequins floating there like a bindi. They still hadn't fixed the vacuum and her sequins were everywhere but the mother liked that they were there. They were a little off-putting in their quantity, but cheerful, like the ladybugs that appeared in their apartment each July.

They sat in the waiting room, the mother in maternity workout pants and her unflattering apple green breastfeeding shirt and the nanny resplendent in a long peach skirt strung with sequins, a pale purple peasant blouse and beaded pointy Moroccan slippers. She always looked so rested and sparkling. The mother smelled her clothes before putting them on to see if they were clean or not, her small repertoire of nursing rags. And strapped to her feet, these terrible lesbian monstrosities she got for the sciatica of pregnancy. She'd seen them on the feet of another mother in the playground, they'd smiled conspiratorially at each other – so comfortable! – and she'd sworn to herself never to wear them again. Yet here they were on her feet again! Her bed sheets smelled of old leaked milk. There was never food in the house and soon the baby would be eating solids.

They had never been out together before. Although the mother had occasionally planned to propose a spontaneous outing – let's get manicures! – she had never actually gone through with it, and all their interactions had been in the apartment, the mother wrapped in the yellow towel, and the nanny looking so bright and put-together, almost joyous.

She had watched her in the park several times, talking easily to the other nannies. She had told the mother all about them, especially the one who turned out to be from the very same village where she was born! The mother had been to the playground dozens of times herself with the baby and had never made a single friend.

The mother looked each woman in the waiting room over, considering their chances. She hoped each and every one of them was completely infertile, in case that would improve the nanny's odds. Two were speaking a foreign language to each other from one of those icy blonde countries; the doctor's patients traveled to him from all over the world; there was a block of rooms permanently reserved at the Helmsley. One woman, who seemed to be there for her sister, had a little boy with her who looked to be about three with a mass of hair like ramen noodles.

The mother felt terrible that she had brought her own baby. How insensitive to rub it in their faces like that. No one wanted to see a beautiful baby when they were sitting in a place like that. The pain of infertility was like the pain of labor; when you held your baby in your arms in the end, you got amnesia. Her heart pounded. In just a few minutes she would see Dr. Heiffowitz again.

"Are you nervous?" she asked the nanny.

"Yes, I am nervous."

"I'm sorry if I got you into something you didn't really want," the mother said. It was an enormous relief to say it. She'd dreamed the night before that she had gotten her period, wiped herself and shown the nanny the blood on the toilet paper.

"Nobody ever talked about this with me before you. I'm very thankful. This is the kindest thing anyone has ever done for me."

"Well, I was very lucky and I just want you to have the same opportunity. Money shouldn't stand in the way …" The mother swatted back tears like tiny stinging gnats. She really did feel enormously relieved.

"You know I didn't get my period this month," the nanny said.

“What!” The mother reeled with excitement. She would give her all the baby’s outgrown gear.

“Yes, I feel very hopeful,” the nanny said.

The nanny’s name was called and the mother and the nanny both stood up. “I’m sorry the doctor will only see the patient alone,” the woman said. “Is that okay?” she asked the nanny.

“Okay, yes,” the nanny said.

“You sure it’s okay?” the mother asked, wide-eyed.

“Yes?” the nanny said.

“What about questions?”

“I wrote some down,” she said.

Of course. The mother remembered the Post-it. “Okay, I’ll wait here.”

“She’ll be in there at least three hours,” the woman said.

“Fine. I’ll just go home with the baby,” the mother said, feeling a little confused. “I’ll see you Friday.” Friday was the last day before they would both be leaving for their vacations. “Don’t be nervous …” There was nothing more she could do. It was out of her hands. The nanny followed the woman out of the waiting room, through the doors to the other side.

The mother sat back down for a moment, grabbed her purse from the seat next to her, and was about to stand up again to leave, when the little boy with the blonde curly hair started running recklessly around the waiting room in a circle. In the terrifying manner of Duck Duck Goose he began pointing at each woman as he passed her chair, screaming, “You’re my mommy, no, you’re my mommy, no, you’re my mommy, no, you’re my mommy.”

His mother begged him to stop – Pickle, no! – but he kept up the game. Each time his finger landed on her, the mother’s heart raced with joy, and each time he sped off to the next waiting prospective parent her heart clutched in desperation. All eyes were glued to the little boy. The women sat frozen, waiting to see how it would all end.

The mother went to the desk to pay. It was $1100 for the first visit and series of bloodwork. Feeling like she was in a 1950’s sitcom, she put it on her debit card so her husband wouldn’t find out.

“What did the doctor say?” the mother asked when the nanny walked in the door on Friday.

“He said I’m in menopause,” she said, and burst into tears. “I told my husband I wish we had gone to the doctor sooner. I didn’t know this was happening to me.”

“Wait,” the mother said. She couldn’t believe what she was hearing. There had to be a solution. But a great despair overcame her. “Do you get hot flashes?”

“Yes,” the nanny cried. “I get them so bad every night.”

Why hadn’t she told her that! “But you’re only forty,” the mother said, almost begging. Her own eyes had filled up with tears. She felt like she might get hysterical. She didn’t know what to do. “It’s still possible to get pregnant,” the mother said. Even now, she couldn’t stop herself. She should leave it alone, not say another word, but, “Plenty of women get pregnant after they’re in menopause.” The mother thought of the birth defects chart, the number forty written in red.

"I'm so sorry," the mother said. "This is terrible."

If she hadn't been illegal, they could take her with them to Paris. And she wouldn't just make her stay in the hotel the whole time like other mothers did with their nannies, they could shop together in the Marais while her husband stayed with the baby. But what if the trip coincided with her ovulation and she was taking her away right when she should be home conceiving? But of course that didn't matter now.

The mother went about her day completely flattened by the news. Menopause. The word echoed in her head mercilessly, making her sick to her stomach. She had the image of a man in a black cape swooping. A sort of grim reaper. Hot flashes. A missed period. Having no blood was the bloodiest ending of all.

All day she had the strange, clutching feeling of being abandoned.

She rushed home and felt relieved to see that the baby was fine in his exersaucer. The nanny was still there. The mother didn't know exactly what she was expecting, but she didn't think the nanny would be her same cheerful self, just going about things as if the end of the world hadn't happened.

"What are you going to do on your vacation?" the mother asked.

"My husband and mother-in-law and brother and I are going to Niagara Falls," the nanny said.

The mother was surprised. She had assumed the nanny would stay home depressed. Niagara Falls was where honeymooners went. It seemed so hopeful. But such a long drive and for what? Just to have a lookylou. It seemed so pointless. "Oh that's nice, it's beautiful there."

"Have you ever been?"

"Been, no."

The nanny took her envelope of cash from the cushioned bench, zipped her pocketbook and went to the door. "Okay bye then."

The mother thought of her and her family, probably in her brother's cab, singing songs and laughing, talking about cricket, sleeping in a cheap motel, eating delicious food they'd brought from home.

The nanny went to the door and opened it.

"Have a good time. Don't worry …" the mother started to say, but she was gone.

The mother stood alone, a feeling of panic setting in.

She could, the mother thought, run to the door and call to the nanny who was probably still waiting for the elevator, and ask if she could go to Niagara Falls with her. Inside, she felt like she was straining against something, grunting with effort, like the baby trying to break through the straps of his car seat. "Take me with you," she whispered.

She and the nanny – both still young! – standing on a ridge, wearing bright hooded rain slickers, laughing as the white foamy water sprayed their faces and frizzed their long hair. She sobbed, wiping her eyes with the flap of her nursing shirt. There was so much to do. She had to pack for Paris and give the baby a bath all by herself. Slowly, she dropped to the floor. Then, crawling on her hands and knees, she began to pick up the sequins one by one, in every room in the house. She lay on her stomach and stretched her arm underneath the crib, to get the last one.

Thalia Field

Anna Kingsford, Clothed in Clouds (1846-1888)

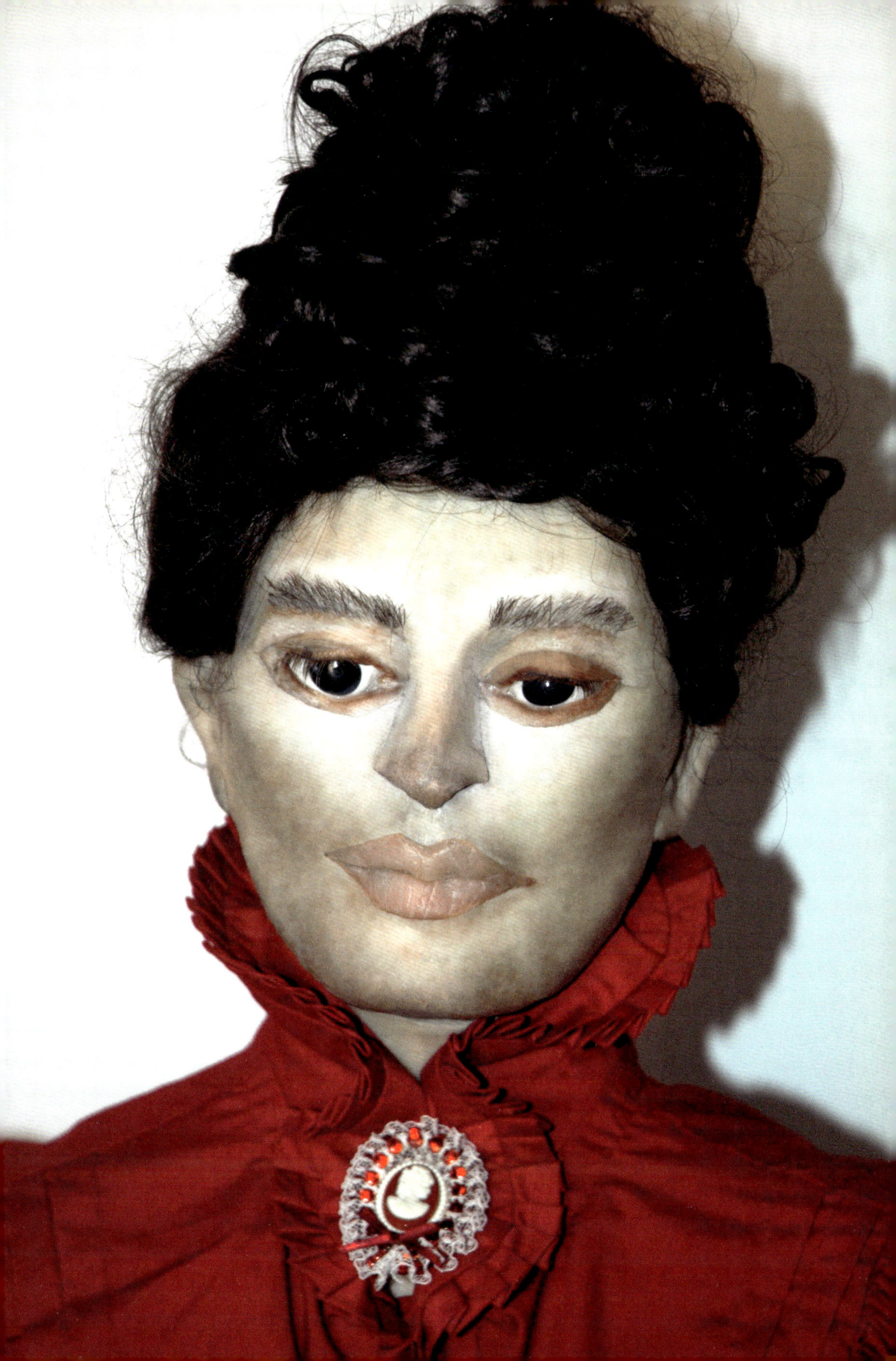

Anna Kingsford you were not quite made of skin. You told your story through a man's mouth. Or did you? It wasn't your husband, or lover, it was the divine touchless Adonai.

Anna Kingsford, clairvoyant, what could you see? Unconscious cerebrations, clothes in clouds, garments of intertwining threads.

How did you do that doctor's degree, with private tutors, and without going to the operating theater?

Anna Kingsford, you couldn't breathe, or could you?

Pain is pain, no matter the subject. Injustice, injustice, no matter the victim. Anna Kingsford, you knew the experience of the hunt on the fox. In Stratford in Essex, you were a fox named Annie Bonus, collapsing from exhaustion.

Anna Kingsford, a woman with horns, the beauty of an animal, the weakness of an animal. She had the strengths of an animal strapped to a table.

Anna Kingsford, a moon wandering to hell. You wrote a book at age seventeen, of a saint Beatrice "left almost alone, an orphan and a Christian, in the midst of a pagan people."

Annie Bonus, young Anna, with a habit of freezing the narrative to study Beatrice in a striking pose: the "motionless figure" tinted by moonlight "with a hue that made it appear rather like a piece of exquisite statuary than a living form."

Anna Kingsford, chasing oracles in dreams. "The night time of the body is the day time of the soul." Testing the influence of fasting on lucid dreams, which come in the waking hours of dawn, in the second sleep.

Dr. Anna Kingsford received her real teachings in these illuminations, in Paris during the years of her medical study, 1870's.

O the gadfly stings me again! I must move on, mad in the study of pain.

"If torture were indeed the true method of science, then would the vaunted tree of knowledge be no other than the upas tree of oriental legend, beneath whose fatal shadow lie hecatombs of miserable victims slain by its poisonous exhalations, the odor of which is fraught with agony and death!"

Anna Kingsford, you made appeal to the people of Paris.

Anna Kingsford, wife with a wife, child with a child, carrying your guinea pig, Rufus. This is not medicine as anyone would know it. You people the animals in their transcendent refusal. Animals are knowledge, and people should know how to rescue knowledge from the wrong questions.

Anna K, white cow crossing the night sea. Bosphorus.

AK, famished and fainting. Where does the frenzied road take you?

Doctor Bernard you are no doctor, no teacher of doctors, you are the gadfly which drives her mad, and madly she wanders the country to speak against your methods. Doctor or no doctor, she talks of white Magians, the knowledge of a pure soul, which cures the body's ills.

"An abominable crime is every day committed in your midst. Your magnificent city, which should be the support of civilization, is today the center of the most barbarous practices. Under the pretext of studying physiology, men devote themselves to the most cruel torture of inoffensive creatures who work for you and who love you; they inflict upon them the endurance of slow and painful agony in order to obtain, as they say, knowledge useful to humanity."

AK, you wrote your dreams and had stories.

Doctors, you are provoking a sick soul to madness with your tormenting. You are pursuing a wretched girl with your inflictions of suffering.

How can I help the animal escape this experiment? How can I not be such an animal cleaved with pain? Mask of a dog, tongue all the way out.

Anna Kingsford you thought you were Io, bigger than life, without the chance to breathe easily, an asthma forever pressing you to the ground. Move to higher ground, dryer ground. Rufus on your lap.

Anna Kingsford, accompanied. A husband for letting go. A man beside you, another older widowed man, to write your bio, to tell stories of Io.

Anna Kingsford, London can't train you as a doctor. Paris boasted. Anna, your daughter Aedith seems incompatible. What is it about her that you find so irritating? Rufus will go with you. A motherless creature and a mother without a child.

Io, lithe and beautiful. She made love with clouds. She was too much a man, she was hidden in a cow. She was never enough mother, she crossed the rivers. A horned virgin, mad-moon in a clearing sky. But other women felt jealous, she was a beautiful cow. A cow in heat. Lecturing on ugly things.

Anna Kingsford, does anyone love your fainting face? Does anyone love your angry face? You would kill some men but you will not cut into flesh.

The doctors assail her with animal screams, goading her forward.

Dr. Anna, or your mouth-man Edward Maitland, writing your diary with two right hands: "what of life remains to me I will live in doing my utmost against every form of cruelty; but it would be cruelty in me to condemn another like myself to the fruitless strife. So at least it seems to me. More and more every day it appears to my mind that I am not of this world. Visions float about me in the night that seem to warn me of some unknown change perhaps awaiting me. I do not know; but my state of mind of late has been singularly clear and expectant. I fancy that there is a Future, and that I am meant to have some special work beyond this plane of existence, something for which I have been put to school here."

Anna Kingsford, what is your rule of life?

"It seemed as though suddenly all the laboratories of torture throughout Christendom stood open before me, with their manifold unutterable agonies exposed, and the awful future an atheistic science was everywhere making for the world rose up and stared me in the face."

To win against the "modern inquisition," Anna Kingsford you had tongue and pen out – you longed for the words, "Mort de ..." Richet. Bert. Bernard. Pasteur.

"A method which is morally wrong cannot be scientifically right. The test of conscience is the test of soundness."

Anna Kingsford. Seizure. rue Jacob. Your first. Living as the niece of an unrelated man. "My malady has resolved itself into three symptoms – bleeding from the lungs, sickness and weakness."

Anna Kingsford, you know there's no cure in curare. "Not that, but for administering to horses and dogs hyperaesthetics, and for inflicting on them, when in this state of exalted sensitiveness, what is described by one of themselves, Claude Bernard, as the 'most atrocious suffering the mind of man can conceive.'"

Anna Kingsford, losing all consciousness in the fall to the floor. Lips ash-white. Heart stilled. What can you see from the floor as your body is rubbed back to life?

When you hear of Claude Bernard's death, murderous vindication, you might think the affliction has ended, the gadfly is dead.

Prometheus: "It is worth it to indulge in weeping over evil doings if one is likely to win the tribute of a tear from the listener."

Anna Kingsford, when you hear of Claude Bernard's death, you think you had much to do with it, your powerful will, and white magic.

Io: Zeus inflamed by passion's dart has called upon me to unite in divine union. Hiding in the pastures, I became animal, and spurred by the gadfly now toil with revealing this body of truths.

When she spoke, she heard herself moo. When she looked, she saw a cow and tried not to choke at this fat ugly version. Anna, did you like your jewels?

Chorus: What a tale to strike our ears with sufferings so hard to look upon or hear about; grievous to endure. We shudder to behold the plight of an animal.

Does it not seem that Gods are violent in their desire for union with the mortal maid – and in making her sick and vexed and galloping?

Anna Kingsford, called monstrous. Not-woman, not-man – they said – she couldn't pass the exams the first time. Wild grief lowings. Oestrus, the lunacy she mastered, in the mastery of esoteric interpretation.

Io: "Oh! Oh! Alas! Once again convulsive pain and frenzy, striking my brain, inflame me. Harrassing me. I am stung by the gadfly's barb, unforged by fire. My heart knocks at my ribs in terror; my eyeballs roll wildly round and round. I am carried out of my course by a fierce blast of madness; I've lost all mastery over my tongue, and a stream of turbid words beats recklessly against the billows of dark destruction.

[She departs from the company of Prometheus.]"

Half-woman, half-animal, Anna seizes in terror. Maddened by Claude Bernard's knives and straps, scalpels and muzzles, ovens and poisons.

Io: "Stung, sting, stung, torment of animals, to push her onward."

To amble, gad about, knock around, straggle, traipse, trek, tramp, roam, amble, bat around, meander, range, saunter. To live the apocalypse? To know a new age?

Anna K, you won't touch flesh. To cut or eat. There is a problem in the epistemology of the science: a girl unveiling – naked white stone for the eyes – a statue at the foot of the stairs – training in the medical school.

Dr. Anna Kingsford, you passed your test. "You may inform your opponents that, so far from your informant having failed to pass his examination – he – meaning she – has passed with the highest note, save one, attainable."

AK, your body barely moves as you seize.

Anna Kingsford, did you really have those dreams?

"This question of vivisection, which should be a burden upon the public conscience of nations, cannot be left to the caprice of men of science, and above all to a class of specialists who, professing materialism, boast of suppressing conscience, and of being independent of that which human morality may be able to sanction."

"Perhaps it will be said to you: 'This is a question of which science alone can judge, she only can decide its importance; public conscience has not part in this scheme of investigation.'"

"We maintain that the truth is contrary to such a proposition and that when science forgets what she owes to civilization, the public conscience must intervene to remind her of it."

"It is not a question of the public having not acquired the scientific spirit; it is, on the contrary, the case that scientists have lost the spirit of morality."

"We feel assured that you will join with us in bringing to an end a state of things which sullies and infringes public morality, and which will be the shame of our century."

Anna Kingsford you caught a cold, or some Karma, or you caught pneumonia visiting the labs of the devil Pasteur, rue d'Ulm, in the pouring rain. This malady lasted a good year, while your writing and lectures took you away.

Anna Kingsford, aka Rosamunda the Princess, aka the Virgin, aka the Martyr, aka the Hermetic Mystic, aka Killer of killers, aka Joan of Arc, aka Faustine, aka.

Anna Kingsford, your last days all bedsores and morphine and sleeplessness. "One of her last utterances was that she could carry on the work better from the other side, where she would be free of her physical limitations …"

The work of an animal is done to be just. Anna, you chose a cow. Did you like the paradox, being cursed by a god and chased by a question, a genius, an aeon?

AK, finally, you wrote with the power to persuade. Even a cow was someone's child, once someone's mother, the mother of all animals, she saw the problem clearly:

"It is precisely the subtle but enormous differences existing between the manifestations and characters of the nervous system as we see them in man and as we see them in other animals, which distinguishes the former from the latter, and which endows vivisectors with the legal right they now posses to inflict on anthopoid apes injuries and mutilations which, if they inflicted the same on men, would be held to render the perpetrators guilty of crime. When, therefore, it is understood that this occult nervous differentiation is capable of constituting a distinction so vast, how is it possible to suppose that the study of biological function in the beast is capable of explaining satisfactorily the mysteries of human life?"*

*Anna Kingsford, "Unscientific Science: The Moral Aspects of Vivisection."

Mei-mei Berssenbrugge

The Four Year Old Girl

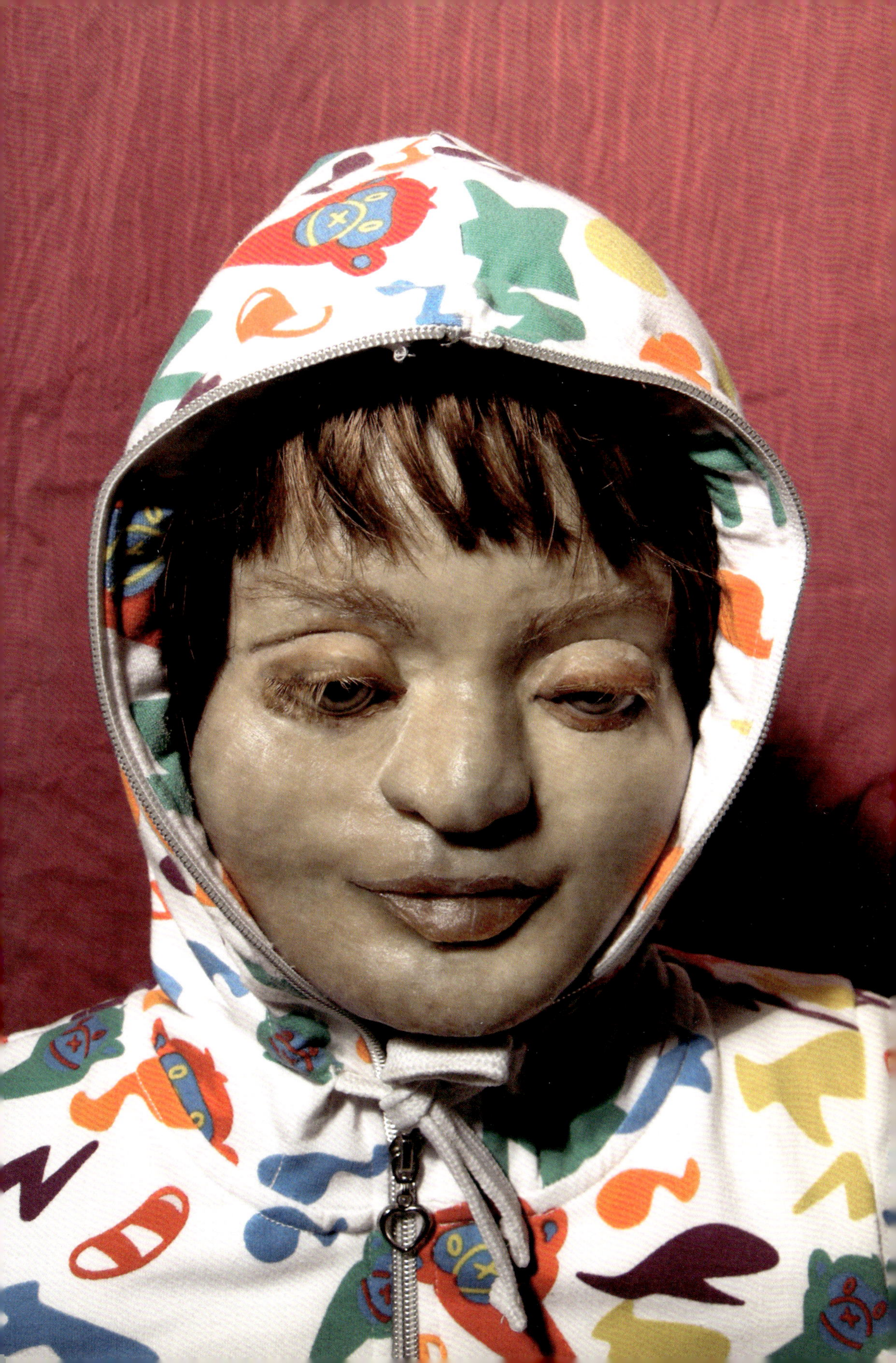

1

The "genotype" is her genetic constitution.

The "phenotype" is the observable expression of the genotype as structural and biochemical traits.

Genetic disease is extreme genetic change, against a background of normal variability.

Within the conventional unit we call subjectivity due to individual particulars, what is happening?

She believes she is herself, which isn't complete madness, it's belief.

The problem is not to turn the subject, the effect of the genes, into an entity.

Between her and the displaced gene is another relation, the effect of meaning.

The meaning she's conscious of is contingent, a surface of water in an uninhabited world, existing as our eyes and ears.

You wouldn't think of her form by thinking about water.

You can go in, if you don't encounter anything.

Though we call heavy sense impressions stress, all impression creates limitation.

I believe opaque inheritance accounts for the limits of her memory.

The mental impulse is a thought and a molecule tied together, like sides of a coin.

A girl says sweetly, it's time you begin to look after me, so I may seem lovable to myself.

She's inspired to change the genotype, because the cell's memory outlives the cell.

It's a memory that builds some matter around itself, like time.

2

Feelings of helplessness drove me to fantastic and ridiculous extremes.

Nevertheless, the axis of her helplessness is not the axis I grasp when I consider it a function of inheritance.

Chromatin fails to condense during mitosis.

A fragile site recombines misaligned genes of the repeated sequence.

She seems a little unformed, gauze stretches across her face, eyelids droop.

When excited, she cries like a cat and fully exhibits the "happy puppet" syndrome.

Note short fingers and hypoplastic painted nails.

Insofar as fate is of real order here, signifying embodiment, the perceived was present in the womb.

A gap or cause presents to any apprehension of attachment.

In her case, there's purity untainted by force or cause, like the life force.

Where, generically, function creates the mother, in this case it won't even explain this area.

She screams at her.

A species survives in the form of a girl asking sweetly.

Nevertheless, survival of the species as a whole has meaning.

Each girl is transitory.

3

Her focus extends from in front of her into distance, so she's not involved in what she looks at.

Rhodopsin in the unaffected gene converts photons to retinal impulse, so she sees normally for years.

The image, the effects of energy starting from a real point, is reflected on a surface, lake or area of the occipital lobe.

You don't need the whole surface to be aware of a figure, just for some points of real space to correspond to effect at other points.

There's an image and a struggle to recognize reception of it.

She sees waves and the horizon as if she were water in the water.

The mother's not looking at her daughter from the place from which the daughter sees her.

She doesn't recognize abnormal attributes.

The daughter resolves her mother as fire in the woods, red silk.

In the waiting room, she hopes a large dog will walk up to her, be kind and fulfill her wishes.

Between what occurs by chance and, "Mother, can you see I'm dying?" is the same relation we deal with in recurrence.

Is not what emerges from the anxiety of her speech their most intimate relation, beyond death, which is their chance?

Obedience to one's child is anxious, heartfelt, but not continuous, like a white mote in her eye.

Within the range of deteriorating sight, in which sight will be her memory, disobedience moves toward unconsciousness.

4

Her skull is large and soft to touch.

The thoracic cavity small, limbs short, deformed and vertebrae flattened.

All the bones are under-mineralized.

Bluish light surrounds her.

This theme concerns her status, since she doesn't place her inheritance in a position of subjectivity, but of an object.

Her X-ray teems with energy, but locked outside material.

One creates a mouse model of human disease by disrupting a normal mouse gene in vitro, then injecting the mutated gene into host embryos.

DNA integrated into the mouse genome is expressed and transmitted to progeny.

Like touch, one cell can initiate therapy.

The phenotype, whose main task is to transform everything into secondary, kinetic energy, pleasure, innocence, won't define every subject.

The mother's genotype makes a parallel reality to her reality, now.

She stands over her and screams.

That the exchange is unreal, not imaginary, doesn't prevent the organ from embodying itself.

By transferring functional copies of the gene to her, he can correct the mutant phenotype, lightly touching the bad mother, before.

5

On her fourth birthday, a rash on the elbow indicated enzyme deficiency.

Her view folded inward.

Ideas about life from experience are no use in the unfolding of a potential, empty and light, though there's still potential for phenomena to be experienced.

A moment of seeing can intervene like a suture between an image and its word.

An act is no longer structured by a real that's not caught up in it.

Instead of denying material, I could symbolize it with this mucus and its trailings.

The moment the imaginary exists, it creates its own setting, but not the same way as form at the intuitive level of her mother's comprehension.

In all comprehension, there's an error, forgetting the creativity of material in its nascent form.

So, you see in her eyes her form of compassion for beings who perceive suffering as a real substrate.

6

Mother must have done something terrible, to be so bereaved.

Ambiguity of a form derives from its representing the girl, full of capability, saturated with love.

If the opposite of possible is real, she defines real as impossible, her real inability to repeat the child's game, over and over.

Parallel woven lines of the blanket extend to water.

Just a hint of childish ferocity gives them weight.

At night, inspiration fell on her like rain, penetrating the subject at the germline, like a navel.

Joy at birth, a compaction of potential and no potential, is an abstraction that was fully realized.

Reducing a parent to the universality of signifier produces serene detachment in her, abstract as an electron micrograph of protein-deplete human metaphase DNA.

Its materiality is a teletransport of signified protoplasm across lineage or time, avid, muscular and compact, as if pervasive, attached to her, in a particular matriarchy of natural disaster, in which the luminosity of a fetal sonogram becomes clairvoyant.

The love has no quantity or value, but only lasts a length of time, different time, across which unfolds her singularity without compromising life as a whole.

Elizabeth Hand

Up North

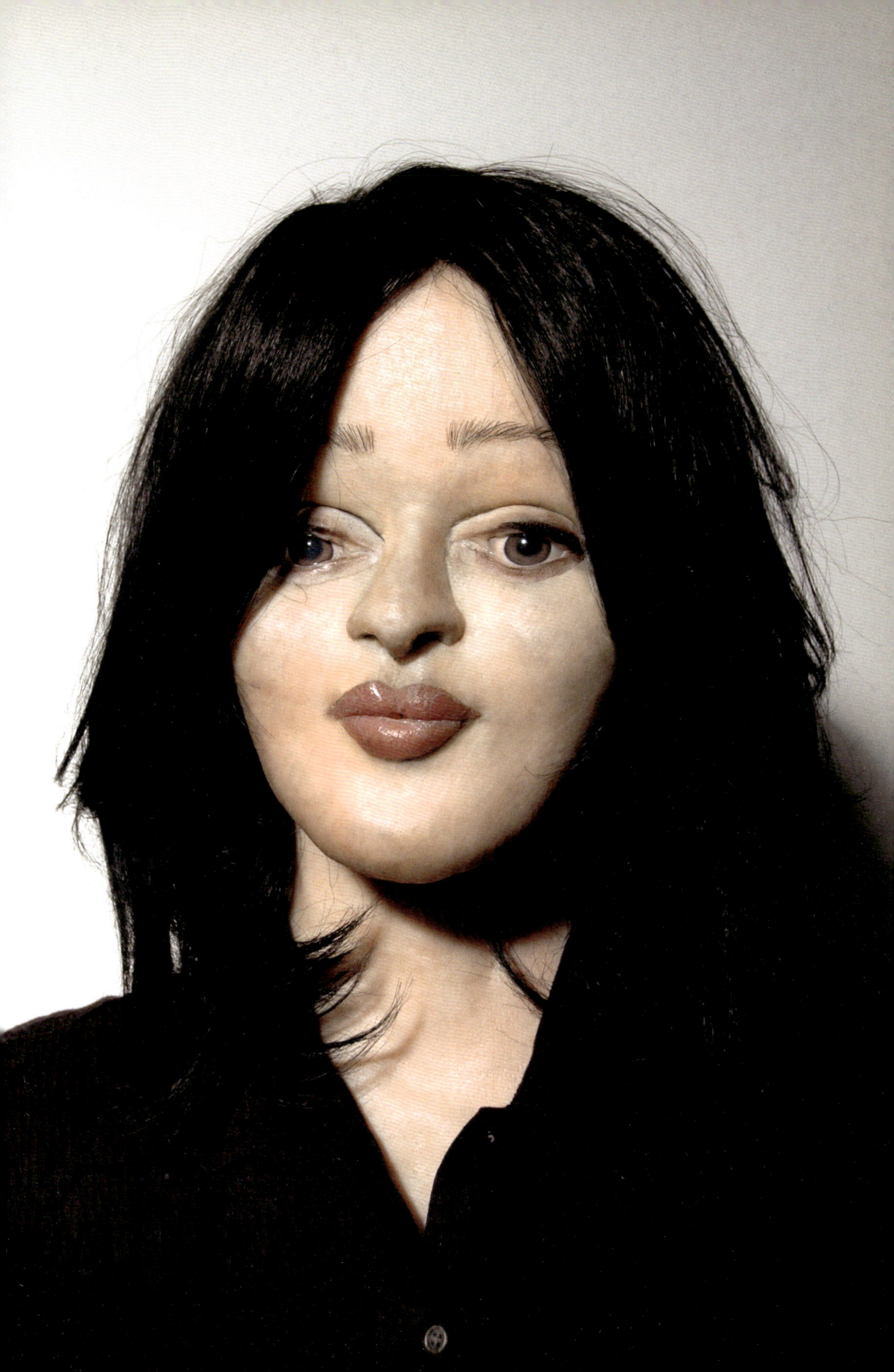

She left him in the hotel asleep, curled in bed with his fist against his mouth, face taut as though something bit at him. Cigarette ash on the carpet, laptop's eye pulsing green then fading into darkness.

Outside on the sidewalk, shards of broken glass. The night before the streets had chimed with the sound of bottles shattering, laughter, men shouting. Women stumbled along the curb, boys pissed on storefronts.

This morning, nothing. The broken glass was gone. There were few cars, no other people. The sky was gray and rainlashed, clouds whipped by wind so strong it tore the beret from her head. She stumbled into the street to retrieve it then stood, gazing at a rent in the sky that glowed brighter than the sea glimpsed a few blocks to the north, between blocks of apartments and construction equipment. Overhead a phalanx of swans hung nearly motionless, beaten by the gale. With a sound like creaking doors they swooped down. She saw their legs, blackened twigs caught in a flurry of white and downy grey, before as one they veered toward the ocean.

She headed east, to the outskirts of the city. The streets were narrow, cobblestone; the low buildings a jumble of Art Deco, modernist boxes, brick spidered with graffiti in a language she couldn't decipher.

In the windows of posh clothing designers, rows of faceless mannequins in hooded black woolens, ramrod straight, shoulders squared as though facing the firing squad. No dogs, no cats. The air had no scent, not the sulfurous stink of the hotel shower, not even diesel exhaust. Now and then she caught the hot reek of burning grease from a shuttered restaurant. There were no trees.

As she approached the central intersection the gale picked up and rain raced through the street, a nearly horizontal band that filled the gutters to overflowing. She darted up three steps to stand beneath an awning, watched as the cobbles disappeared beneath water that gleamed like mercury then ebbed as the rain moved on.

In another half-hour she reached the city's edge. Beyond the highway, a broad manmade declivity held a stadium, scattered concrete outbuildings, a cluster of leafless trees. She stood for a few minutes, watching SUVs barrel past; then crossed the street and started back to the hotel.

She had gone only a few blocks when the wind carried to her a sweet, musky smell, like incense. She halted, turned her face toward the sea and saw set back from a row of houses a tangle of overgrown hedges, their formless bulk broken by a dozen or so trees. Frowning, she tugged at the collar of her pea coat, then walked towards them.

In the distance she could see the frozen lava fields that ringed the city, an endless waste of ragged black like shattered tarmac, crusted with lichen and pallid moss. Here, sidewalk and cobblestones gave way to sodden turf ringed by skeletal bushes thick with plastic bags, crumpled newsprint; spotted, diseased-looking leaves that rattled in the wind.

Yet despite the coming winter, the trees – birches – had shafts of pliant green growth at their tips. It was these she had smelled, and as she drew nearer their scent grew so strong she could taste it at the back of her throat, as though she'd inhaled pollen. She coughed, wiping her eyes, looked down and saw something in a tufted yellow patch at the base of one tree. A dead bird, a bit larger than her hand and lying on its side, head bent toward its breast so it formed a pied comma, roan and beryl-green. She crouched to look at it more closely. Her tongue cleaved to the roof of her mouth, the taste of pollen froze into copper, saltwater. She picked up a twig and tentatively poked the small form, instinctively recoiled though its sole motion was in response to her prodding. Its skin jeweled with scales that gleamed palest green in the light, tiny withered arms folded like a bat's wings against the russet hollow where its chest had been eaten away by insects or rodents. Its face sunken, eyes tightly shut and jaws parted to bare a ridge of minute teeth and a black tongue coiled like a millipede. When she stroked it, strands of long reddish hair caught between her fingers. Long afterward, her hand smelled at once sweet and faintly sour, like rotting apples. Where she touched it, her finger blistered then scarred. It never properly healed.

Diana George

Diment and Wondratschek

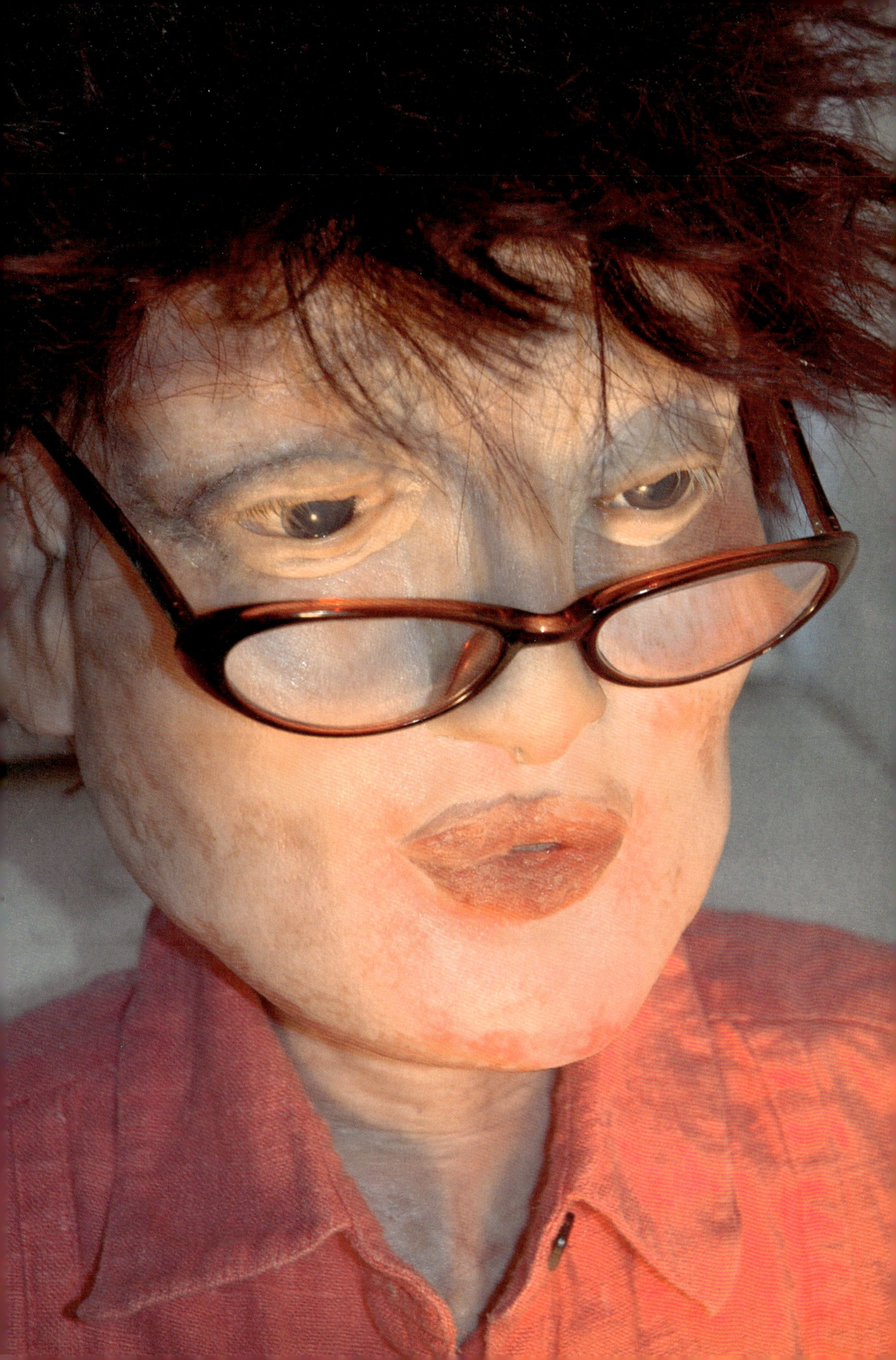

Both of us had settled for hospital work. Alone in our stenograph closets, we listened to the proceedings of operating theaters and consulting rooms. We were careful to distinguish speech from sobs, as instructed. We asked ourselves why we ought to transcribe the one but not the other.

We took to spending the lunch hour together, throwing rusks to the filthy canalside gulls and planning our conjoint future: a house in the country, a modest living, time enough for books and study and conversation. "How much there is to know!" we exclaimed. "How much there is to research!" When we had no more rusks, the gulls chivvied and cried. The conclusion presented itself as always: "Making a living takes all our time," we said. Under winter's dim noonday sun, we walked arm in arm past bare, pollarded chestnut trees and over the bridge that led us back to our separate hospitals.

It was a mistake to let Eduardowa persuade me to leave the city. In the cafeteria of Eduardowa's hospital, the Veterans', I nibbled at a prune torte while Eduardowa made her case. Nibbling, too, was a mistake, considering what we have since been expected to choke down: the chaff, the rinds, the cloudy reeking whey.

"Listen to me, Irini," Eduardowa said. "A new dynamism is at work in the world. A new electricity, so to speak. In a word, privatization."

I demurred. There were thieves of every kind, inside the government and out. My downstairs neighbor had shot himself again. That was the kind of thing. It was more like chaos than electricity.

"Misery only confirms what I am saying," Eduardowa said.

Had I not been miserable, all those hours alone in my stenograph closet? I agreed to leave with Eduardowa. A host of further mistakes followed.

Diffuse glare filled the sky the day we arrived at Ore-Works Hostel. The horizon blurred under soughing exudates of industry: ash and slag of mines, smelters, railcar factories, nuclear generators. Only the ore-works stood idle.

A mile of rutted road separated works and hostel. Even when new, the works had not merited construction of its own dormitory, nothing modern in cement or stone, only this wood-framed quondam manor house that listed further with each spring thaw. Gutter-spouts had yawed free; rain and rot left mineral-white streaks down dark clapboards. Above the doorway, a sign of enameled tin was nailed to the lintel, "Ore-Works Hostel." Stapled to the door a yellow notice proclaimed a grade of "3" during the hostel's inspection last autumn by the Tick-Borne Infections Institute.

There were no guests for us to see to that first day. The hostel would often be empty, Eduardowa explained, "due to conflicting logics of production, plus time." Eduardowa said such frequent idleness would suit our rhythms of study and discovery; the less we worked for the hostel, the more we could work for ourselves.

Even without guests, hostel work would not be easy. Vapors issued from the drains. Chimney fittings had loosened or flues stuck; there were smuts and soot-drifts in the corners of the rooms. We noted these and other difficulties, but did not apply ourselves to them right away. Eduardowa claimed the attic for our quarters and laboratory, and there we shook out a counterpane and took our rest.

Eduardowa convoked our first research meeting the next morning. Our laboratory was sparsely appointed: from the Veterans' hospital Eduardowa had filched some surgical instruments, including one that looked like a lyre and another like a bellows done in dull steel. I hoped one day we might have nameplates on our desks, such as doctors have, or a sign on our door:

I. Diment & E. Wondratschek
RESEARCHERS

"To begin with, we will observe you," said Eduardowa. "What are your ideas, your sensations? You yourself hardly know."

I looked out a gable window partly obscured with a mottled coating of ore-dust. In the distance were the works' pale tanks and silos, stippled with corrosion. I hadn't known we were to choose a research topic in advance. I suggested studying a society in miniature; we could observe ants, or snails.

"I don't see any use in observing ants or snails," Eduardowa said.

I did not mind conceding the point where ants were concerned; their teeming and roiling did not really interest me, either. The observation of snails, however, might have been rewarding. Given its creeping pace, snail society must be without war or commerce as we know them; only later, coming upon glittery traces in the leaf-mold, does one snail sense another's long-past presence, a passing gravely acknowledged with the slow dip of a horned head.

"What are you thinking now?" asked Eduardowa. "What do you feel?"

I did not know what to say.

"Come," said Eduardowa. "You want solitude, to sharpen your self-awareness." She headed down the stairs, and I followed. On the second floor Eduardowa stopped before a sealed room and began removing electrical tape from around the doorjamb.

"Are you sure?" I asked.

"Solitude will return you to the inwardness of childhood, which is the age of genius," said Eduardowa. "You'll be much more keenly aware of your ideas and sensations." With her left hand now encased in a bulky mitt of tape, she motioned for me to enter the room.

She shut the door behind me.

What would I say later, when Eduardowa asked me to report? I was not thinking or feeling anything; a fretful nullity had overtaken me. I walked the length of the room, along a row of iron bunk beds. The mattresses had been folded in thirds and bound with twine. The research was going wrong already. I had pictured myself performing experiments alongside Eduardowa: hours of companionable silence in the laboratory, evenings of long debate before the hearth. I paused by one of the top bunks to tug at a piece of twine; a bullet-headed insect crept out from the mattress and down a rusted coil. I thought about how, later, I would say to Eduardowa, "A fretful nullity overtook me." I heard, without hearing, my voice catch and break as I described the loneliness I had endured. Eduardowa would say, "Hush, hush now," and bring me a chipped mug of milky tea. Already my tears welled up in anticipation of Eduardowa's tenderness.

Eduardowa came in.

"Get hold of yourself," Eduardowa said. "We have visitors downstairs."

"I am Mr. Trutschlow, the assistant," said one of the men at the front door. He leaned forward, a cane in each hand, his right trouser-cuff loose around a peg of steel capped in rubber like the canes. A second man stood behind him, younger, heavier, and dressed in a stained white smock. He towered above Trutschlow, if only because he stood straight.

Trutschlow moved each cane and leg and peg singly, checking for purchase. The younger man followed, resting one hand on the back of Trutschlow's neck and the other on Trutschlow's right hip. When both men had crossed the hostel's threshold, the younger man abruptly stepped away, releasing Trutschlow. The younger man wore a look of satisfaction, as if Trutschlow's remaining upright were a parlor trick that redounded to his, rather than Trutschlow's, credit.

"Mr. Trutschlow's leg was lost," said the younger man. "At sea."

"My nurse, Nana," said Trutschlow, making something like a gesture of introduction, but without letting either cane leave the floor. The half-gesture induced a wobble; the nurse stilled it, stroking him.

"You will let me know if you require assistance," said Trutschlow. "Or if you have anything at all to turn over to the ore-works consortium: receipts, inventories, an account of how you are using your time."

"We are making observations about solitude," I said.

"Oh?" said Trutschlow.

Eduardowa did not give me a chance to elaborate. She said, "We'd like to know when the consortium expects to re-open the ore-works. Has a date been set?"

"The works are 'open' now, in a sense. Value is being extracted in a different mode at present. You will be kept apprised, if need be. Meanwhile, I hardly need remind you, this is not free time; you have a job before you, readying the hostel for workers. Some of the rooms have not been opened since the last fumigation. – Nana, I am ready."

The nurse undertook a complex series of maneuvers to get Trutschlow turned around and out the door again.

So this was hostel-keeping; I thought I had acquitted myself well. Later, Eduardowa explained to me what I had done wrong, and I was given more time in the solitude room, to learn from my mistake.

A winter with scarcely any snow passed into an uncommonly wet spring on the plain, and still the works did not re-open, though other, more distant factories choked the air as before. Wolves, ill-nourished, insomniac, coughed and yipped all night in the rain. We, too, had begun to suffer: The meat was gone and the groats had spoiled. The requests we handed over to Trutschlow were many; the remittances and assurances he brought us, few.

Of my solitude, I continued to report only "nullity" and "loneliness." These did not arouse Eduardowa's sympathy, nor did they dissuade her from sending me into the solitude room. Eduardowa assured me this was a phase; in me, something was preparing itself to be born, something rich in possibilities for research. "As the outside world recedes, so your inner world will develop," Eduardowa said. To this end, Eduardowa bound a sash over my eyes and stuffed my ears with paraffin-soaked cotton wool. I spent entire days so, and not only in the solitude room. All vision one black-green, all audition dull percussion, I awaited my inner world.

I was just where Eduardowa had left me, on a bench in the hostel's muddy courtyard, when I heard a muffled voice. I removed my blindfold and earplugs. Trutschlow was seated next to me.

"… and he will end by killing me," said Trutschlow.

"Who will?" I asked.

"Nana."

"A strange name for a man," I said. A pullet stood with unnatural stillness by the front gate. To economize, we had fed the hens the spoiled groats. It was not long before a rheumy flux streamed from the hens' beaks. They gasped, as if on the verge of speech. This pullet alone had survived the brood's descent into cannibalism.

"He makes me call him Nana," said Trutschlow. "The humiliations he forces on me – the degrading acts! You cannot imagine."

"Perhaps you had better find another nurse." The pullet did not cluck or strut or scratch. I had the impression it wanted to lie down.

"Nana is the consortium's creature, not mine. I asked for medical leave; I got Nana instead. I dread his crooning solicitude, his ministering hands, his 'treatments.' How healthy my former state of sickness seems to me now."

Trutschlow thrust his prosthetic leg straight out before him; its foot or tip was clotted with mud. He tried to use one of his canes, also muddy, to prize away the clots, but the array of limbs overmastered him, and the cane slipped from his grasp. I retrieved it just in time; Trutschlow was listing.

"You do have difficulty getting around," I said. "Don't you find Nana helpful?"

"Nana does not help; Nana harms. How do you think my leg was 'lost'?"

Eduardowa and Nana came out the hostel's front door together. Nana went to Trutschlow and ran his hands over Trutschlow's stump, plucking, tugging, smoothing. He chided Trutschlow for sitting improperly and letting his asymmetry worsen. Eduardowa leaned down to me and murmured a scolding; I ought not to have removed my earplugs and blindfold.

That night Eduardowa served a roast for supper – a scorched and shriveled beet.

"Your inner world is turning out to be something of a blind alley," Eduardowa said as she carved. "We must stop forcing it, at least for now."

Here was another chance to contribute to the direction of our research; I was again unprepared.

"We have focused overmuch on ideas, to the neglect of sensations," said Eduardowa. She handed me a notebook. "I have made a system of signs; learn it, and then we can begin the new phase of our research."

I opened the notebook. On the first page were two columns: signs and words. The caret meant "dull"; the doubled virgule, "sharp"; the vertical line, "stabbing"; the horizontal line, "aching." There were signs for radiating pain, for throbbing, searing, and crushing pain. I turned the page; on this and all subsequent pages, two figures had been drawn, two women, simply and without any detail. Or, a single woman in two views, front and back.

Our days were busy with experiment from then on.

Difficulties beset the research almost immediately: There was no provision for marking the little figure with a suffering perceived as "delicious" or "annihilating." Then, too, Eduardowa hadn't invented any middle notes, hadn't anticipated that between the searing and the crushing pain we might need symbols for plainer sensations, such as "knouted, soundly." We adjusted the system, more than once, and went onward.

We could not keep ourselves from the laboratory, not for a single day. Even when I was too saturated to endure anything further, there were still results to annotate: swoons, and lineaments, and the sensation of having my heart outside myself. Often the just proportion of sign and figure could be hinted at only by blacking out the entire page.

Eduardowa was witness to all my sensations twice over, in the laboratory and in the notebook. Just one thing rankled me, and that only a little: that I had to endure and observe at the same time. As on gray summer days when you cannot decide whether you are hot or cold, I suspected that I was unhappy, but I was not sure.

We had Trutschlow and Nana over to supper. We served the pullet, boiled, along with the very last onion. Trutschlow and Nana brought fermented whey. A fire sputtered in the ore-stove. No one spoke of the works' re-opening. For some time now, we had stopped giving accounts and requests to Trutschlow, just as he had stopped promising to relay them to the consortium. All these renunciations brought a terrible gaiety to the evening.

After the meal came an entertainment of Trutschlow's devising: a pantomime of *Robinson Crusoe*, with Trutschlow and myself in the principal roles. We went into the kitchen, the better to make an entrance. Trutschlow showed me his right hand. His little finger had been excised and the stump wrapped in dirty gauze.

Trutschlow said, "You have to get away from Eduardowa. And you have to take me with you."

"I am not like you," I said.

"But I was once like you."

I told Trutschlow it was curtain time. We entered the dining hall, and I helped Trutschlow onto a table where I covered him with a sheet. Crusoe, played by me, stood on the deserted shore, nothing but a rock in drapery for companionship. Crusoe cycled through shock, anguish, and resolve. Then, as had not occurred in rehearsal, Trutschlow remained upright while he flung off the sheet to reveal that Crusoe was no longer alone. Now Friday went to work: Friday farced the whale pemmican; Friday built a palm-thatched folly; Friday put knife to whetstone and bade Crusoe sit and be barbered. The gestures were somewhat vague, but Trutschlow gave an unmistakable impression of purpose.

Trutschlow had written an unfair number of interior or mental actions for me to pantomime. Crusoe, witness to Friday's labors, suffered a master's "debilitating ennui." As Friday repeatedly approached and evaded Crusoe's domination, ennui overflowed its channel, became "something else." In Crusoe's soul, an "obscene rubbing" began.

For the climax, Friday gripped the knife and Crusoe rose from the barber-chair. The two castaways stood facing one another. Trutschlow's script called for the greatest stage-craft here. "The neutral expression is the height of pantomime," he had told me during rehearsal. "It is best achieved by concentrating on the phrase, 'Nothing in the eyes, nothing in the mouth.' " We would hold our neutral expressions a very long time, and so plant these questions in the spectators' minds: Why this death-bound theater of mastery and surrender? Could not all our hardening and melting have some other end?

I do not know what seized me. Against all miming precepts, and against Trutschlow's script, I called out, "Nothing in the eyes! Nothing in the mouth!" The audience of two applauded. Crusoe helped Friday climb down from the island and into the sea. Trutschlow, enraged by my betrayal, fled to the kitchen, where he remained while I returned for two more curtain calls.

Eduardowa opened the ore-stove and doused the fire with dregs of whey. The embers hissed. The night's gaiety recommenced, still more terrible than before.

Even with the help of the notebook, I do not remember everything that happened after I ruined Trutschlow's pantomime. I recall a clarity of purpose, and a pleasure neglected since our days as hospital stenographers. I recall sitting next to Eduardowa, the notebook open across our laps, as Nana brought Trutschlow back to the stage. While Nana made ready, Eduardowa crossed out the heading at the top of her page, "Irini: Pathography," and on my side of the notebook I did the same. The little figure was feminine and was not missing any limbs, but it would do.

As Eduardowa and I transcribed, everything was suspended in air like motes, like spangles: the word "cut," the word "shatter," sensations of pain and terror and dissolution. The motes grew heavy and began to fall. They covered us like a snowdrift and sealed us in our destination.

Svetlana Boym

X-treme Intimacy

Excerpt from the novel *X-treme Intimacy*

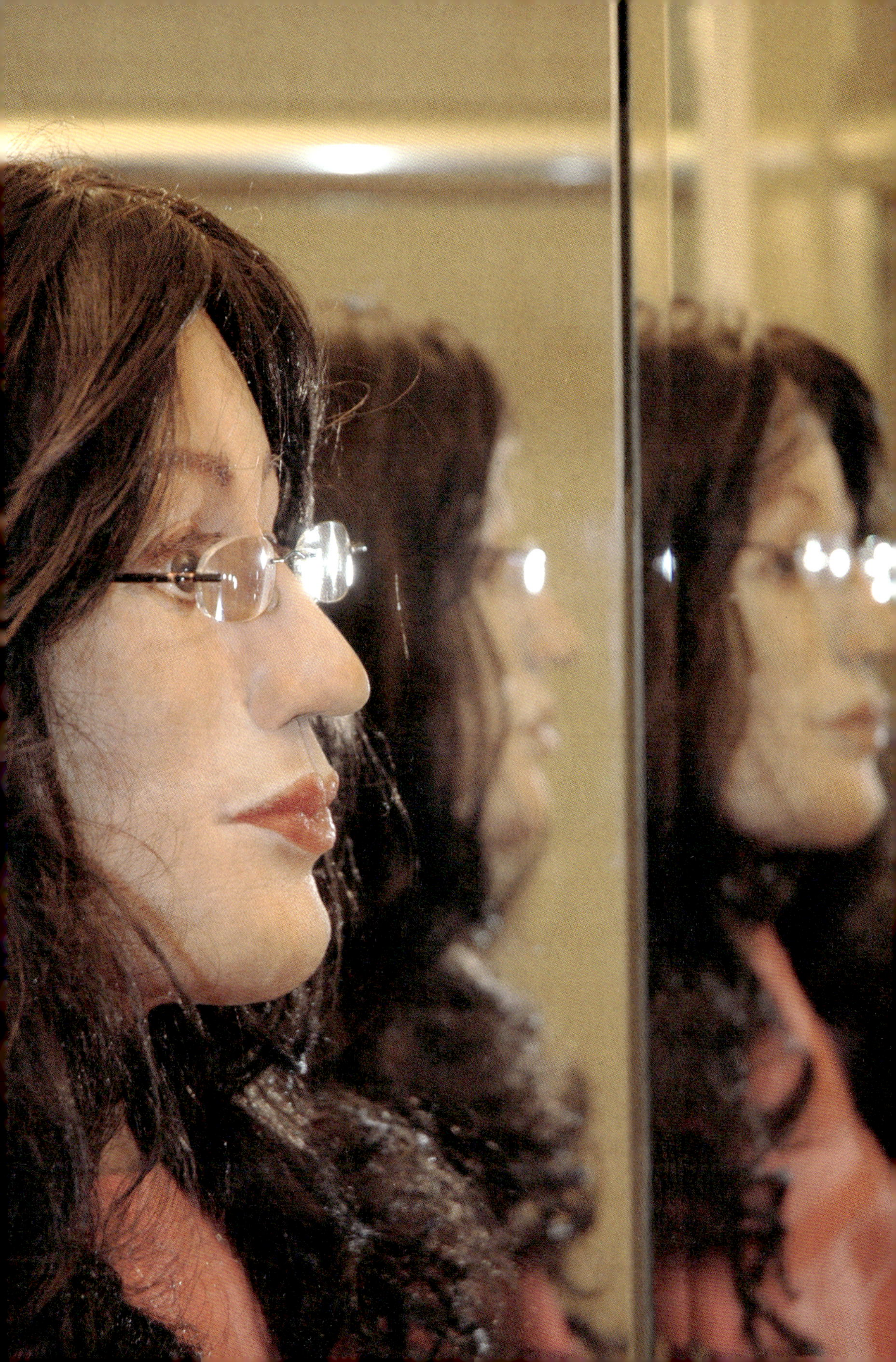

– You know, we met before, says a perky radiologist.
– Are you sure?
– Yes. I recognize your bones.

There are extreme makeovers, why not extreme intimacy? Let me offer you my X-ray on the first date. The connective tissue forming the major portion of my vertebra is in front of you. I have nothing to hide. It is semirigid, I admit, but porous too, leaving space for hope. Sometimes excessively so.

In the old days the doctors were looking for a nostalgic bone. Wherever mine is, it's badly broken. Don't get me wrong. Broken heart has nothing to do with this. I am not nostalgic for my riverside hometown half-drowned in its own reflection, I long instead for all the escape trips that never came to be. Now that my fractured right leg lies high up on three pillows defying the force of gravity in excruciating pain, I have to resign myself to the safety of virtual wanderlust.

Dear busy friend, no need to get distracted by the penumbra of my flesh. Forget the shades of grey and prickly nerve endings. I am not offering you superficial intimacy, skin-deep and time-sensitive like affections of a moody lover.

I know that you want to go to the marrow of the matter and examine the bare essentials. Hold on to my X-files, see for yourself. Examine the crooked timber of my off-white tibia. Next time I stumble upon you on the crowded riverbank, you could look straight through me and say: "We met before, I recognize your bones."

1. The Diary of Pain

Handout. (For hospital use only.)

How would you grade your pain on a scale of ten?

10 – 9 *The worst pain you've ever had. This is the kind of pain that would prompt you to call an ambulance to bring you the emergency room*

8 – 7 *Horrible. Pain that is present when you're sitting still. You don't even want to eat (possibly can't sleep)*

6 – 5 *Distressing. Pain that interferes with fun and also with work*

4 – 3 *Moderate, pain that interferes with doing fun things*

2 – 1 *Mild. Very little pain. The types of minor aches and pains that most people associate with getting old.*

0 *No pain at all.*

Pain Symptoms for Patients who Can't Communicate

Facial expressions*: Grimace, frown, eyes closed tight*

Verbalizations*: Moan, groan, grunt, sigh, call out, breathe noisily*

Body movements*: Rigid, tense, fidget, pace, restricted movement or change in movement or gait*

Behavior changes*: Restless, agitated, not sleeping, refusing food*

Mental status*: Frequent crying, irritability, confusion*

Determine Patient Pain Control Goals

How would you grade your pain on the scale of ten?

– Akh …

– Is it that bad, honey?

– Nurse … Susan …

– It's Marion, dear. Susan works the night shift

– Nurse … Marion, it hurts lots. No, no. I do speak English. I am verbalizing. Morphine. Please.

I push the button by the left side of my hospital bed and feel the warmth of morphine going down my veins. I can talk to you for six minutes before the pain returns.

The nurse lifts the mummy of my leg, moves it around in a matter-of-fact way, arranging the pillows underneath and offering me a "fanny," which I first mistake for another friendly caretaker with permed hair and kindly wrinkled face. My leg has an existence of its own outside my control, I feel that I'm lying in bed with a bundled up voodoo doll that shoots exclamation marks into my body.

– Oh dear, says the nurse. Your X-rays are just back. You've got a tibia and fibula fracture in your right leg. Ten weeks in the cast and ten more for the full recovery … five months if you're lucky. It's like in that black-and-white movie with Jimmy Stewart … Remember, he looks out of the window and things just start to happen … it's right there on the tip of my tongue but I won't remember it now. He's a photographer or a journalist.

What is it that you do for living?

– I'm … a journalist … a foreign correspondent

– Oh that must be very exciting. I'd love to get out of this place some day. Well, you won't be going very far, honey, not on this leg. Maybe it's better this way, with all those bombs blowing off out there. (She gestures towards the TV)

The TV monitor, however, shows no explosions. Instead it projects something familiar and disturbingly uneventful. A twilight hour on the riverbank, not much of a landscape there, just the naked branches entangled in the air like in children's puzzle books (do you see a profile there?) aimless clouds taking shape and dissolving, and a winding path leading down the muddy slope … You can't see it but there are some roots here on the ground, treacherous, the way the roots are. They keep you in place, or if you try to escape, they make you trip and fall. I witness the beginning of the blizzard, slow and quiet. I can't say if the flurry is real or if it's just TV snow, a problem with signal. This is not a regular programming, but channel 0, a real-time recording made by the hospital web-cam right outside the building, perhaps to compensate for the claustrophobic view from the window onto the corner parking lot.

Strange thing is that I am staring at the scene of my accident.

– Really, that's where it happened? Says the nurse. I go there sometimes, just to get out of here … Just saw a jogger kissing a roller-blader there today. They were right there on my way. You know usually they don't get along.

I am not saying much, waiting for the pain to fall from "distressing" down to "moderate."

– So what happened to you? Did you stumble into someone? Anyone pushed you?

– Not as far as I know.

– Oh dear … What were you thinking? Where was your head? How could you fall there? Two days before Christmas? You were walking and suddenly …

– Yes.

– Were you power walking or something?

– No, just walking.

– Well, well …

Her face expresses incredulity mixed with pity. She makes me bite the thermometer, cleans the "fanny." But in fact she cannot take her eyes off the TV screen. It is captivating and still. A black bird flies across the still frame, occasional jogger here and there, a few flurries swirling in the wind. Somebody could have watched me fall right here in the left corner of the frame. They could see me trip and slide down the slope beyond the viewfinder.

– Look, says the nurse. The blizzard is starting. I can see it in the air. They promised a mixture of snow and rain for the next two days all the way till Christmas. How will I be able to get home today?

And then she remembers me and chuckles: "Oh, poor you, you aren't going anywhere tonight. You got what you need, right? Here is your "Diary of Pain." Please fill in the blanks in the handout. Make a list of what you need. Here is your pen. Make sure you don't stain the sheets.

Wait, nurse … Marion? A little more painkiller, please. I remember it now … the break up …

My diary of pain.

10 – 9 Worst pain imaginable, I am shattered and cast off like an old bone china with the cracks of age and tea stains. I am falling apart, barely ambulant. No, don't spare me your emergency caress. My skin is a web of nerve endings laid bare. *Ending*, did you say ending? No, I never did. *You* said it, not me.

7 – 8 I am lying still. Time is still. Space has shrunk. There's nothing to look forward to. The supple and expandable world that we shared is no more. No ripples on our horizon. Remember how walls turned into doors for us? You'd always discover unmarked entries, like on that day when you pushed a glass wall on a dead-end street in Chinatown and found the little bar that saved us from rain. Now that door is unhinged and discarded and you are forever off-the-hook. Our private country no longer exists. I live in the three-dimensional real world, a dreary, plain background without a figure. Once I caught a glimpse of you in a subway car but *la niña de tus ojos*, the pupilla-doll of your eyes had a glazed look.

5 – 6 A throbbing sensation. *Nel mezzo del camino di nostra vita,* life is capsizing into its later half, I'm stooping a bit, when I talk to you in my head, tripping on the New York side walk, bumping into a family of hydrants with chained nipples. Remember how we laughed at them together ... You liked the green one with the pipe shaped like a question mark. It's gaping into my face now. Why?

3 – 4 – 2 – 1 Time blurs the outlines of your image, develops tender callous on the site of the break, cures acute symptoms. I don't cry anymore, but there is still a lingering afterimage in the corner of my eye, that wrinkle that I owe you. Otherwise, just minor aches, must be age-related. . . . What did you expect? The patient has to set realistic pain control goals. Remember that armless mannequin in the frozen shop window that framed our reflection? Her chopped lips are almost smiling.

0. No pain at all. Artificial snow in a glass ball. Flying and falling, up and down, up and down.

Heather Hartley

Colomba, La Camorrista

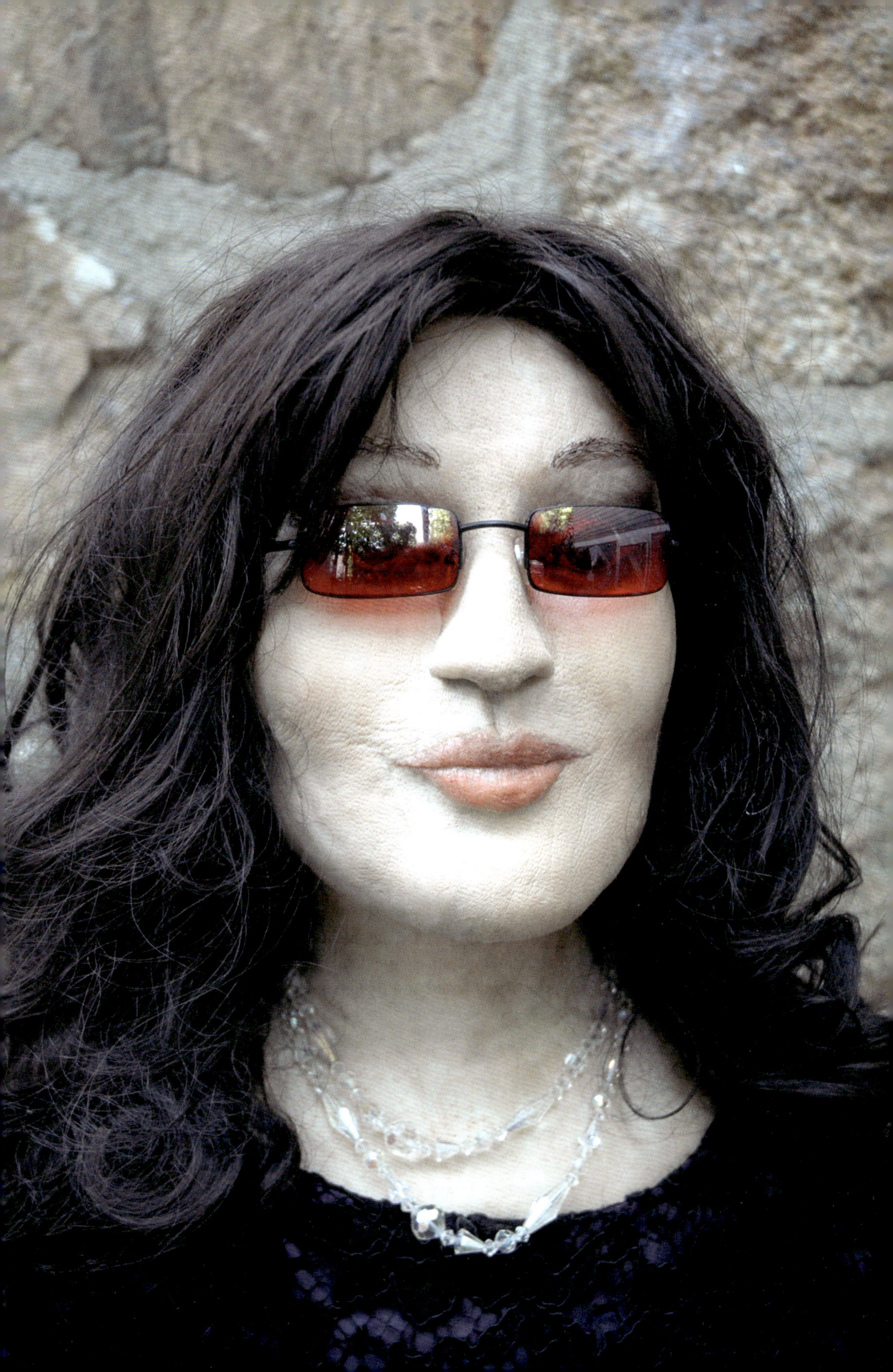

Puttana, strega, troia. Whore, witch, pig. She eats pasta with meat sauce. More than she should. Immacolata, the sister, the one in the shadows, says, *Watch out, Colomba, it's a dark time. It would be easy for them to strike.*

Blood is a dirty business. See the white laundry drying out on the balconies – not enough sheets to stop up the holes, to sop up the blood. It can get to you. That's when you remember who you are.

Think of the bitch who suckled Rome. The two baby gods drinking her up. She's the one – not the men. The men are just meat in the end. All good she-wolves bring out their guns and fangs. It's a question of territory, of honor – a question of the gut. Immacolata would say, *That bitch holds all the balls.*

It's September soon and if the Saint's blood boils, the season will be good for all of us. Pray to the Madonna dell'Arco, our Lady of Situations, touch your tits, kiss the cross – it's all for *scaramanzia* – luck – good or bad.

Here comes the funeral horse – for whom? You forget. Because the dead replace the dead. Little ducks in a row. You forget the math. You turn off the TV – the widows spitting on the ground, people clapping and crowding – the hum of the Vesuvius biting at your back.

I was born this way – with death in my hand. It's a question of birthright. *A fucking trademark,* Immacolata says. This is our city, Napoli, this is the city where we eat our young.

Sunday Slaughter in the Ongoing Sacro di Sabila War

– article from a local newspaper
Monday, June 16, 1980
Napoli, Italy
In what has come to be known to locals as the "Sacro di Sabila War," a veritable massacre occurred yesterday when four members of the D'Ambrosio clan including one child and one woman were shot dead at the first communion celebration of Colomba and Immacolata D'Ambrosio, daughters of Salvatore "La Smorfia" D'Ambrosio, boss of the Sabila area of Napoli.

At 9.13 pm, five men from the rival Riccia clan opened fire on the seafood buffet, immediately killing D'Ambrosio's wife Giuseppina and their only son Stefano, eight years old. Alfonso and Flavio D'Ambrosio, cousins of Salvatore visiting from Puglia, were also killed. In addition, twenty-one people were injured.

Long known as one of the bloodiest and most gruesome feuds in the recent history of the Camorra, the Neapolitan branch of the Mafia, the Sacro di Sabila War has now reached a new level of violence and has the local police and carabinieri extremely concerned.

"We are deeply disturbed by the intensity of violence," said Renzo Mancini, head of the Anti-Mafia league for the city of Napoli, "We are doing everything in our power. This butchery just can't go on."

"Blood was everywhere. The girls [Colomba and Immacolata D'Ambrosio] were screaming, screaming for her [their mother]," exclaimed one shocked first communion guest speaking on condition of anonymity. All that purple and red splattered all over the place. We are killing our own."

Local church officials released a statement today condemning the killings, calling them "barbarous acts against the will of God and the sanctity of the first holy communion. These brutal and bloody acts will not go unpunished."

Due to heightened security risks, no church service will be held. Only the traditional black curtain will be hung over the main entrance to the Cattedrale di Sabila. A private family gathering for the burial will take place on Tuesday morning at 6.00 am in the strictest confidence and under the vigilant eye of the Sabila police force and the carabinieri of the city of Napoli.

Colomba's Confession

My dress was from Paris. My little white dress with a matching hat and veil, Nonna's white lace gloves. My tiny beaded purse. Immacolata knew I came first – for everything. I was the bride of Jesus that day.

Candles everywhere. Singers and solos. Applause. Women touching my hair. So happy. Lobster, squid, oysters, shrimp, clams – *A fortune in sea-fucking-food,* Papà said, *eat up, bella. This is for you.* Men kissing one another on the cheek, laughing, and everyone, everyone looking at me.

At first, I didn't see the blood. Then I heard it in my sister's eyes, her eyes seeing everything. I saw the face, faces, Papà made – *una smorfia*, a grimace.

Mamma's body hit again and again and her body blasted in the air, raining food, tables flying and the screaming screaming. *I'd do anything for my children – my little nuts, my sweetmeats,* she would say to me at night. Immacolata knew I came first.

Blood is a thirsty business – a question of birthright. You can't stop drinking.

Thyrza Nichols Goodeve

The Wind is Here
And My Head is Not

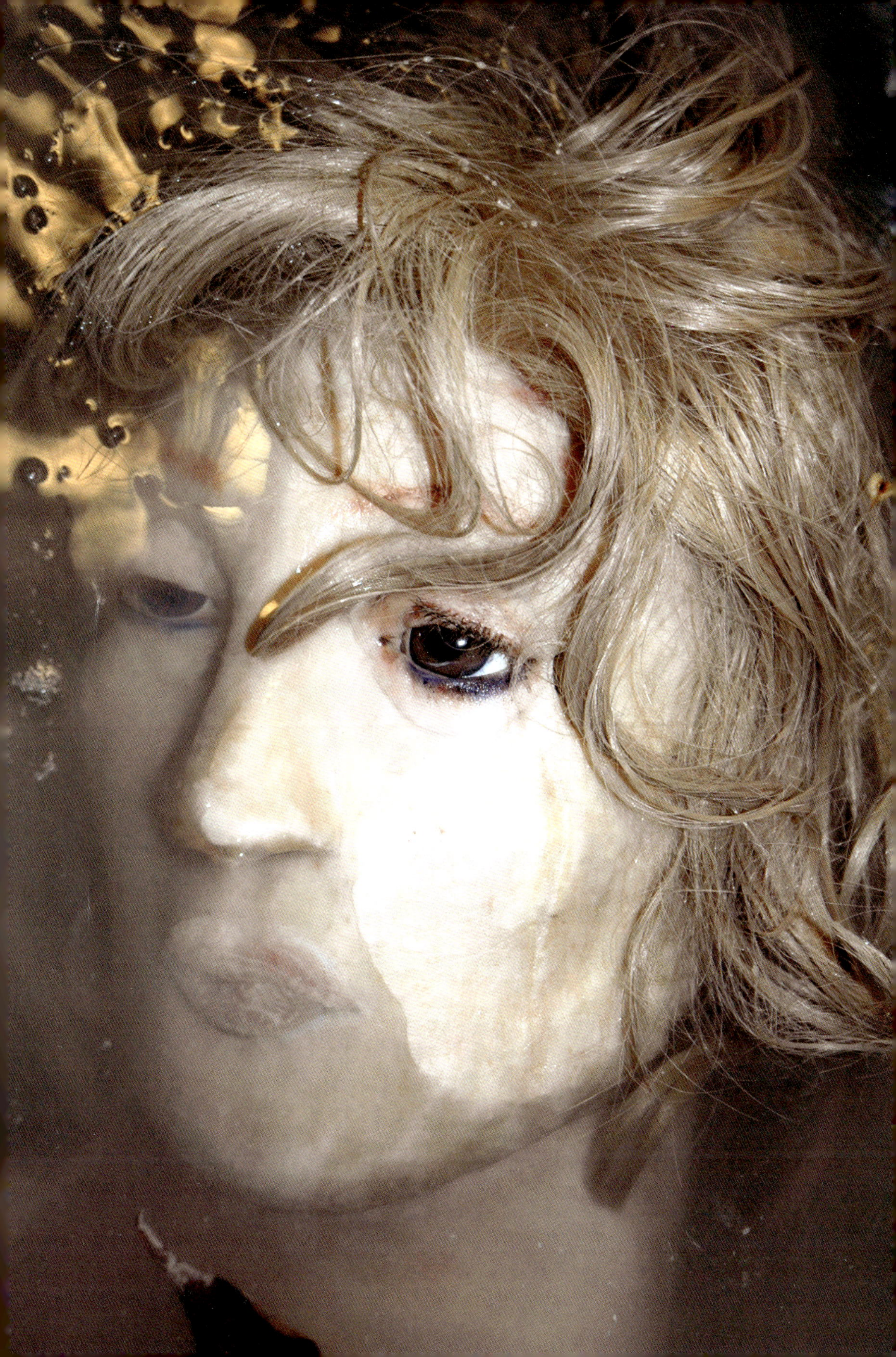

Saturday 6.30 pm. Patio Café

The wind is here. It is quiet. I am lonely tonight. Not for people but there is something in the air that is missing. A sound. A smell. It is the war. It is too hot. I am waiting. Is that him? No, another. It looks like him. So many do. I wish he didn't look like everyone else. But then he does. Where is he? My hands are damp. My eyebrows ache. Where is the wind now? Is this sweat I feel breaking from my skin? Maybe the weather will change. Maybe it will get cooler. If it does will he be here by then? He said he would. Look, there is a shadow where the sun was. A bird flies through it. Someone has left a dog tied to a table. The waiter is quiet. When he arrives he will run his hands through my hair. He tells me it is full and fluffy and feminine. He is good with his hands. Men are wrong. They think love is in their penis when it is in their hands, their skin, their eyes, and yes the lips as they travel gently across the surface learning how to penetrate and when. It is all in the rhythm, the knowledge, the intimacy, the exchange. There are no maps of love only paths – new each time – some become patterns, others are lost until rediscovered. Just right. Balanced yet crazed. Brave and gentle. His hands holding my face, stroking my neck. I have never known an American who could make love with his hands. Where is he? Will he come when the shadows dissolve and all is black and the candles on the tables are lit? I will relax. The air is cooler now. It is from the river. The dog sits patiently. He follows my gaze as I scan the air. Both of us are waiting. The skin around his eyes is worn and white and scarred. Bite marks dapple his cheeks and nose like bits of salt. His ears are torn. His eyes are those of a bait dog not a fighter. His tail wags with the anticipation of the moment when a human, its human, the human, returns. His leash strains against the metal table he is tied to. Muscles ripple. His eyes shift to look at me. He is aware I am not the one but still he looks at me as if I know. We both wait. We both look. A form arrives in the distance. Is it him? The dog tenses. I push my hair away from my face. As the dog uprights itself, distended nipples come into view. It is a female. A mother. How old are her puppies? I tense and close my eyes. I want the surprise. Do I hear his steps? I listen to the sounds of the dog's excitement. She whines and is all muscle frenzy and jingling chains. My eyes open. It is not him. The dog is quiet, breathing rapidly, lips curled back in that expression we humans interpret as a smile. A man is kneeling, holding, stroking, joyous. The air goes out of me. I watch. I watch the caressing and the licking and the love that passes between. There is trust and gracious understanding. Nothing strained or sharp. I am struck by the depth of their bond. How long has he had this dog? What has he named her? What does the dog eat? Is the dog's loneliness the same as mine (for him) when she is without her human? Although I am alone and cold and waiting, I smile. Is it important to the man that the dog is female? At this moment, something light strokes the top of my head.

"I am happy to see you." He says pulling his chair close to mine, althought my attention is still drawn to the man and his dog. Michel places his hands on either side of my face and guides my gaze until it is locked into his. I love the way his eyes search my face. I feel as if I am a question he is trying to answer. We kiss. His lips are soft and comforting even when he is emotionally distant. The dog gives out a long sigh.

"May I have a beer?" the man says to the waitress. "And some water for my dog?"

Michel strokes my face and cups my chin with his hands. It is during these moments I like to think of him as Alain Delon. It is a joke between us. I am Monica Vitti to his Alain Delon. He, the ambitious beautiful stockbroker in Antonioni's *The Eclipse*. I, the ever-anguished full-lipped Italian blonde. We sit and look at one another as if in long black and white takes. Michel has Delon's skin and smile. "All of my girlfriends have always complimented me on my skin." He said in the shower after our first night together. "But your eyes, they are the eyes of Monica Vitti."

We order wine and wait until the waiter brings it to the table before we talk. There is no reason. It is just what we do when we meet like this. He fills the time until the bottle and glasses arrive by checking his messages. I sit absorbed by the reflection of the dog in the window. The waiter uncorks the bottle.

"Did you have a dog as a child?" I ask.

"Of course, didn't everyone?"

"Not necessarily."

"In the Riff Mountains we did. They were work dogs. We used them."

"Did you love them?"

"I suppose so. We needed them."

I smile. He is looking over my head across the patio observing the man and his dog.

"Is needing something love?"

"It is a bond. It means the dogs were indispensable to us."

"And how is that love?"

"Because it was our responsibility to find every way we could to make sure the dogs were not hurt or killed."

"They had to die sometime."

"Well … until it was their time to die."

"And how did you know it was their time."

"When they were no longer of use to us."

"I'd call what you did care, not love."

"Okay we cared for them."

"How did you feel when you had to hurt them?"

"Don't we hurt everything?"

"I guess so. But, with animals, hurt so easily turns into abuse."

"But don't we abuse each other?"

"But we stop. We know when it is not right."

His lips pursed, his head jerked back and twisted as though fighting off a bad memory or smell. Was he saying no?

"When I was training a dog I may have had to do what you would call abuse but, it was not to hurt the creature as you say, it was to teach them to obey. Dogs learn discipline when there are physical and mental consequences. Sometimes one must be violent in order to get one's beliefs across. It's the same with people. I learned that in the military."

"You liked being in the army didn't you?"

"Yes. I did. I found it a valuable model. There the balance between discipline and violence is rational and controlled. You know where you stand. You're told what to do."

"And that means you liked it?"

"'Like,' 'like'. You home-bred Americans … always interested in whether people 'like' things. That's not something we really think about where I come from and it's certainly not why I volunteered to fight in this war – 'your' – war. So … have I 'liked' the army I guess yes, somehow I must. That doesn't mean I would do it for the rest of my life, nor that I was happy the whole time nor that I *like* the fact that I might be called back for a third tour at any moment. But all in all I am glad. Really glad. It makes me wonder what I would have been without it."

8.30 pm. The restaurant. Tangier Buzzless Flies

"It was important to come here tonight," he says. "I need the food, the language, the arguments with Mohammed even if he is the kind of *motashadded* I came here to get away from. It feels good. Soothing. My childhood. That other self – the Riff Mountains and The American School of Tangier. Both sides. Europe and North Africa."

When our waiter, Mohammed, arrived at the table with food Michel immediately began to speak with him in Arabic. Mohammed was from Tangier as well but they had not known one another there. Although Berber and originally from the Riff Mountains, Michel's family was well off and Europeanized. They lived in a modern house above the town. Michel attended the American School of Tangier where he acted in plays directed by Paul Bowles while Mohammed's family was poor, strict, and mostly stayed in the Medina selling carpets to tourists. Until he was fourteen Mohammed had been the "runner" in the family – the one who met the boats at the port and then guided the tourists through the dark narrow labyrinth of the Medina back to his family's shop.

One evening we discovered a connection with Mohammed that had nothing to do with Tangier. Michel's first tour of duty for the special forces was in Afghanistan fighting, for those first months, Al Quaeda. He was stationed in the south, which was heavily Pashtun, meaning Taliban. One night while he was on guard a small tribe of Taliban kidnapped and held him for months. He has never sure how long. When he was released, a family took him in, helped him get better, and brought him back to the U. S. military. Somehow through their conversations they discovered Mohammed's mother who grew up in Afghanistan, had talked about the kindness of this same family. Although the connection was slight, the coincidence was mighty. It felt like a river of blood had passed between them.

Tonight Michel talked with Mohammed longer than usual. He seemed intent on getting something from him. He was excited, almost agitated. As we left, Mohammed handed him a small package. Michel looked at me, smiled, and shook Mohammed's hand. Because it was small – and represented something between them – it didn't seem right to ask what was in the package.

Wednesday 7.30 pm. The Patio Café

The wind brings with it so many smells – of long conversations, of tension, of exhaustion. The dog is sound asleep. So is the man, his mouth half open. Michel has taken an interest in the dog. He is now the one who sits absorbed.

"It was while I was in Afghanistan that I learned to hear the way dogs smell."

It was an abrupt statement.

"I don't understand. I know they teach soldiers to hypnotize goats to fall over as if dead but why to hear like a dog smells? It makes no sense."

"No, the army does not teach it. If they did, why would they?"

"I don't know. You brought it up. You have an acute sense of hearing that is truly a talent, perhaps more than just an average sense, I guess as good as the way dogs are able to know things through smell and maybe that could be useful in combat."

He takes his eyes off the dog.

"But combat is noisy."

"Well, in pre-combat. When you're looking for the Taliban?"

"Yes, but anyone can have that kind of hearing. This wasn't a military thing. It's something I learned from the dogs, from being there in Afghanistan."

"I thought they didn't like dogs over there."

"They don't. That's why you learn from the dogs. They know things because they are hated. And since their strongest sense is smell, their nose is their brain, smell is their knowledge, their encyclopedia, it's how they think and strategize …"

"And …?"

"So, my brain became my ears because the Taliban are mean to animals and women in very specific ways. So when I saw a bitch's nose poke at the air in a specific way I knew it was the Taliban, and then I knew I had to stay invisible, to listen for the Taliban the way the dogs were smelling them."

"And all this time I just thought you were a genius."

"But it was more, something about being there on the level of the reviled creature, learning to think like it thinks with a sense not a brain. I felt like the monster in *Frankenstein* only I wasn't learning language, philosophy, Western civilization, I was learning how to hear with the intelligence of a dog's nose."

I think this was his genius. He heard things everywhere, all the time. Not voices. Not the obvious things we all hear. Little shifts in the planet's atmosphere, rifts in the air, moments when parallel universes wrap one over the other. The sound he said colors make was the most surprising. Not all colors, just red. Not blood but red pigments and dyes like paint or lipstick. It was something that started to happen to him after he had been with the Taliban. I think he may have tried to talk to Mohammed about this because Mohammed also found red disturbing. His wife wore a very pale shade of lipstick.

Five days later. The Patio Café

The man is reading the paper and keeps wincing. The news is about the evacuation of families from Fallujah, from their homes, because our soldiers are going into the city to clear out the insurgents. Does this mean my house will be destroyed if I am one of them? I try to imagine being told to take my things (but which things) and go to that "somewhere" people go when they are told of these evacuations. It is just unimaginable to us and catastrophic for them and yet to read it in the newspaper is our routine. A wince and then we turn the page.

The dog whines every so often as if in pain. She is looking at me as usual but tonight her gaze is different and her nose keeps twitching. When Michel arrives she growls. "That's strange," says the man.

Everything is different tonight.

Michel has brought me a gift.

"My god Michel. How could you? But I thought … It makes you sick?"

"I've been trying to get over that. Mohammed has helped me. You are so beautiful. You should be able to wear lipstick once in a while. It shouldn't be for the Taliban to make such decisions."

It was the first time he had ever mentioned the Taliban in passing.

"So you've actually been researching?" I teased.

"In a way. I asked Mohammed what his wife wore."

"Why?"

"The color must be less loud, less pungent."

I smelled the lipstick and then put it up to my ear.

"Oh Michel, this lipstick doesn't smell, or scream!" I laughed and went into the bathroom to put it on. As I left the dog jolted and pulled at the leash. The man leaned down to calm her. It was as if something really strong had passed through the air.

"So, how do I look? You've never seen me this way?"

He smiled at first. "Beautiful. So beautiful. But it does change you. Would you mind?" He didn't look very well. "Please take it off. I know I just gave it to you."

"Does it really look that funny to you?"

"I tell you, this lipstick won't work. It was a mistake. I am not Mohammed. We must get rid of it. We must go."

The dog was tugging hard at the leash and yelping helplessly in our direction.

"Stop it." The man said and removed the leash. The dog ran and jumped all over me whining and licking. It reminded me of that first day. Her emotion was more hysterical than affectionate but it was a bond nonetheless. Michel pushed the dog away violently, hitting her hard with his fist. She flew across the deck slamming her spine against the railing.

"Michel! Oh my god. What the hell are you doing?"

"That bitch. We've got to get out of here. It's the insects. They're screaming. The bloody pregnant females."

He tore my shirt as he jerked me off the deck hauling me down the stairs to the path. A waiter from the café came out. "What is going on?" I struggled with Michel. I had to know if the dog was alright. She was on her back with her head turned towards us watching as we disappeared. She knew.

Night. A few days later. The Riverbank.

It's been a few days. The wind is here and my head is not. Michel took it off and put it elsewhere, which is where I am now. Near the river but where, exactly, I am not sure. I think even he doesn't know. I feel the chill at the base of my neck where my body is no longer. You'd think that would be impossible but it isn't. I don't know why. Nor is it uncomfortable. Just that beginning with my neck and moving out into the world it feels as though there is no air.

It's been a week

The dog is the one who found my head and placed it here. He had smelled the threat rising in Michel before Michel had even given me the gift. The lipstick *was* too pungent, the color too loud. What Michel heard was not wrong. He had indeed heard the crushing of pregnant female cochineal bugs, a white flat bug that lives on the leaves of cacti, which, when crushed produce the crimson that has colored everything from the uniforms of the British to the lips of the modern female. Since I knew this is how they make the color red it did not surprise me to hear him screaming what to someone else would have sounded like madness. I knew Michel was not crazy, just gifted. The sound of thousands of tortured pregnant insects dying at frequencies that hit the ears in ways beyond anything we could hear must be painful. That was rational. That made sense. But as we walked, and Michel tore at the color on my lips, I realized it was not the death of the innocent insects that was producing the frenzy, but the sound of the red, of the pregnant, of the female, *the female, the female and the red and the lips and …* the woman and words in a language that wasn't English or French or Arabic. Michel was shouting in the language of the Taliban. The Taliban were in his head, in his ears, coming out his nose spewing nonsense about the evil of woman, our bodies, our sex, the red on our lips. It was their discipline and violence he had heard and learned so well. A discipline of hate so loud and clear and mean and intolerant that just a touch of pale red lipstick provoked him to cut off my head and throw it onto a riverbank where the only animal able to find it was the one he had learned to listen from, to listen with the same acute perception that it had learned to use smell because it knew what it was to be hated as he had learned what it was to hate.

Lo Galluccio

Denebola

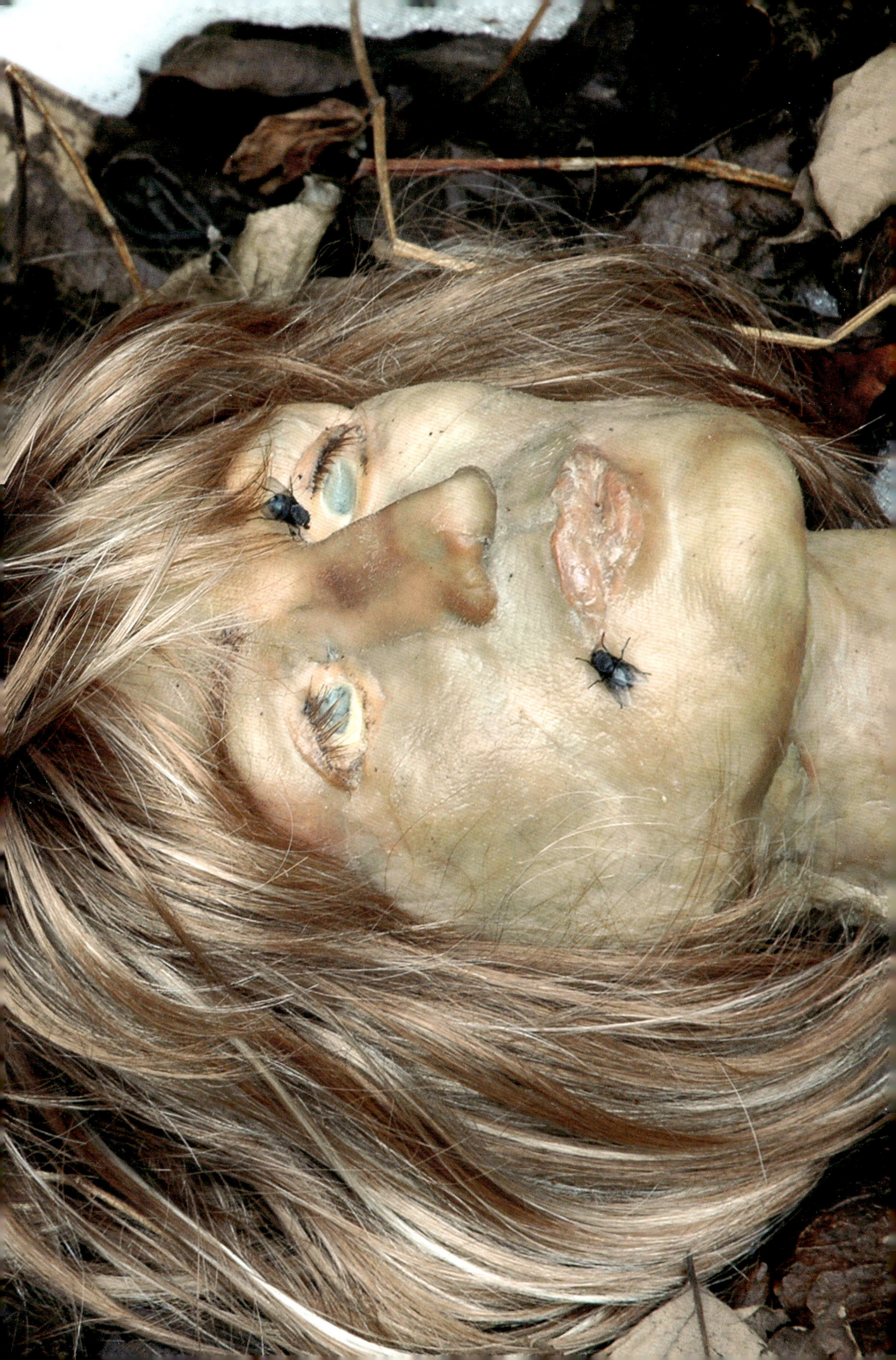

I once dreamt I was a starfish with four arms; Ophelia flying the earth with dry sand in her fists; a child-swan with a coppery neck, broken. I once dreamt the moon was in my bathroom mirror with the name of a healer across it – she was a flamenco dancer named Lucia. Without her I would drown like Alice in my own tears.

My father thought I could not swim as a child. He was right. However, one summer in a pool by a motel on the Maine coast I fell in love with the turquoise waves and insisted, at five, on trying to test the water. The red buoys seemed like a necklace of jewels. What lay beyond the shallow end seemed like more than just adult thrashing and pleasure. For me that pool symbolized beauty itself.

I was named after a star, the star Denebola, because my mother worked for astrophysicists. It was my father, however, who worshipped the sun.

When I started to drown that first time, I can only remember a strange feeling of not belonging to the element that held me spellbound. The others' legs beat like mechanized parts as mine seized up. It must have been only a few minutes of gasping for oxygen from under the waves. It was not my father who saved me, but a young woman who had seen me going under fast. I don't remember her name and perhaps will never know it. However, her arms grabbed me like angel wings. She must have been a sturdy angel of chlorine.

At 17, my father died. It was then I discovered my lust for men and my ability, despite the first drowning episode, to swim fast. My father's funeral was like a dark tunnel speeding me into the earth. It seemed like the death of water. I remember only that I would pull my baby sister, with her dark curls and fat calves, out of the wake parlor again and again. My father had wanted to be cremated – his ashes sprinkled over the cold green Atlantic, but his mother wanted a conventionally Catholic funeral and burial. This upset me very much. But it was tears, once again, and not assertive words, that came to me in the face of my father's corpse. My grandmother sat with me, her lilac perfume and starched dress heaving too, as we both sobbed for the loss of my father. My mother stood in a receiving line in a simple black dress. She was named Nancy, after Nancy Sinatra. One aunt reprimanded my tears – "Be strong for your mother," she warned. But my only honor was dragging my little sister out of the nightmare of my father's stiff repose.

By 21, I was in New York City, becoming an actress. I lived in a brownstone walk up in Hell's Kitchen near a cupcake bakery and the wide expanse to the west of New Jersey. The building was famous because a great cabaret singer had thrown herself off the top landing at 47, believing her career had ended.

That day many flowers were strewn in front of the sidewalk where occasionally you could find a used heroin needle. By day I worked as a secretary in nylons at various financial companies and auditioned, when I could, for plays by Ibsen, O'Neil, Shakespeare and the Greeks. It was in the early spring one year that I was cast in a Greek tragedy – *Iphigenia in Tauris*, by Euripedes.

Maybe you know the myth. Iphigenia was sacrificed by her father Agamemnon to win the Trojan War. He pushed her over a cliff as a sacrifice to the gods. Then Athena would unleash the winds and let the boats of the Grecians sail to Troy, where the deceitful demi-goddess Helen was being held in a bondage of sensual love. Artemis, according to Euripides, rescued the girl in mid-fall, like Superman does in the movies now. Iphigenia was spared by this wild goddess of childbirth and savagery. She must have seen something of herself in the girl. At any rate, Iphigenia was placed on an island with her sisters, 7 of them, all her double, and made to pay penance to Artemis for her safety.

In the play we spoke in three languages, and the set consisted of two rows of beds from which the Iphigenias would wake up nightmared by her father's war. Then the girls would intone prayers to Artemis as they dressed and avoided the wrathful tricks of the island's ruler.

I was haunted, on our tour, by my younger brother, Antony, who I had separated from after my father's death. One day, sitting at a mountain-side café, I wondered for hours about what my brother dreamt. As Iphigenia's brother is pursued by the furies, my brother's ghost pursued me. In a fever I stole a silver ring from a cliff-side tourist shop in Athens and wrote, "My brother, what is it you dream?" I wrote in my journal, "The moon is one pregnant pearl dressed for the void." There I was in Greece, with the air sublime and yellow, enticing all memory, writing again about the moon.

Then, by the mountain near the Acropolis, I saw my own death rise like a mist before me. As if Cassandra the seer were issuing a prophecy. It's said that oracles only tell what will come to pass, but not what you can do in reaction to these events. But if the event regards your own death, I wonder, then, what chance you have to elude it?

I saw an image of myself with my skin like tattooed leaves. My eyes were blazed open but murky from river water. I was lying prone like a felled maple tree. The gray sky made my copper hair look like an apple you could eat.

My eyes reflected the moon in loops of forever. Denebola, eclipsed. I didn't know from this image how I had come to be drowned like that. I only knew that the image would probably come true and this was my one occasion to see it.

Upon leaving Greece, I sat alone in the amphitheater crying. I missed my father, the real one, not Agamemnon. For I was always able to wake him up after my night terrors, and we would sit alone in front of the TV static till I felt calm enough to go back to bed.

I wanted someone else to know about my vision on the hill. Yet, I couldn't seem to bring myself to tell it. I left my Greek lover, Achillas, behind and while my theater mates slept on valium on the plane back to the States, I watched two Italian children run around the cabin and scream.

These words crossed my mind: Who will kiss the blasted bird past a limbo of leaves?

In the paper it will be written, "She died in the river, but dries in the sun."

As the plane crossed the ocean, we swerved several times and I gasped for air, believing this was my fate: a plane crash into the sea depths. Would that explain my vision on the hill? But no, hours later, we arrived safely at La Guardia Airport.

It was the Hudson River I looked toward. As my luggage rounded the conveyer belt I made up a plan. There was a place I would run to over the summer near the meat market, where the prostitutes would stake their ground in shiny purple tights and tight leopard skin dresses – to thrust their breasts at businessmen and smear pussy into their cheeks. Stones lined the river bank and a pier extended out into the oily ripples. Fate drew me there when I had only a day or two before my sublet was up. I had no place to go, and the vision from Greece had replaced all practical scheming for survival. I had nearly drowned once, then learned to swim. I went, at midnight, to be mesmerized by water. I dressed in a white tunic that I had purchased at a dress store near our rehearsal site at a Lyceum in Athens. I dressed purely for the river.

Natalie Wood. Virginia Woolf. Ophelia.

Perhaps, I mused, Iphigenia had never been rescued by a goddess, but had fallen straight from the cliff into the sea.

I remembered Achillas' mouth, my father's eyes, my brother's absence. The river would entangle me like a feather boa. The river would resolve.

I wondered if an autopsy would be performed. I wondered if pagan eels from deep in the river would etch their tiny teeth into my body. I wondered if Christ would dribble wine into my mouth from the Heavens for all my childhood communions. The prostitutes would open their thighs for money in the background. I would fight the urge to tread water or swim. I would be drugged by my dream.

By morning I would be like a bluish doll.

This is my river. And so, at five minutes past midnight, I walked toward it, like a pirate on the plank.

Iris Smyles

Agnes, The Treatment

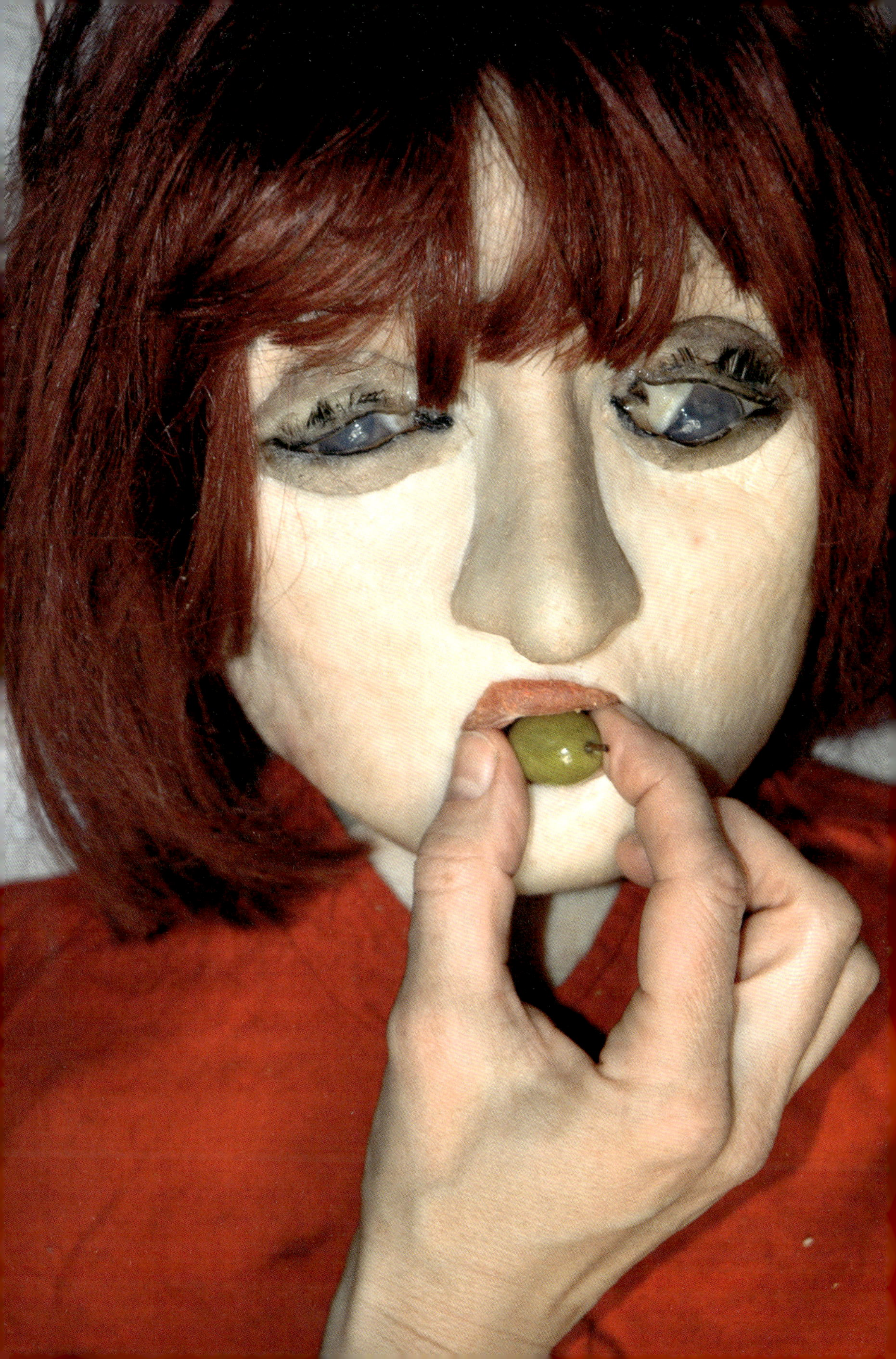

There is a red splotch on my cheek where I accidentally scratched the skin off. If we ran into each other you'd ask me about my face, and I'd tell you it was a funny story actually but that I didn't have time to explain.

I did it because I'm crazy, obviously, and you've already said that, so why the dumb questions about my face? Don't you remember when I peeled all the skin from my fingers; you complimented me on the style of my band-aids, bought me a drink, and then introduced yourself.

I'd thought I had something on my hand, I'd explained. And so I scratched until it came off, I'd continued to you charmingly. I'd had dreams about things growing on my hands – giant welts in the shape of tiny animals, secret mathematical formulas puffing up from the skin, and skyscrapers that kept getting higher, and so when I woke up I scratched and scratched until it was raw.

Seeing what I'd done I dipped the whole hand in a sink full of peroxide. The way it fizzed white like soda when I put it in and stung me all the way to my eyelashes, I knew I was doing the right thing and they were clean.

Later my parents made me visit a doctor because I didn't want to die just yet, not before I found love and wrote a novel on a paper napkin anyway, or at least obtained a good position typing, and a boyfriend who'd pay for dinner and say something nice about the dress I chose to wear.

The doctor looked at my hand, and I looked at him concerned. He said it was only scar tissue. "But underneath, underneath!" I said. He said there was nothing underneath, so I stopped scratching and it healed.

Remember when I couldn't open my mouth all the way and so I had to mash bananas through the small opening between my teeth when I felt hungry? The doctor said it could be TMJ, so I told you I couldn't hold your cock in my mouth anymore because it placed undue stress on my jaw, and I felt I should leave my retainer in all the time if I wanted those years of braces to be worth anything. Later on, when I was leaving again for a long time and you were staying behind at the bike shop, I told you I couldn't kiss you anymore because we weren't getting married, and I didn't want to anyway, but would always love you even though I didn't like you anymore, and hated the way you came near me in the bed at that seedy motel after your cousin's wedding.

We haven't seen each other in a while, and I couldn't respond to your letters because I woke up the morning after my last birthday with paralyzed arms. I figured they were probably just asleep from the way I had been lying on them, not wanting to stress out about it, so I slammed them against my bureau and desk and walls to get the feeling back, but it didn't work so I went into the office that morning but couldn't take notes. The numbness is mostly gone now, which is good because it was winter and it was hard to button my coat.

I've been seeing a chiropractor who is trying to right my spine, because it all comes from the spine, he says. He twists my neck till it pops, like the way they kill monsters on TV with one swift stroke. It calms me down seeing him three times a week. I'm not supposed to carry anything heavy, and I bought a new chair for my desk and special wrist splints to wear while typing and sleeping.

I saw a neurologist before that, and he asked if I had been doing anything funny before it happened, sustained any trauma. I didn't mention the drunken roller-skating down the incline in my apartment because I didn't fall or anything, and there isn't enough space to pick up enough speed that it would be so bad or inadvisable, and how would I explain it?

The chiropractor tried to get to the bottom of it, and he asked me if I was under any kind of stress or if I was sad, if anything had happened in the last few months or year, and I said no, not at all, and never thought for a moment of you of all people and my jaw felt tight suddenly, which was weird because my jaw's been fine for years now. "No, nothing," I said, as he pressed me. He told me I was only deceiving myself if I tried to deceive my doctor, because that's part of the treatment and it all goes back to the spine. He left the room to get the X-rays and I started crying but really fast, so when he came back he couldn't see anything.

The other day I saw a pink spot on my cheek and started scratching it and applied peroxide and various creams I found in the medicine cabinet. And then this morning I accidentally scratched all the skin off so it's raw and it hurts a little.

My face is all messed up, which is why if I saw you on the street I wouldn't tell you all this but turn around before you saw me and not call you back if you called and stop seeing you once and for all, all together.

You've been calling all week. You probably love me now that I'm gone, because you think I've stopped thinking about you and I'm beautiful when I'm not looking at you. All the photos you have of me in profile. The one with my eyes closed you say is beautiful. I don't think about you every day, sometimes it's all I can do.

I don't go out anymore, and I wouldn't be lying if I said I was busy last Wednesday; I had to stay home because I wanted to, and because there is a lot to keep me busy at home. I stood on my head for an hour to see what it felt like, to see how it might affect my alignment, and to see if it would work to get me back to the way I was before I met you. My back still hurts, but I don't mind the treatment, and the doctor has noticed an improvement in my mood, though he hasn't asked about the splotch on my face, steadily growing and taking over. It's new skin. Maybe I can get all new skin.

I'm not seeing anyone. I could, but I find it too boring. I'm too busy. Yesterday, I pulled all my eyelashes out thinking I wouldn't need those wishes anymore. I have to stop wishing that you'd call and say that you love me rather than "do you love me?" as you would if I answered.

I pulled them all out and dipped both of my hands in peroxide, and covered my face with toothpaste, and cracked my neck, and stood on my head. Then I did it again. I listened to the fizz of my hands sizzling cold in the peroxide and dreamed about how you'd stop calling eventually and how that's what I want.

Katia Kapovich

Betsy

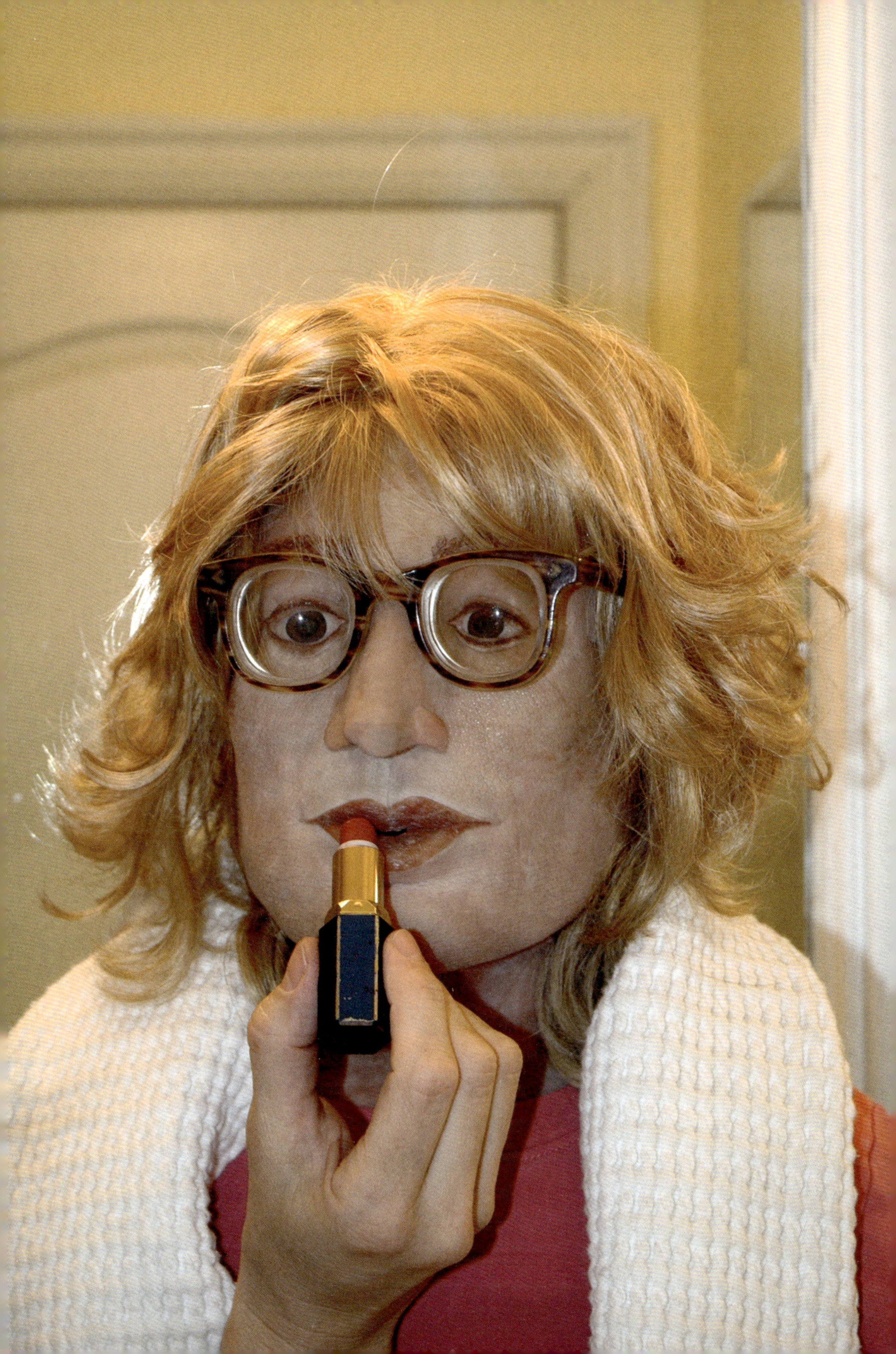

A friend of the bride gave me a lift. All the way there we talked about destiny and love, and agreed that what works for some people doesn't work for others. She, herself, divorced her husband a year ago. "When I see him I understand why I married him, but I also understand why I divorced him seven years later." "So you have no regrets, no pricks of conscience?" "No" – she answered simply. I looked at her gorgeous profile with dark cloud of hair falling to her shoulders.

Her driving was excellent and we made it there in two hours. "I'm staying at the hotel, but I believe your headquarters are across the street in the Emerald House." I had no idea where they put me up, and the bride's friend called Tina. "Yes," she said. "Tina told me to drive you to the Emerald House." "Is it an inn?" "Bed and Breakfast," I guess. "The host's name is Betsy."

The Emerald House wasn't so emerald by color. Maybe it was emerald once, but it was long ago. It was green though. The bride's friend helped me with the few things I brought with me and drove away. I waved her "bye" and looked around. I was standing on the porch of the two storied house, my suitcase stood a step ahead of me, and there were woods and woods around. A beautiful winter day swayed them back and forth but it wasn't wind that moved the trees. The sun did it. When it entered the cloud the woods leaned against the blue wall of air. Then the trees bowed again though there was nobody but me standing on this steep porch to salute.

I forgot to mention how I happened to be invited to this wedding. I had known the bride for years. She was actually one of my students, one of my very favorite students. We still say a few words in Russian now and then. When Tina started dating Fire, she called me and asked for my advice. Perhaps I sounded a bit too critical.

"What kind of name is this? Why is he called Fire?"

We had this conversation in a bar on a very loud Friday night. Tina explained that Fire's parents were hippies, and he was raised in a Native American settlement.

"What's his real name?" I shouted. A dart flew by my ear and hit the board. The table we sat at was in the corner.

"His other name is Ferdinand, but he doesn't like to be called that."

"Jeez, it's getting better and better." I thought. I was very fond of Tina. She was bright, intelligent and talented. She worked in movie production, that's why she moved to New York after graduating from BC. She told me that Fire, alias Ferdinand, broke her heart on a cold December night. They were leaving a party at the same time. While they were waiting for their cabs downstairs, she asked his opinion about Woody Allen's movies. I know Tina. She asks questions and listens patiently. She deliberately does it to make another person feel better. Anyway, the groom plunged into the subject. At first, he named all Woody Allen's movies, then he catalogued them by year. One of the two cabs was sent away, and they rode in the same cab, because he was trying to organize the movies in order of excellence, of original plots, of good acting, of his favorite jokes. When they woke up next morning, he told her that he forgot to mention one aspect of Woody Allen's movies that make them universal.

"What's that?" She asked putting on her coat. She was about to leave for work.

"Love." He said. "I think I'm in love with you." Fire said.

So two months later he proposed to her. He had rented a limo, and the limo was waiting under her window while he was steadying himself with Champagne. She showed me her ring.

"Why did he rent a limo?" The ring was ok.

"He said later that he wasn't sure I would accept it. If I had said "no," he wouldn't need it."

"And you said 'yes.' "

She nodded.

"We were carousing on the limo all that night visiting different bars and talking and getting drunk like crazy. Nobody treated me like this before."

I thought it was a bit of showing off on his part, a bit too theatrical. My whole life experience made me suspicious of big gestures. My stepfather won my mom when he showed up on the stairs of the high school with a hundred white roses in his arms. She was a director, her salary was 150 rubles. An uptight Soviet citizen who didn't think much of herself, she lost her husband in her early thirties and raised me alone. My stepfather knelt when she came out of the door and kissed her feet in thick brown stockings; the roses fell and covered three stairs below them. Two years after that he made away with her secretary after stealing all my mother's golden and silver rings. There weren't too many of them, her family souvenirs. She never reported him to the militia, she was too proud.

I took a last look at the transparent winter woods, at the sky above them and at the empty road reflecting the blue with the enthusiasm of the neophyte. It was a rare day for the middle of January, after all.

When I buzzed the door I heard the dog bark somewhere in the depths of the Emerald House. The shuffling of the slippers on the hardwood floors didn't materialize immediately. Through the window to my left I could see a wall with paintings and part of the piano in the corner. The woman who opened the door also didn't look like Baba Yaga.

"Betsy," – she said. "And you are …"

"Elisabeth."

"It's very nice meeting you, Elisabeth!"

She was in her fifties. Her straw hair was trimmed short leaving an inch of pretty plump neck. Betsy was dressed in a fluffy sweater and a woolen skirt. She wore no make up. When she bent forward and lifted my stuff from the threshold I noticed that her hands were young and the fingers were long. I tried to protest but she insisted on bringing my suitcase upstairs.

"Make yourself comfortable, dear." She ordered and closed the door behind her.

The bed by the bright window, wide and flat, was covered with a pastel quilt. Two coffee-colored pillows mounted on it like two pyramids in the desert. The walls were painted in the same pastel colors. It all looked very nice. I took off my coat and dropped it under the coffee table in the right corner. My suitcase felt heavier than I thought. Something happened to it, it gained gravity. I pulled it closer and opened it. Of course, my flannel pajamas were on the top mixed with two pairs of shoes. I was never good at packing. A week before Tina had called me and repeated her soulful invitation. Her desire to see me at her wedding finally convinced me and I agreed to come. Right after that I started packing and I packed for a week. One leather shoe had a whitish nose covered with black marker. I didn't see these shoes in the daylight for several years. Tina graduated in '99 and the next year I was laid off. Since then I hardly ever wore my "official" leather shoes. Maybe on one of the occasions when I had to give a paid lecture I extracted them from the closet and seeing that one had turned bald I put this last minute amateurish makeup on it and forgot about it. The second pair looked better, not so worn out. It was a synthetic golden boat shaped pair of shoes. The problem with them was that they made my feet sweaty and cold. But given the beautiful weather outside it wouldn't be much of a problem, I surmised. I dug out my nice skirt, navy blue silk running through fingers like warm water. When did it come into my possession? As usual I didn't remember its origins. Some clothes came from friends, others had traveled all the way from Russia and survived due to their ability to hide in the corners of the wardrobe. Also, I never moved from place to place. Once in Boston, I always stayed in the same small and dark one bedroom apartment. At some point I was hoping for finding a more spacious place, maybe even with a balcony, but after loosing my job I stopped. The landlord never raised the rent; after ten years I paid the same seven hundred dollars and felt thankful.

The difficult part was to find a top that fit both the synthetic golden shoes and the navy blue skirt. I dug yet further. My fingers came upon a hard paper package on the bottom of the suitcase. What the hell was that, it weighed a ton. It was a large size Gzhel ceramic plate I had bought at the Moscow art and crafts exhibition during my last visit. I wasn't even sure whether it was me who put in the suitcase. On the other hand, who else could have put it between two sheets of cardboard, tied it with a string and stuck it in the suitcase? Could it be that the thing had been there initially? Had I ever taken it out? I had no recollection of taking it out.

I honestly tried to prepare for the wedding after that call Tina gave me on Monday. I bought her a present, an amber necklace. I gave my wardrobe a serious inspection. Some things needed ironing and I ironed them with passion, laying out a cotton blanket on the kitchen counter. Now and then I filled my mouth with water and blew it out the way my mother always did when she was getting ready for work. Not all of the spray was the right size; some came out as big as a spit. Dark wet spots produced much steam. After an hour of ironing perspiration and vapor covered my face as if I had undergone a complicated surgery. At least, I thought, I fought. I fought and fought. I hung the ironed clothes on the bottom of my suitcase. It was a mistake. I stared in the suitcase. The clothes were crumpled again. Plus they didn't match; my desperate attempts to look appropriate became even more obvious in this nice countryside room with a large window. "Enough is enough," I said, and at that moment saw a very delicate white top with laces on its short sleeves and a neat triangular cleavage. It was also wrinkled, but the wrinkling was intentional. My boyfriend made me buy it last summer as we took a stroll in the shopping district. We didn't plan to shop. I guess we had to meet with somebody there. The thing was on sale. It didn't cost much, something around twelve dollars, and it had style. That's what he said the fourth time I tried it on in front of the mirror the other night. He couldn't come with me. He was absorbed with his problems. But that was all right. Now, as I was done with the clothes, I could relax. I still had two hours before the wedding.

Downstairs, on the porch the two brothers of the bride, Lake and Corn, their girlfriends and Betsy shared a bottle of Chardonnay. As I was passing by looking for a clock they called me in. It was already dark outside though it was only 5 pm, and Betsy brought out two oil lamps. I hadn't seen oil lamps in many years. My memory of them goes back to the sixties when our family lived in a shabby clay cabin. Even then we only used them when there was a short circuit. When Betsy put the lamps in front of me on the table I recognized them. The fire played in them, and a long shadow pulsated on the wall. Some soot on the inside of the vessel made its glowing more mysterious.

Both brothers lived in California. Lake was older than Corn by four years. He worked as a system administrator at UCLA. He was bulky, his nose was pierced in several places; his head was molded to a perfectly round shape, a globe with an Africa of very short hair protruding into the ocean of his large forehead. Corn, who already wore a wedding suit and a white shirt with cuff links, was different. As long as I observed them from my corner in the gap between two oil lamps I couldn't catch any resemblance between these two young men. Corn was lanky, light footed, didn't have the energetic facial features of his brother. He was busy in landscaping, setting lawns and flowerbeds for the city. Their girlfriends, both very young and pretty, went to change for the wedding, and the four of us moved our chairs closer to the table.

Betsy asked resting her hand on her dog's neck:

"Who do you know – the bride or groom?"

"The bride." I said.

"Have you ever met the groom before?"

"No. Never." Suddenly I realized a simple fact, which somehow eluded me for a long while. We were sitting on this dark porch lit only by two oil lamps, lost in the midst of woods because Christina insisted on having her wedding in her native town. That's why we were sitting here and not in New York where she lived now, or Boston where she studied, or Washington where her parents lived. The sound of wind came through the woods like a slow train. I knew Betsy heard it too.

"The weather is going to change. It will finally snow tonight." She said. "You, guys, better get yourself all clean and ready."

They nodded and excused themselves. Lake had yet to change, and Corn wanted to see how his girlfriend was doing in terms of dressing up.

"Lake, don't forget the rings!" Betsy shouted when the brothers were upstairs. The door shut, and their presence was reduced to low muffled sounds after the much brighter voices of their girlfriends.

"They are good boys, all three of them." Betsy said reflectively.

One of the lamps soon turned dim. Betsy took off the glass part and straightened the wick with her fingers.

"Isn't it hot?" I wondered.

"Not so hot." She was silent again. It was a nice and comfortable silence that this woman radiated around her. I felt refreshed after fifteen minutes of sitting here with her and drinking wine out of a large water glass. I didn't even care that the Chardonnay was warm and bitter.

"Who are you? Are you a family friend? I mean, do you know Tina and her parents?"

She has known them for a long time, she said in a friendly way and pushed a plate with a piece of cheese a little closer to me.

"I'm the groom's mother."

We, sixty people, stood in a large barn brightly lit by three hundred candles. The air was arid dry from their burning on haphazard shelves above our heads. Two waiters were serving hot spiced wine at the table placed behind ten rows of plastic chairs. After fifteen minutes of brisk walk through the cold owl-black woods it seemed the best place to be. Thanks to Betsy who led our small expedition amongst the swaying trees we made it on time. Her flashlight unraveled the dirt road peppered with snow with confidence; she seemed accustomed to such endeavors. As soon as we stepped off the main paved road she took me by the elbow, and the brothers and their girlfriends followed us. When we were half way from our destination a man with a flashlight stepped out of some bushes. He breathed carefully in the large woolen scarf from which his voice came.

"Lake? Corn?" Betsy and I waved our hand. "They are behind us."

"Did anybody see Uncle John?" His voice came out heavier than this puny silhouette in its long coat and white scarf would make you expect. I couldn't see his face because he kept his flashlight turned down, but I noticed that he carefully avoided Betsy's eyes.

Nobody, as it happened had seen Uncle John, and we proceeded.

"Who is this funny guy?"

"That's Garry, their dad and my ex-husband. He is looking for his brother John. John started celebrating yesterday … By now he probably fell asleep at the hotel."

I looked back, and seeing that the young people were a good seven feet behind us ventured to start a conversation.

"I'm sorry for being invasive, Betsy, and you probably think that I'm a total stranger here but, in fact, I'm not. I'm very close to the bride."

"Oh, don't be silly! We all know that. She is very fond of you. And we know who you are and that you were her teacher. And we also know that she insisted on your coming to her wedding … "

I wanted my voice to sound as delicate as possible, but I also knew at that point that Betsy didn't really care about the form of my interrogation. In my defense, I should also say that I was never nosy.

"I noticed that Garry was stiff with you."

"Why are you saying that?"

"He didn't look at you while he talked."

"You're right. We're not on speaking terms. Which is very unfortunate."

"When did you two separate?"

"Long ago. We only stayed together for three years. Weren't married officially.

Then we had a son. I left them and went to New York City."

"Why?"

She sighed but didn't stop walking.

"I fell in love with a famous pianist who lived in New York; I followed him during his concerts all around the states. Garry never let me come back."

"What happened to the famous pianist? Was he in love with you too?"

"He was and he wasn't. He married me …" She gave a deep sigh and stopped. In the moonshine I saw her face filled with sorrow and immediately knew that the story of her love wasn't over. And I was right.

The brothers caught up with us.

"Rosemary lost her glove!" Corn declared.

"I've found it!" Rosemary yelled, and we took off. The dirt road started widening. Soon we could see the clearing in front of us.

"You are the mother of Fire, but not of Lake and Corn, is that right?"

She nodded.

"Actually, I just met those two when they came for the wedding. As to their own mother, she died when they were in their teens."

They seemed pretty comfortable with each other, Betsy and the two younger brothers of the bride groom, and she was certainly proud of it.

Why, why, I thought, people are doomed to make such horrible mistakes again and again. Betsy and Garry. Me and my husband. I knew this sadness and remorse that she was gripped with. They were obviously meant to be with each other, the man in the long overcoat with a large scarf around his face and this very calm fair woman. But no, something came between them; some wretched power took her away. In my head I called these insertions of destiny "invasions." So many books have been written about them, and still people are unable to recognize them when it comes to their own lives. But now, after the invasion is over, I thought it was yet even more unfair that they couldn't come to terms with each other.

"Betsy, look, I want to be perfectly honest with you. I belong to your tribe. Believe me, I know what you feel right now." She lifted her large brown eyes at me having no idea what I was talking about.

"I abandoned my husband too. I too experienced the invasion, and went with the wind." As I expected, she only said: "Oh, dear." She wasn't much of a talker anyway, but she appreciated me saying this.

"Do you still love him?" I squeezed her soft hand. We were already moving down the paved lane toward the barn.

"I never stopped loving him." She murmured. Other guests kept moving from both sides of the road. Candles in tin cans lit the snowed-covered lawn showing the direction.

"Then maybe it's not too late to change it once again, to white out the mistake. I'm talking about having done with your own past."

"Garry is a bitter man. He won't even talk to me. Which is unfortunate." She said it firmly and smiled with one corner of her mouth.

"Do it and see what happens. You never know what some will say until you start the conversation."

"Oh, dear!" She helped me to get rid of my suede jacket. "People don't talk much in America. We don't live in a Dostoevsky novel here. More like in a silent movie."

"People don't talk much anywhere … And nobody is suggesting to wander into a Dostoevsky novel … What I tried to tell you is as simple as this: just talk to Garry …" She didn't say "no," she put a warm hand on my shoulder and I realized that it was quite time to fall silent.

The bride led by her father walked to the front isle of the barn. Passing me, she leaned her head and I saw a flicker in her eyes acknowledging my presence. Then I saw the groom, who was accompanied by Garry. Fire had Betsy's eyes, the dark eyes of a silent movie star. I immediately knew that he also wasn't much of a talker. But unlike Betsy, whose body had no gravity, a tumble weed, he had an anchor. What the hell was I trying to do, I asked myself. Had I made myself look like a fool? I hardly knew the woman on my right side and my acquaintance with the groom's father was even slighter. The music stopped, making room for the ceremony to get started again. The words were said, the oaths were given, some guest laughed, some cried. I didn't see much of Fire behind the crowd of people in front of me. But I could follow Tina's ritual movements with my eyes. She looked very sweet and gracious. "All is well, all is well, Fire is the one …" I mused and then a question came. "What makes you so sure?" "I don't know. They are from the same sandbox, as they say in Russia." At that point I started noticing the strange looks people were giving me.

"Oh dear, you talk to yourself …"

When half an hour later I entered Travelers' Castle most of the guests had already taken their seats in the dinning hall. The weather by then was changing outside, and the snow flew in from all four sides of the dark. The father of the bride was the first to pronounce a speech. He was a stiff tall gentleman of ordinary looks. It was difficult to imagine that this casual guy, with wrinkled forehead and square soldier's chin, with the slightly red nose of a drunkard was an American ambassador to several Eastern European countries for twenty five years, that he had personally met Leonid Ilyich Brezhnev, Josef Bros Tito, Ion Ceausescu and some other notorious leaders of the Soviet Block countries. In his speech accompanied with shy bursts of laughter mixed with embarrassment he counted the merits of his daughter and demerits of his new son-in-law. Tina was stunningly beautiful, extremely impractical, talented in the arts, trustful and universally loved. Fire was shorter than his wife by two inches, was poor as a church mouse and had the doubtful profession of a sitcom writer. That was kind of rude, but funny. Mr. Bart made me laugh to tears. He drained his glass to the bottom and sat down without looking at the guests.

"Fire grew up the Native American settlement among simple hardworking people, most of them farmers. I was a single father, never had much time for him. He taught himself how to read and write at the age of five, and the next year how to cook his lunch and wash his clothes. He was a trooper, he is a trooper." Garry had a mellifluous Southern accent. Two burning almond shaped eyes lifted above the guest's heads addressing a plump fair woman in the corner of the dinning room. Betsy sat in her chair in a very straight position. Her strong young hands lay on the white tablecloth in front of her. Moonshine played around her face. "When Fire met Christina Bart and fell in love with her, he called me on the phone and asked my opinion. I suggested that he took her to the town where he grew up for a vacation. "Why should I, dad? It's boring out there," Fire told me. I explained that boredom is the best test of love. And he did. For three weeks they lived among our folks camping in the prairie, making food on the old stove, taking care of each other when both fell sick with a flu. When Fire and Tina got back to New York they knew they were meant for each other. I hope, they are right about it. But what do I know? I'm a surgeon, I'm not a psychologist" he finished and lowed himself into his chair. Many of the guests were moved to tears. Garry's speech, charged with sadness made everybody hungry, and the clinking of silverware filled the large room. Waiters were still serving between the tables, bringing wine, when I stood up. I wasn't quite sure what power pushed me up to the center of the room. There are moments in life when you don't need to consult reason. Anyway, I experienced an almost religious sensation of separation from my own earthly flesh, which stayed at the table while another me reached the focal point of the sixty people in the dinning room in one leap. The last thing I remember seeing was Tina's look. Her long neck leaned toward her husband's shoulder swaying all the way forward, her face blushed with alarm.

"I wanted to share with you my love experience." I said, and without knowing what I did, I took a bottle from table number four and filled my glass. "Look at me, dear guests! Stop chewing and look up! I'm a forty year old writer, an author of seven books of poetry and two collections of essays. I'm also a professor of Russian literature. I'm jobless temporarily but never mind. Two days ago I received a prestigious award …" I heard applause and waved my hand. "Stop it. It's zilch, nothing to me. I'm openly unhappy, dear friends and relatives, dear newlyweds, dear parents of the beloved celebrated couple! In a minute I'll make myself known to all of you. Just listen. Many years ago I fell in love with a wonderful man and married him. He was a talented physicist, very well known in his field. He loved me more than anything in his whole life, he wanted to spend every free moment with me, he abandoned his friends and surrounded me with care and understanding." Now, as I had the full attention of the audience, I started realizing the goal of my strange talk. Not that every other person shared my understanding of the moment. But I knew that Betsy followed me, and Garry whom I could see in my peripheral vision, became pale. "I did a bad thing to him, I betrayed him in the most horrible way. Being almost three months pregnant I had an abortion, packed my suitcase and left. If you had asked me 'why' then, I wouldn't be able to give you one intelligible reason. But later I learned the sad truth. And the sad truth is that I felt imperfect next to that great, loving, righteous man. In other words, I wasn't ready to accept the gift of love. Years passed, I lived here and there, I suffered and rejoiced. I grew as a human being as a result and thought that now I could go back and look for him. I bought a ticket and came to the city where he lived all these twenty years without me. He had never married after I fled, as it happened."

Joanna Howard

Helene, Draft of a Girl

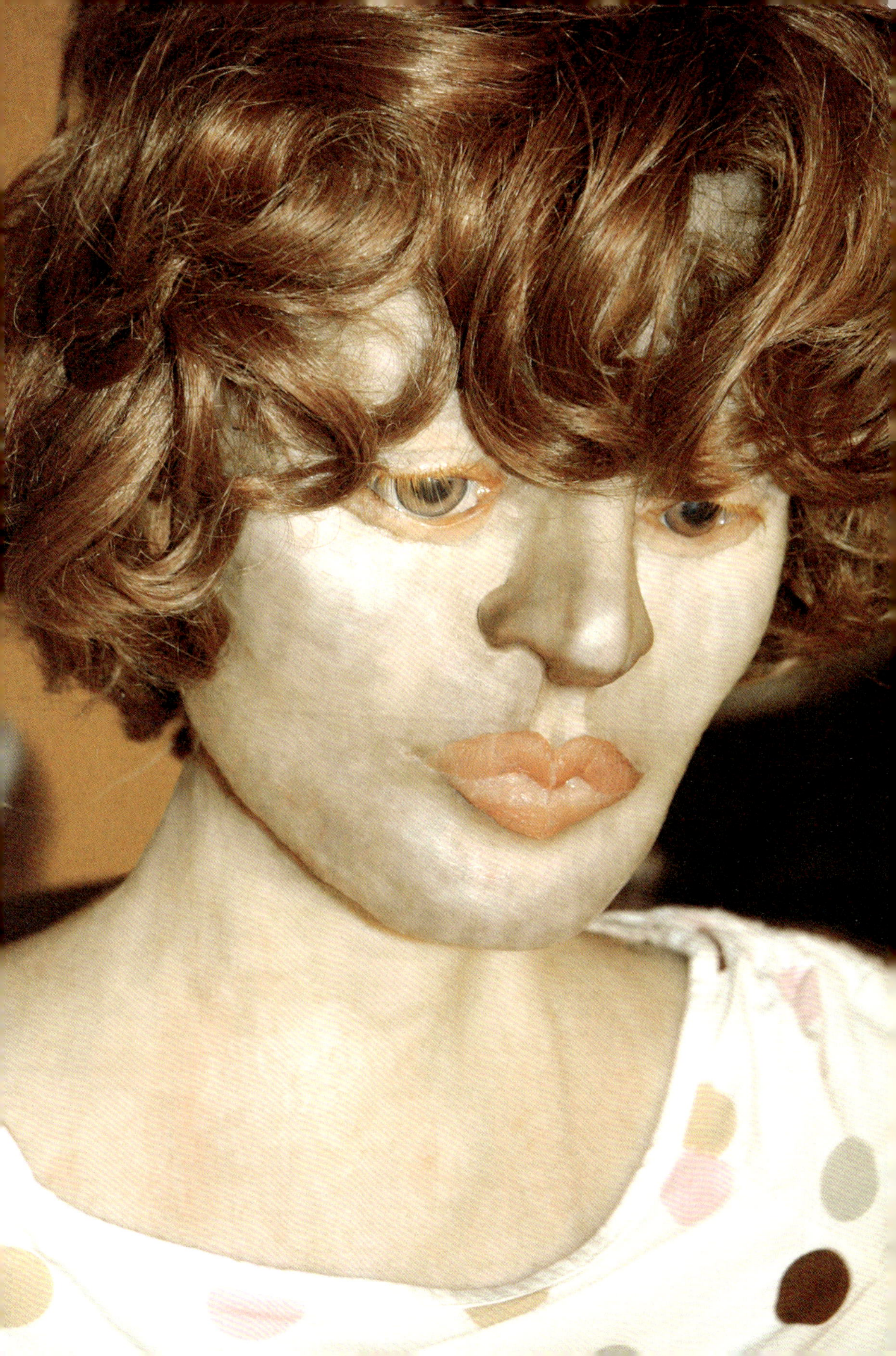

To begin an emblem, I offer the shorthand of my life: My arrival came quite late. Recently this fact reasserted itself. After a long day of driving to a picturesque inn on the Cape, I arrived much too late. The restaurant was already closed, and inside only a faint light emerged from behind the potted palm. The party had already dispersed. My girlfriends, what was left of this meager group from the deep past, had forgotten to mention several specifics of the reunion. I doubt it was spiteful. It was simply that it didn't register on any of them to be careful in arranging things with me. And the ladies were not waiting. Though this was no surprise. Even on the long drive along the coast, I had been unable to image any other scenario than one in which I was left here alone on the dark sidewalk. It had been so many years since the four of us had been together, or so it would seem, *together with me*. (They had of course been together without me for many years.) Outside the restaurant, the empty streets of this fashionable tourist district were quiet and quaint. Fairy lights dangled in the lindens. Dainty and high-end shops kept tasteful vitrines. I attempted to look beyond the faintly mirrored glass of the restaurant window to a place deep within where some scrap of movement seemed to betray a person. A rap on the pane, and then the quick flicker of the last man slipping out the back. I breathed a certain relief. He escaped out the back door, and I dashed off across the street to my car. In our opposite retreats, we had a similar thought in mind: only to get back to the safety of a quiet, if empty, home.

Had there been a time when I still loved them, the three old girls? Yes, but it had been nearly 20 years. And I do remember it, if not well, at least *well enough.* There were four couples at the rented cabin in the mountains for the holidays that last time we were all together. For the first few days, we exhausted ourselves at various outdoor sports in the thin, cold air: long hikes, skiing, and an assortment of rustic house chores in this far-from-modern locale. On Christmas Eve, the men attempted, for the first time in their lives, to roast a leg of lamb. We assorted wives were grateful for the evening, and with our children raucously occupied with each other, we sat about lost in our own minds. We scattered about the cabin with books and knitting. Only one, the best of my girlfriends, stayed in the kitchen on a bar stool, making helpful suggestions, and in general being one of the boys in a way that men seem to find appealing. Inevitably, when chaos ensued, and a column of smoke came up from the burner of the stove, in her drunken good humor, she grabbed up a hot pan only to drop it instantly on the floor. From the living room, where I knelt before a coffee table, I watched as my own husband swooped naturally over my friend and collected the boiled potatoes in the palms of his bare hands. They were both blatant and blithe in their complicity. He dropped the potatoes back into the pan, and then glanced over his shoulder in my direction, but I continued on, flipping through a book of photographs. I adjusted the rather uncomfortable blouse my best friend had given me for Christmas, something which was much more in that woman's style than in my own: low-cut, feminine, in general open and revealing. At the time, I couldn't quite put all the pieces together. Exuberant laughter poured out of the kitchen and several of the other wives put their heads up almost long enough to suggest that they cared what their men were about. I suppose, it was in this instance, as in so many before, that I tried to remain unmindful of the coming onslaught.

On New Year's Eve, that same year, we followed the European tradition of dropping molten lead into a crock of cold water. The others melted filings in the bowl of a bent spoon over the flame of a candle, and then each in turn, with a quick snap of the wrist, dropped the liquid lead into the water. The shape that emerged predicted the future, though only with careful interpretation. One by one, they extracted magnificent mounds from the water: jagged, faceted indications of their lives to come. When my turn finally came, my gesture was off completely, and the metal burst apart on the surface of the water into so many slight drops. The fragments I pulled from the water could certainly not be reassembled. I wanted to try again, but fate rarely has more to offer the second time around, and what could be worse than confirming one's future in shards? And somehow, letting them know that I actually believed in this ridiculous ritual seemed far worse than whatever was yet to come.

In those days, my mind easily snarled. I could pace for hours, and never resolve anything. It was one of my least attractive qualities. My husband had told me so many times before. On our last day at the cabin, the men went off on a long walk through the woods, and I watched from the balcony. As they all gathered around my husband, one of them held his elbow as he moved through the trees, another kept stopping him, moving into his path, and then as if remembering himself, continued on along beside him. They made a pretty set, all of these fit professional gents in their jackets and scarves, and their country gumboots, with their thick dark hair poking out beneath stocking caps. In a way, I could tell that they might very well be interchangeable. It had yet to occur to me that we girls might also be interchangeable, though no one seemed to be looking my way. From the bottom of the hill my husband watched me pacing in my shawl, before he finally got it off his chest. This first major schism, the first parting of ways. I would no longer see any of them, not for a very long time, even in passing.

Now, it is later in life than ever before, and my youngest daughter rests all her sullen weight on a campus bench in the Berkshires, while the college band marches through the quad playing a fight song. It's lurid New England fall, and it's parent's weekend, and there are all too many of us, trying to mingle with students as though a memory of youth manifests itself physically when called upon. Quite a few fit-looking dads attempt a pick-up match of soccer. This unfair distribution of spirit is alarming. My ex is among them, with cut and bloodied knees making a display of his potency. I don't know who he is trying to impress, but it is certainly not me. It really does not occur to him to feel that this is an awkward event, for the three of us. That shows how totally he has erased the effect of me on his life. If he regards me, out of the corner of his eye, it is only as a novelty. That something about the making of him, the forming of who he is today, is somehow tied up in our years together, is likely the only positive emotion he can possibly offer me. What I make of myself, or what I have failed to make of myself, is my own problem.

My daughter, now in her late twenties, has never really managed to blend into her generation. Perhaps because I had her so late in life, or perhaps, because for so long, I have forced her to be my best friend. If only the rest of her could be so delicate, so porcelain, as the fingers that now rest against her temple, instead of cakey and startled. She remains, even in this enormous group, unaccompanied. When she speaks, she speaks in her usual ugly way, about betrayal and trust, before sinking into a sweatered lump. Her periodic complaints about her father, however terse, are perhaps a gesture in some way toward caring for me. I have no idea if she talks to him. Certainly, a part of me would like to think that at *some point* she becomes animated. Some part of her wants to spend our time together roughly silent. All that is forthcoming from her end is another blocky reminder of myself. The less said, the more remembered. And that is something I'm firmly against. I have no desire to let my memory have the upper hand.

Rather, I prefer to hold onto only the few brief moments of my life worth noting. For good or ill. Namely, that in my girlhood dreams walked tyrants and invalids from films. Such memories are just the memory of a fantasy, once so real it occupied my mind entirely. For instance, in the dim flicker of the cinema, while my head began to ache from the shuddering light, I recall only a wagon train, and an attack, and that when the damsel's shoulder was pierced and held to the wheel, there was someone to cut away the fletching. And, in lighting gunpowder in the groove of the shaft, the hero (gunslinger, outlaw, sheriff) could draw it through this precise hole in the body, and cauterizing, seal the wound from the inside out. Oh happy fantasy.

Or, there is another memory. That in the beauty of my youth, in another country, the country I was born in and in my parents home, in the last year of the war, there was a day when the phone began to ring, and in the distance was the sound of something falling from the sky. Then a greater sound. The staircase collapsed beyond the open bathroom door: glass strewn, uncrossable path. A beam, from overhead, had joined me in the tub. I remained in the bath for a time, until, with sovereignty, I passed over this newly bejeweled field. The house was now open-aired looking onto the scrap of a courtyard. I had broken something, and beyond this, something had entered me. This memory of shrapnel and shards in the body, and my foot which, in turning, turned a bit more than before, this stays with me. A gammy leg I would carry forward. This bit garnered for the duration.

Or, there is a correction of one final scene in that other country that I knew so well, a memory shortly from before the bombing. A parachutist, whose chute had failed to open, who I watched falling into my father's freshly plowed field. Every bone in his body was fractured by the fall. I watched him through the faceted colored glass of the staircase window.

Is it my memory or my fantasy that returns me there now? For it seems that at this moment, I can finally drag him inside to care for him. The dark figures may not emerge from the wooded edge to claim and allocate. Nor later, the distant report of the pistol may not call out in rejoinder. Better still in this final possession, as I put together the two memories I have of this house, this war, as in a dream we connect the disparate and forge a new narrative, I finally may meet him on his own ground. We two cross the shattered courtyard, ruptured, fractured, unable to move in space ever again as we had before. He has gained a curious new aspect, his features in new alignment intersect, and the organs of my body have now been replaced with stained glass. In light of this, they must be held very carefully, very gently, inside me.

Carol Novack

Crazy Broad

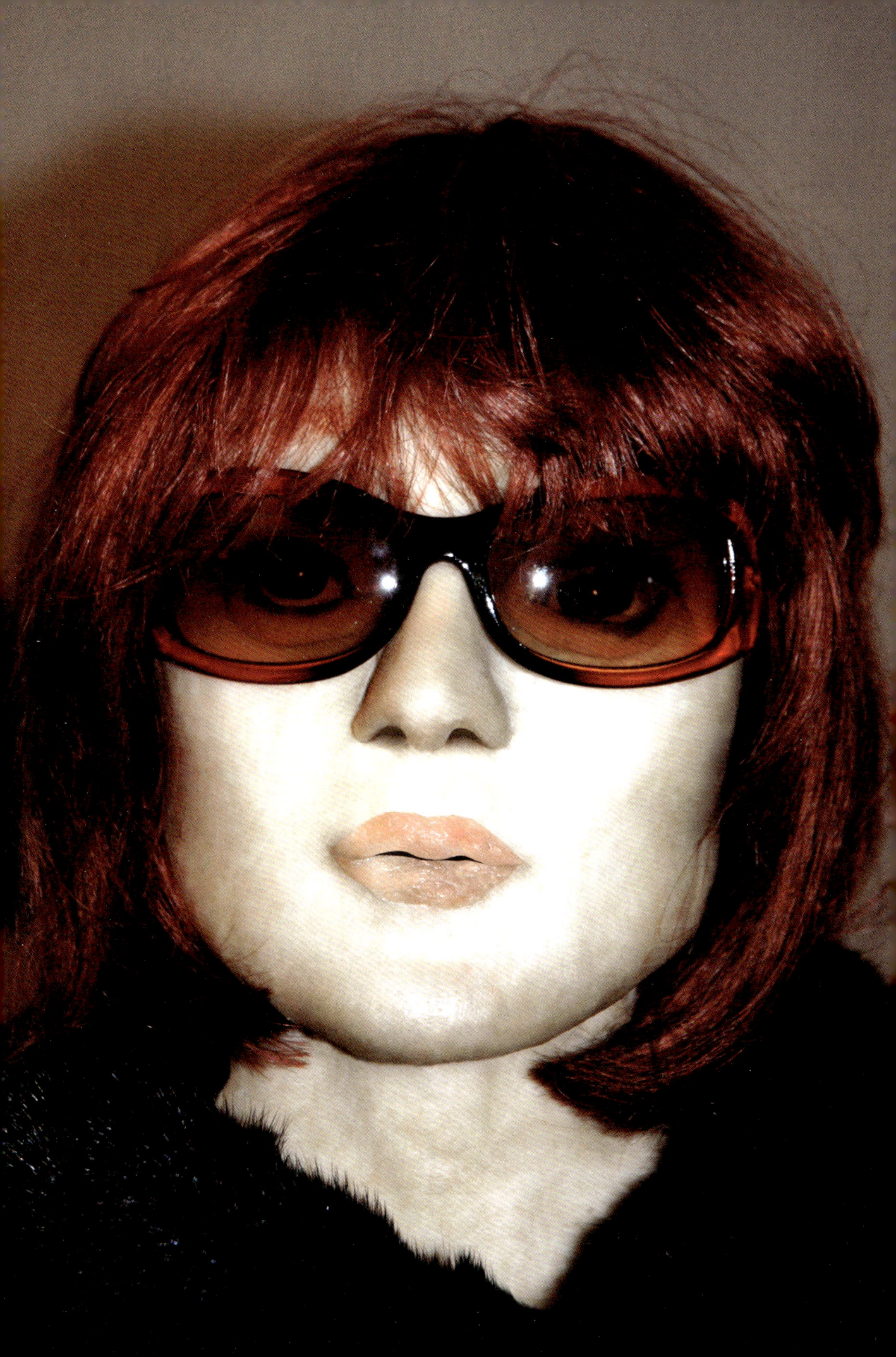

The young woman has a job editing articles for a trade magazine. Theoretically, she could tell you anything you might want to know about camping equipment. Actually, she doesn't read the stuff; she checks for grammar, punctuation and spelling, and has to cut out words and phrases so the copy will fit. She tries to eliminate phrases like "maximum comfort," "economically priced," and "guaranteed for life." She knows next to nothing about what kind of tent you should purchase if you're going to be camping in Yellowstone National Park with your ho-hum dog and three kids, so don't ask.

Truth is she doesn't want to go anywhere and doesn't want to be where she is. She split up for good with some guy over three months ago after one of those on again off again agonizingly prolonged attempts at permanent pairing, ho-hum. She can't decide whether she hates the man more than she loves him or whether she ever liked him or loved him anyway, but she's in a black hole over it. The thing she thinks about most is when she'd make his favorite roast chicken and he'd complain she hadn't cooked it long enough. And he'd complain about his crazy mother who'd never cooked him anything. Calling the guy a bastard is too easy. She's trying her best not to fool herself too much.

On this hot and irritatingly humid summer Friday, the young woman and her boss take off a little early and go to a trendy new bar that's supposed to be a replica of an 1880's saloon. The boss is fashionably anorectic with a voice like a cello's and has an after hours habit of swinging her long chestnut mane languorously from side to side; she also has a matching, chestnut colored Siamese cat. It seems that whenever they go out together, the young woman ends up alone at one end of a bar; she's the one wearing the long, black, high-collared cotton dress, even in August, wearing it because she feels fat and worn and believes that black makes her invisible, although she also thinks maybe black makes her look sexy 'cause that's what it's supposed to do.

So the young woman's nursing her third or fourth sex on the beach which nobody bought her, of course, and the boss is talking to this immaculate specimen of American maleness sitting next to her, you know, Wall Street navy blue suit, light blue striped shirt and red tie with tiny blue amoebas. His face is composed primarily of horizontal eyebrows and a mouth like two pickup sticks and ho hum he's been buying the boss Sapphire Blue martinis with little white onions, no umbrellas.

Next thing the young woman knows she's into her sixth or seventh sex on the beach and her boss isn't in sight; she might've said something about leaving a while ago, but the young woman isn't sure, so she gets down from her stool and makes a grand tour of the bar. By this time, the crowd is thick, sticky, and predictably boisterous. Somewhere a jukebox is featuring one of those pop stars with a babyish voice singing *oooooh ooooh babeeee do me like you done me.*

The young woman would prefer Otis Redding sitting on a dock. She's nostalgic for her college years and all those people she may never see again, but she can only vaguely recall them anyway, particularly the guy with the red hair who drank Southern Comfort and tripped on LSD while he was playing jazz piano. Pathetic, she thinks ho hum *really stupid.*

Actually, the young woman's starting to feel as if she were standing at the edge of a subway platform waiting for the right moment to jump, just that moment when you see the tracks pale with the light of an oncoming train. She can't call the old boyfriend 'cause that horrible "girl" he's been seen with might answer the phone and she shouldn't anyway, and she's not ready to go home to her studio apartment which she hasn't cleaned in weeks, and she can't call her best friend who just got engaged. That's just about when one of the ugliest men she has ever seen starts talking to her, if you'd call it that, like *talking?*

If you asked her now, she'd be unable to remember his name and his features are a blur. She recalls he's on the short stocky side, with greasy dirty blonde hair, blotchy skin, and eyes of no discernable color that look as if they belonged on a corpse. Definitely off eyes. But she might be hard pressed to identify him in a lineup with other ugly men. Another drink before she allows herself to launch into an incoherent conversation.

What they speak about is mostly him. He says something about painting houses or doing construction but she's not really listening, trying to extricate herself politely; after all, he can't help looking that way and being boring too. He won't go to foreign films because he hates subtitles, talks incessantly about baseball teams, and thinks it's "cute" that she goes on protests. So she tells him she has to leave, she's hungry, and she has to visit her aunt in the hospital. He spends the next half hour or so trying to convince her to go to his place in an unfamiliar and scary neighborhood she's avoided; she'll get to ride his motorcycle and then he'll feed her. Then they'll listen to his fantastic collection of disco records and he'll give her a ride home after all that. The guy hasn't bought her a single drink and the thought of disco unnerves her.

Well, by this time she's thinking why not if he feeds me. There's something about this whole person that's awry but she can't put her finger on it; and at this stage she's not sure that she really gives a damn what happens to her. She really doesn't; she can't get the point of herself straight. She feels numb, as though she's been sleepwalking for years. The mirror behind the bar reflects a face hardly recognizable as hers. The face appears to stretch across the entire length of the glass, streaky as a poor paint job.

The guy lives on a street of vacant lots and dilapidated brownstones. His apartment's on the first floor of one of the brownstones and smells like stale cigarettes and rotting food. There's a guy watching a small television in what appears to be the living room. He grunts at the ugly man, who steers her into his bedroom "to show" her "things." There's a dart board over the apparently unused fireplace, which is cluttered with cigarette stubs and newspapers. The single bed is unmade; the window shutters are drawn. She thinks the poster above his bed is meant to depict the Madonna on a crucifix, but the woman looks like a female version of Superman stripped of his pants; a burning bush encircles her vagina, which exposes a pulsing, red clitoris.

The ugly guy points out a framed award he received from some vigilante gun club for being able to shoot straight. She doesn't see a single book in the room, just lots of motorcycle and girlie magazines. He chooses a record from a heap on the floor and places it on the turntable of his stereo system, which dominates at least a fourth of the room. He adjusts the volume, plays the disco loud. He's squatting to fiddle with the knobs; for a moment, she thinks he's a goat.

The young woman suggests going into the kitchen to fix something to eat. Reluctantly, he leads her there and opens the refrigerator. She peers inside, sees something that looks as if it might've been cheese, two six packs of Pabst, a bottle of ketchup, and a nearly empty jar of mayonnaise. He hands her a beer and extracts what might've been a head of lettuce from the vegetable bin. "No good," he says he'd thought of making tuna fish salad. But there's scant mayo and no tuna fish. She can hear sitcom laughter wafting obscenely from the television.

The next part of the evening is even more of a blur than the preceding part. Somehow they're back in his bedroom sitting on the bed and then she's lying on it, pinned down by his arms.

The young woman knows she must've said "I have to go home now" several times and struggled to get away from him. She knows she must've been polite, and she must've attempted to explain she didn't know him well enough. She might've said, "I think I've had too many drinks," "I have to visit my aunt," "I have to go to an abortion rights demonstration tomorrow morning." Whatever she said drew no response.

Next thing she recalls is her panties are off, he's pulling his pants off, and he's forcing himself into her. There's no point in struggling; he's stronger and it doesn't matter anyway. She now knows why they call this sort of thing "screwing"; she's so dry it hurts like hell. He hurts like hell grinding into her and the room is spinning around the blasting bare light bulb hanging from the ceiling and she can't get away from this maniac and how did she let herself get into this, let him get into her.

What an idiot I am, she thinks.

After the guy's finished, he lies beside her, lights a cigarette. He says, "Why don't we go away together? I've been saving some money to go down south and start a turkey farm." He says, "I know you'd like that, but you're a little spacey, you know. I don't know …" She lies there, wondering if she should humor him. She can't seem to move. At some point, way into his monologue, something about his cousin doing time in Alabama, she manages to sit up and find her underpants. As she's putting them on, he puts his hand on her shoulder and asks her where she's going. He lets her go to the bathroom. The young woman sits on the toilet, hunched over, elbows on her knees. She can't pee and is wondering if – when she does – she'll pee blood. He's standing in the hallway by the door when she comes out. He grabs her by the waist 'cause she looks as though she's going to fall.

Back in his room, the ugly guy tells the young woman to lie down on the bed. She closes her eyes and tries to think up pleasant childhood memories while he's screwing her but all she can think of is the time she apparently said or did something mean to a girl at camp and got stung by a wasp when she put her hand in her pocket. She tries to pretend she's swimming in the ocean. She tries to pretend she's hallucinating this guy. She tries to pretend she's in love. But the guy's skin smells a bit like asparagus pee and his every touch bruises a different part of her.

The young woman looks at the ugly guy, who has fallen asleep. The cast of sleep has lent an innocence to his face, a startling perspective, possibly absurd. But she doesn't look too long, dresses as quietly as possible. She's about to leave the room when he asks, "Oh, you're going?" "Yes," she answers, "go back to sleep, I'll see you soon." "Crazy broad," he responds, but he doesn't stop her.

The young woman doesn't know if or where she can find a cab. She actually considers returning to the apartment to ask the guy to give her a ride. If you were to ask her how she got home, she has no recollection.

No matter how hard she tries to forget, she recalls, sharply, her awakening the next afternoon. "I felt like a fish that has swallowed one of its own bones." That's the only way she can describe the pain. She recalls her awakening, makes light of it.

Lydia Millet

Sexing the Pheasant

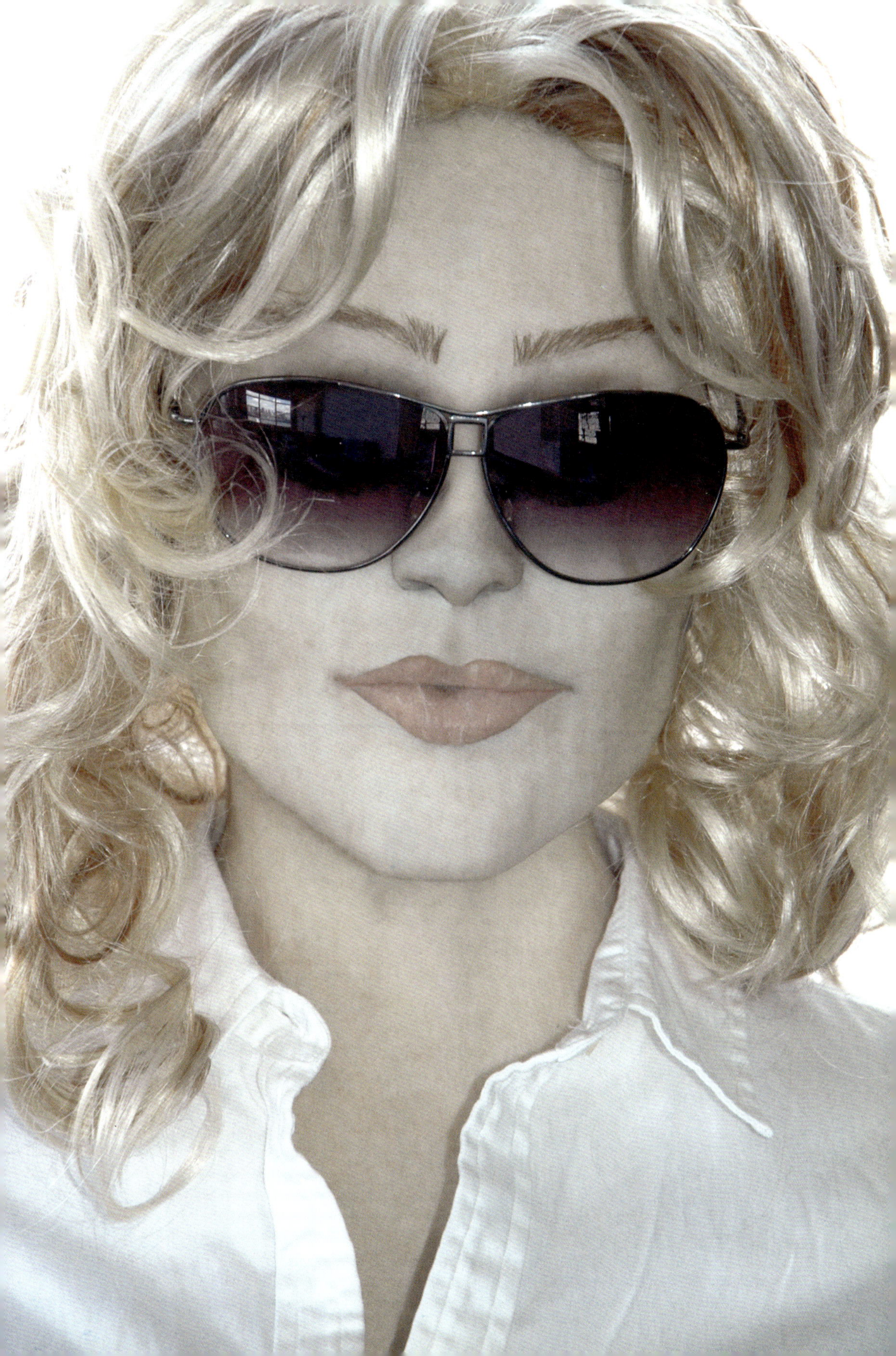

When a bird landed on her foot the pop star was surprised. She had shot it, certainly, with her gun. Then it fell from the sky. But she had not expected the actual death thing. Its beak spurted blood. She'd never really noticed birds. Though one reviewer had compared her to a screeching harpy. That was back when she was starting. What an innocent child she was then. She'd actually gone and looked it up at the library. "One of several loathsome, voracious monsters. They have the head of a woman and the wings and claws of a bird."

She did not appreciate the term *pop star*. She had told this to Larry King. She preferred *performance artist*. She was high art and low commodity, and ironic about how perfectly the two fit. A blind man could see her irony. She was postmodern, if you wanted to know, pastiche. She embodied.

What, exactly?

If you had to ask, you just didn't get it.

The bird feebly flapped and made silent beak-openings. Where the hell was Guy when she needed him? The London tabloids still called him Mr. Madonna, even though she had tried to make clear on numerous occasions that he wore the testicles in the family. She wanted to yell at them: giant testicles, OK? Testicles! Huge! ("Large bollocks." Use frequently.) He was back there somewhere in the trees. Easy to get separated on a thousand acres. She was an English lady now; not to the manor born, but to the manor ascended. So she was the American ideal, which was the self-made person, and the English ideal too, which was snotty aristocrats. Not bad for a girl from Pontiac, Michigan. These days she just said "the Midwest," which gave it more of a cornfed feeling. Wholesome. In that *Vogue* thing she said Guy was "laddish" and she was "cheeky" and Midwestern. Later she learned "laddish" was pretty much an insult, actually. Well, eff 'em if they couldn't take a joke.

She should step on its little face and crunch it. But the boots were Prada.

Should she shoot it again? No. She couldn't stand to. Sorry. She would just wait for the rest of them; no point being out here all alone and unseen anyway. Shouldn't have strutted off all righteous while they stood there drinking. If he wanted to be a frat boy, let him. Her own body was a hallowed temple. His was apparently more of a bordello/sewer type thing. He was acting out because he was pissed at her. (Self: "peevish." *Pissed* meant drunk in England.) For the shrunken balls situation. No man wanted puny shriveled ones the size of Bing cherries. Still: not her fault. He had to step up himself. If he felt like the stay-at-home wife to her world-famous superstar, he had serious work to do. On himself. Not on her. She was not the one with the self-esteem issues.

Frankly she might as well be doing weights, if the alternative was standing around in the dried-out brown winter grass waiting for idiots. Waste of time. Hers was at a premium. And the abs were a perfect washboard, but in her personal opinion the quads could still use some hardening.

When the rest of the party got here he would take care of it for her. Drunk or sober, he would put it out of its misery. What were men good for if not to crush the last spark of life out of a small helpless creature?

OK. The rabbi had been hinting at this: it was better not to kill animals. For sport, anyway. Before, when she was learning to shoot, she never hit anything. Only the clay pigeons. It was fun and games then. The "bespoke" clothes were good, the whole "compleat" attitude. (Good thinking.) These knee breeches, for instance, were the sh-t. She bent over and stared at them. Flattering. She was "chuffed." (Self! So good!) And guns, let's face it: there was no better prop in the world. A woman with a gun was kind of a man in girl's clothes, a transvestite with an external dildo. But guns had more finesse. A gun was basically a huge iron dildo designed by someone French and classy.

So, shooting: she had liked it till now. Guy looked good with his 12-bore. He was a nature boy. It was sexy on him, esp. with the faux-Cockney stylings. ("Mockney." Use in moderation.) Basically if a man had a gun it was like a double cock. A cock and a replica cock, which was also postmodern. One had the power of life, the other had the power of death. Ying-yang. *Sefirot*. Etc.

Back to the bird. She felt a wince in her throat. It was still struggling weakly and blubbing blood, trying to flap its way up a small rise in the ground. Not much time had passed. All this thinking made the minutes go by slowly. Had she kicked it away? She must just have stepped back. It wasn't on the tip of her boot anymore; it was a few inches off, dry leaves sticking to its bloody side as it wobbled forward and then did a face-plant. Must have a leg broken as well as a wing. Guess she had good aim these days, since she'd really hit it. Madonna: marksman. That worked. Evoked paintings from the Renaissance. ("Re-*nay*-since." Use frequently.) Gentle mother of God done in a Duccio style, or a soft Da Vinci: but then instead of holding the Christ child, sweetly cradling an AK-47.

Consider for next album.

Madge, marksman. That worked too. When the British press gave you a nickname, that meant you were one of their own. Love you or hate you, that was irrelevant. What mattered was being one of them. In the gray steely ranks. The long-gone colonies. Once they ruled the world, now all they had was a better accent. They wore it well, though. An entire country that was basically quaint. Plus less of them were obese. In her closets there were hundreds of those tailor-made tweeds ... but she could still wear the outfits, even if she stopped the killing. Right? You could pull off tweed without actually shooting. Couldn't you?

Esther, marksman ... nah. Didn't work.

She was distracted; she could not focus, could not ... she was cold, standing there shivering. If millions of screaming fans knew she was cold at this very instant, they would rush to her aid. They would bring her their coats. Take the coats off their backs. Yeah, whatever. One thing was for sure: their coats would suck. (Off-the-rack = "naff." Use frequently.)

It had to be dying soon. "Shite!" (Good work, self!) It was taking a while.

She had nothing against the poor thing, but then it rose out of the bushes and flew up and blam! – fell to earth, like Bowie in that seventies movie. (Sternly to self: "Film.") He was like Jesus in that. If Jesus was an alien. Which, let's face it, he probably was. There was no other explanation. Huh: what if Christians were basically the UFOlogists of ancient history? And the Jews were the people who were the debunkers? They were like, "No, the messiah hasn't come, and if he has, where's the proof?" Whereas the Christians were the ones who said, "Seriously, the aliens came down, and we saw them. Man, you've got to believe us!" Except there was only one of these aliens, namely Jesus.

Christians were hopeful, which made them basically insane. They were hopeful about the past, i.e., Christ = son of God, etc. Hopeful about the future, i.e., paradise will be ours, etc. And then the clincher: they figured this particular hope made them legitimate. They hoped they personally would be saved and live happily ever after: and then they had the chutzpah to call that faith. So like, faith was thinking you were great and deserved to sit at the right hand of God. Selfish much?

Jews were more like, Come on. Be reasonable. Here we are on earth, now just try to be nice for five minutes, would you? Can we have five lousy minutes without a genocide? Sheesh.

Course Kabbalah was something else again. It wasn't that you deserved to be saved, it was that God was in *you*. The power of the names of God, the seventy-two names inscribed in figures of light … what if the bird had tiny eggs in a nest somewhere? She had her own eggs, Lola and Rocco. This thing could be a mother too. Poor little thing. Birds were graceful. She wouldn't look that good if someone shot her. Bad thought! Knock on wood. She reached out for a thin tree. Did a tree count as wood?

I mean yeah, she knew that, but for luck purposes?

Actually, if she was shot in the right place, then well-lit, she could look excellent. Kind of martyr concept. Consider. If not shot, crucified. (Good one there.)

Now the eggs would die in the abandoned nest, forgotten. But maybe not, if this bird was a man. Rooster, that is. When it came to pheasants they called them hens and roosters. (Good work, self.) Too bad she couldn't tell. You couldn't check between a bird's legs like a dog or horse or something. A male bird had nothing out there bobbing and dangling. Really no way to know. Unless you were like a bird penis specialist. (Kidding, self.) The poor birds had no dicks. Their sex was in the plumage. Any idiot knew that. Different colors, she guessed, but then there were the young ones, that all looked the same. Piece in the *Mirror* recently called her "an accomplished breeder of pheasant and partridge" – good. Good. In the sense of *manager*, she *managed* the breeding. She didn't sex the things personally, so what. She hired very good gamekeepers. Had to know how to delegate.

She was chosen by God. That was what so many people seemed to completely overlook. What else explained her meteoric rise to stardom? Her continued success? For twenty years now she had basically been a megastar. Try, the most famous person in the world, basically. They said her name in the same breath with Elvis and Marilyn. What, because she was pretty? Just because she could dance, and once mastered a Casio? (Kidding, self, just kidding!) She had talent, even brilliance, even exceptional brilliance ("Brill." Use in moderation.), and nothing's wrong with a Casio anyway.

But that alone would get you to the corner gas station. ("Petrol." Good thinking.) True to her name, which was not even a fake one, she had been chosen. Chosen to embody.

Now and then someone asked her, usually a crazed psycho, "Are you the Second Coming?" Because that was what it looked like, if you were literal-minded. Like maybe she was the Mother of God, Mark II. She wouldn't go that far, of course. There was a reason they called them psychos. But the kind of luck she'd had couldn't really be called luck anymore. Luck was catching a bus, maybe winning a raffle. Luck was a good parking spot.

You had to keep this kind of knowledge under wraps, though, as a celebrity. You had to keep it a secret between yourself and yourself or you would end up a Tom Cruise. Come to believe the sun shone from your sphincter, and go around beaming with the smugness of the All-Knowing Colon.

When all you were, at the end of the day, was a highly paid face.

But she got him basically, the Scientology thing. Not her "cup of tea" (good work, self!) but what the media didn't get, when they made fun of her and Guy for Kabbalah, or Gere for his Dalai Lama or Cruise for his pyramid scheme or whatever the *Dianetics* thing was anyway, was *you* needed to worship too. The fans worshipped you because they needed something: well, what were *you* supposed to do? Well, prostrate yourself before the Infinite. Clearly.

OK, granted, sometimes the mirror suggested it: not your fault if your reflection reminded you of all that was sacred, all that was divine and holy. The world would do it to you. At that point you were the victim. Brainwashing, like with anorexics. Too many magazine covers. But she resisted. She was actually very humble. And of course, it was not wrong to see God in yourself. Anyone could do it. That was where the intellectual part came in. She read the holy books, she read old plays and that ... it helped her, as an artist, to be extremely intelligent. Besides being a savvy businesswoman – she got that a lot, and rightly – even a genius at the marketing level, she was a seeker. A seeker never gives up.

She was pretty sure she remembered there was some kind of bird that would sit on another bird's eggs, hatch them and feed them like they were its own. The Mia Farrow of nature. Maybe one of those little mamabirds would come rescue the eggs of the dying one. She hoped so. Other day she saw that pigeon she told *Vogue* was the reincarnation of Cecil Beaton ... the best fags were all English fags. Englishmen were the Ur-faggots, pretty much. All other fags in the world were pale imitations of real English fags. This was the land of homos; even the straight men were fags here. One reason she liked it so much. In the U.S. guys were basically rapists; here they seemed uptight and formal with their great accents and not showing any emotion, but all the time they were basically daydreaming about nancy boys in sailor suits. Not all of them, of course, I mean what would a sex goddess like herself do without at least a few of the poor "sods" (pat to self!) being genuine heteros, but you know, the default position. ("Benders, bum bandits, ginger beer." Use in moderation.)

Guy was not gay, of course. But he had an edge of anger to him. The ones that weren't gay were often angry about it.

It was a tradeoff, more or less.

OK. The bird was finally chilling out. Lying there. "Effing" dead. (Good one. Use frequently.)

"Oi. Bag one then?"

She jumped. He'd snuck up right behind her. It was the red-faced "bloke" from "down the pub," Guy's new pet "lager lout." (*Self! Ex*cellent!) Pig, as far as she knew. Gave her the creeps. What Guy saw in these losers from the King John with their saggy beer tits ... come to think of it, she liked this one even less when he was carrying a gun. A gun was like a cigarette that way: if you already looked good it made you look better; if you looked crap to begin with it made you look even worse. This particular "lager boy" had a chip on his shoulder about women with power. It hung on him like a stink. Made him actually dangerous.

Best not to challenge him. Alone here in the middle of the woods.

"I guess, you know – actually, I feel pretty bad. You know? I mean it was really suffering."

"Brain the size of a peanut, yeah? How much suffering could there be?"

He was openly contemptuous. Thing about these lager boys of Guy's was, they gave her a reality check. Like, what would it be like to be a regular person again? They had zero respect for her, for her megastar stature. At this point in her career most people she met either had to resist an urge to genuflect or got completely tongue-tied. Often their mouths hung open like Down's Syndrome kids. (Which was sad. The real retards, that is. Come to think of it, retards were among the few that still acted normal.) Once she had cheek-kissed a journalist – one, two, in the English manner – and he fainted and soiled himself all over the place. And that was a guy who was used to famous people, they were his total job. You learned to spot in a second which ones were going to freak out. Point was, the lager louts would have been refreshing if they weren't such assholes. She was sorry for their wives and girlfriends.

He leaned down to pick it up.

"No! No," she said, and put out her hand. "Just – thanks, but you can leave it. I want to just leave it there."

"Defeats the purpose, dunnit."

"I just want to leave it in peace. I don't want to desecrate the corpse."

He snorted.

"You seen the others? Guy? Was he with you?"

"Nah. Went off on me own." He was turning away.

"Wait! Can you tell me something?"

"Mmm?"

"Is it a hen? Or –"

"Rooster! Blimey."

What a relief. No eggs.

He stumped back down the hill, head shaking. Good riddance. She knelt down beside the small body, modest hump of brown and red feathers. It was still beautiful. She put her hand on the feathers. You could feel the slight warm frame beneath them. It was light: almost nothing in there. Birds were like air.

It had been more beautiful when it wasn't dead, though. Before it was shot. Which wasn't true of everyone. Take JFK, even John Lennon. Assassination had matured them like a fine Pinot. If you died of old age, besides not leaving a good-looking corpse, all you died for in the end was living. But if you got shot you were an instant symbol. You must have died *for* something.

She was always completely new; that was her secret, albeit an open one. Sure it was obvious, but no one did it like she did. None of them could touch her, when it came to transformation. That was the key to her longevity. She wasn't one megastar; she was a new one constantly. Novelty was what people lived for. Skin-deep, maybe, but so what? Skin was the biggest organ.

She should envy the bird, actually. Guy said in the wild they died of starvation. Shooting them was a mercy killing. I mean come on, fly, eat worms, fly, lay eggs, fly, starve to death. "Bob's your uncle." (You go, girl.) Life was not equal for everyone. That was another reason she liked it better in England. They didn't stand for that Thomas Paine bullsh-t here, all men were created equal etc. What a crock. One drive through Alabama was all you needed to take the bloom off that rose. One ride in the subway. (Self: "Tube." Good work.) Back home, the second you stepped out of a major city you were surrounded by the remnants of Early Man. Here there were some of those too, but you had to go down the pub to find them. And at least they didn't run the country.

All history was the history of class struggle, right? Lenin said that, and he had style. He had a very sharp look. When the statues came down, she for one was sorry. She always wanted to meet him.

Maybe if she said a prayer. Yes. It felt right.

She touched the red string and squatted beside the bird. She would think holy thoughts about it; she would utter a name of God. She closed her eyes with her fingers resting on the feathers.

This was a problem she had: when she wasn't already tired it was sometimes hard to speed-meditate. Mind kept working, working. A powerful machine. Difficult to rein in. The bird once ate the worms, now worms would eat the bird … every word filled with light. That was how it should be. Desire to Receive. Which name? The name to reduce negativity?

What would help her and Guy, she saw, besides going to the Centre together on a more regular basis, was if Guy understood her more on a spiritual level. If he could just see her interior the way she saw it herself, he would not worry about the shrinking mini-Bings. He would see she was a little girl, secretly. She was a Shirley Temple. She was very pure, despite her sophistication. She believed in the ten luminous emanations. The ladder of awareness. She cherished in the core of herself the beingness of being.

Immortality for the bird, for all things of beauty. That was what the lager louts could just never capiche. It was right, so right to know your own beauty and see it was God's own beauty too. One day the body would be a giving vessel, not just a receiving. Life could go on forever. They might not be able to understand, the lager louts, what she was, what all of them could be if they gave themselves over to the light instead of, say, the Guinness, but that did not mean there was not room in God for them too. The house of God had many rooms. And through the great windows of these rooms the golden beams of the divine streamed in.

Not as many rooms as Ashcombe, possibly. (Joke! Joke to self.) The house of God was neverending.

The word for healing …?

But you couldn't heal dead.

She rose, still looking down at the bird. It was peaceful at last. She had killed it, but she was also sorry. In the end, that was all that mattered. Do not have violence in your heart.

"I love you now," she said.

She heard voices and turned. The hunting party stood at the edge of the trees, too far away to distinguish. But she thought she saw Guy there, with them. Nearby stood the dogs, tails wagging. The men's faces were small white blurs. She saw hands raise. First she thought they were raised in greeting, hailing her from afar. She raised her own right arm and waved back. But then she caught flashes of silver in the sun. Flasks raised to their faces. One of them stepped back from the group, staggering and falling. They had apparently not ceased to drink the whole time. Their laughter was carrying.

She felt annoyed, but then a surge of forgiving. She could not blame them for their alcoholism. They were so small! All of them. It was difficult to be small. Pity warmed her, a generous blossoming.

They would catch up sooner or later. Or should she walk toward them?

Micaela Morrissette

Wendigo

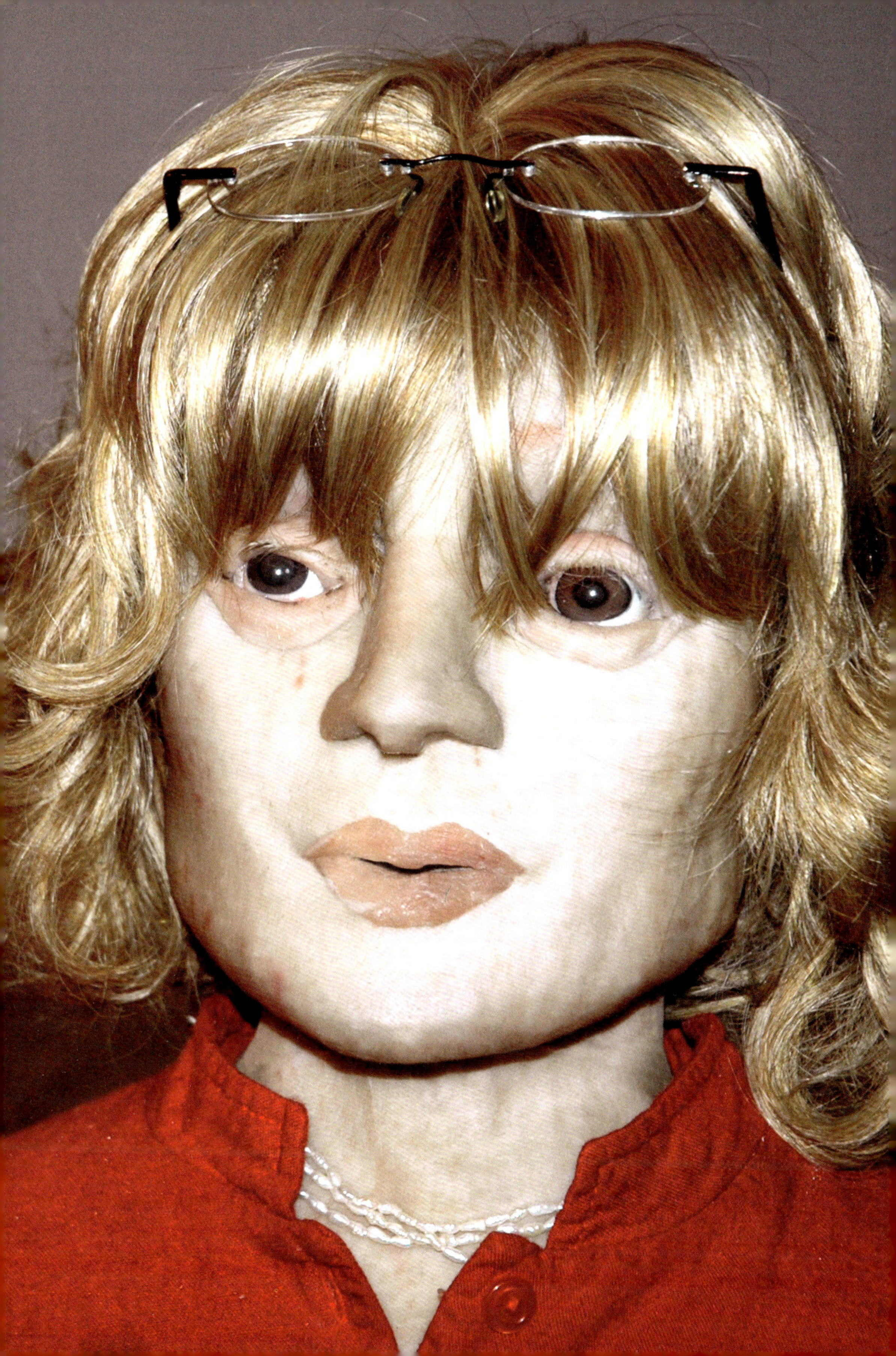

Dinner was special. The candles were miraculous, emanating a light that went oozing into pores, piercing into strands of hair, that found its way inside the thin glass of the champagne flutes, the rough, quartzy crystal of the punch bowl. Nothing glittered, nothing sparkled, nothing shone. Everything glowed, everything throbbed. The other guests did not smile, but they radiated pulses of tender heat in her direction, until her cheeks were mottled red. Each course in the banquet had an aura that hung heavily over the platter, like steam weighed down with globules of grease, thick particles of oily light.

She swallowed the wine that paused in her mouth, clung there, spreading itself. She swallowed the black soup: thin, sour broth swimming with clots that trailed delicate filaments. She swallowed the tempura of cobra lily, and, inside its cup, the pale, limp moth that seemed to sigh and dissolve on her tongue. When the songbirds were served, her gracious companion, sensing her confusion, placed a steadying hand on the back of her neck and guided her head under the starched napkin. She ate the scorching meat, needled with tiny bones her teeth had splintered. She felt little ruptures where they scratched her throat. Her companion was missing the fifth and second fingertips of his right hand, the entire middle finger of his left. Bluntly, blindly, fondly, the stubs knocked against her skin. The manservant brought the baby octopi in shallow bowls filled with, her host informed the company, vibrio fischeri, which sent a faint gold-green luminescence throughout the water. She dipped an octopus in the spicy sauce and trapped it lightly between her teeth. Its small heavings and sucks brushed against the pads of her cheeks like tiny kisses.

The main course was a roast: mild, slightly stringy. Sweet bursts of fat jetted from the sinews as she chewed. The light in the room was so dense it oppressed her; she could barely see through it. Food filled her stomach like air in a balloon; the heavier she grew, the higher above her chair she seemed to float. Her solicitous companion murmured an inquiry; it was decided they would leave before the dessert. She deposited her hand in that of her host. Rivulets of sweat trickled through the plump seams in his palm. He twinkled and beamed at her with his eye; the side of his face where the eye patch adhered remained stolid. In the car, she sniffed at her fingers, still slick from her host's farewell; they smelled like earth newly turned over: fresh, rich, heady. The smell seemed to cleanse her palate: Her eyelids spasmed in the bottomless night; her stomach wrenched in sudden appetite.

In the morning she woke with a head that felt stuffed with cement, cracking and crumbling against the inside of her skull in jagged pressure. Her bedroom was narrow and spare, the walls shrunk tight around the heat that came shrieking and spitting from the iron radiator. She scrabbled frantically at the window; it screeched open in a flurry of dirty paint chips, and the air shoved in, knocking her aside, gnashing at her shrinking skin. She sank down, flinching at the grit that bit her legs and hands, and entered her stretches. Inflexible, she tore tentatively at her muscles, lunging forward with shallow gasps. Compelling her forehead to the floor, she felt frustration lash up her spine and stab the back of her neck like a handcuff snickering tight around her straining.

The bathroom smelled strongly of the new plastic shower curtain. She brushed with her lips pursed around the handle of the toothbrush, preventing the froth from running out over her chin. Her skin was getting worse. Her face, which at sixteen had been so pure and watertight, was at thirty-three beginning to boil and leak. Her virginity, which had been withered, dry, and hard, was beginning to rot and extrude. Like a 1,000-year-old egg, it had softened, become pungent, delicious, disgusting. She tapped against her pubis with one finger. She flattened her palm against her stomach. "Somewhere in there," she said, "like a little dead baby."

She hobbled out in her matted pink robe, cleared the table of its ketchup-caked refuse, cooked three strips of bacon, which she ate with the fat still gelatinous and slightly cool. Her professional wardrobe was consistent: slacks, with leggings underneath to intervene against the scratch of the wool; a cardigan; another cardigan.

On the bus she leaned her head against the window so the jolts of the motor and the road chattered her teeth together. She tried to give up her seat to an expecting mother, but the woman didn't want to sit there. When she entered her cubicle there was an unfamiliar odor: creamy, sweet, powdery. Later in the day she could only smell it by whirling her head suddenly to the side. Her new colleague across the aisle caught her doing it and laughed. He had laughed the day before, too, at her dispersal of pillows: one on the seat of her folding chair, one at her back, two under her feet, one on her desk for her elbow to rest on. He had a gaping laugh, this new colleague, she could see the hole at the back of his mouth, he opened that wide. It was delightful. She thought of smiling at him, but resisted. Her smile, she knew, was crooked: It had a forced quality. Nonetheless, pleasure rocked through her in slow waves at the trust implicit in her new colleague's exposed gullet. She settled for beaming at him with quiet kindliness. When she swung around, she checked her beam in her little round mirror. There was a grimness to it, in the set of the jaw, but something in the eyes, she thought, that was accurate.

Her elegant companion invited her to accompany him to the grocery store, and she accepted. "Dress warmly," he counseled. He drove for hours in the dark, the headlights spinning uncertainly off the broken curbs, the sharp teeth of the stoops, the strobing telephone poles. The supermarket was in a bad neighborhood, but vast, swallowing several city blocks. Homeless were encamped at the intersections of the aisles. They each took a cart and moved quickly to the meat department, looking neither left nor right. The meat department was a gargantuan walk-in refrigerator: the space so enormous and the cold mist so dense that she could not see from one wall to the opposite. They did not leave each other's sides. They did not speak or touch. They filled their carts: chicken, goat, bear, salmon, pork, lamb, conch, squab, rabbit, shark, beef, veal, turkey, eel, venison, duck, mussels, ostrich, frogs, pheasant, squirrel, seal. Tripe, kidneys, liver, tongue, and brains. She suggested the purchase of some lemons and marinade; he reproved her cordially.

She helped him load the boxes into the service elevator of his building; then he drove her home. Outside the door of her apartment, probing her bag for her key, she discovered he had slipped in a small package of pancreas sweetbreads: a token. She tucked it beneath her pillow and dreamt all night of the beating of her heart.

The new colleague sat at her table in the company cafeteria. She had a Ziploc bag of cold shrimps, while he had brought a Tupperware of deviled eggs, each half in its own hollow of molded plastic, which he ate by forking out the middles, then peeling off cool white wedges of the whites.

The new colleague had been transferred from a branch of the firm located in another state. He described himself as "corn-fed." Moving to the city had not been as difficult as he had anticipated. There were lots of ways to meet people. He had joined a church choir and was taking a photography course. The first half had dealt with still lifes; the second was on snapshots. He produced a picture he had taken of her in her cubicle. She looked as if the flash of the camera had struck her across the face. It was flattering. She wished she had known it was happening. "It's out of focus," she said. He smiled. He said, "That's artistic."

"Are you a good singer?" she asked. He used to be incredible, he said, before his voice changed. It had been his whole life. It had given him a kind of spiritual mission, as a kid. He was a very mature child. He felt he had been charged with something. After his voice changed, he felt neither release nor despondency. At that point, he stopped considering things like blessings and missions. He became childlike; he lost the habit of thinking much about himself or the things that happened to him. "What about now?" she said. "Do you wish you had become a castrato?" Behind his tongue, his throat was roseate, and the flesh there jerked with his laughter.

When at the conclusion of the meal she folded her Ziploc bag, sealing in the salty film of pink water, and began to rise, he forestalled her, and took her garbage with his to the trash receptacle. She did not reflect on the contact their hands had made during the exchange until, late that afternoon, she noticed him scratching feverishly at a rash that had swollen across the range of his knuckles. She wished she had remembered beforehand to think of it.

The door of her apartment shuddered with the force of the knocking of her illustrious companion. When she flung it open, he staggered in, holding up his right hand. The tip of his index finger was flapping there on a strap of skin. In his left hand was a plastic grocery bag. "Take it off!" he said, in a voice admirably controlled, if keen in pitch. She got him into a chair at the kitchen table, and placing a skillet under his hand to catch the blood, snipped off the fingertip with her nail scissors. She swathed the stump in toilet paper and tied dental floss tightly around the base of the finger to stop the bleeding. He whistled in relief and pulled a rueful face. He lit a cigarette, picked up the grocery bag from the floor beside his chair, and jiggled it merrily in the air. "Would you care to dine with me this evening?" he inquired.

She set the table while he busied himself at the stove. He had removed his tuxedo jacket and tucked a dishtowel into his collar to protect the pique bib of his shirt. While his back was to her, she glanced covertly around the apartment. But everything seemed to be in place: The sag of the couch springs had a decadent grace, like a courtesan in the half-swoon that succeeds a debauch; the buzz of the fluorescents was textured and complex, a Gregorian plainchant heard from across a great distance. Water stains undulated across the ceiling, like tentacles of a translucent sea-monster half glimpsed through immense currents. The smell from the cooking wove an intricate web from wall to wall; she felt it smothering against her nose and mouth, rich with the scents of ingredients that surely were absent: zedoary, fenugreek, frankincense.

He brought the skillet to the table to ladle the meal, still bubbling, into their bowls. Without ceremony, but gravely, he maneuvered the digit into her portion. Her genteel companion had extracted the nail, or it had dissolved. She speared the tines of her fork through the nailbed and ran her tongue across the pattern of lines on the pad of the finger. She inserted the portion into her mouth and sucked off the dark, congealing stew. Her companion's breaths were audible and steady. She removed the part and considered its form, then inserted it again and began, with small strokes of her incisors, to shuck the nugget of flesh from the bone. There was not much meat there, but once she had it all behind her lips, it seemed to fill the space of her mouth. It tasted like her tongue, her gums, her cheeks. She was nervous to chew; she was afraid to bite down on her own tissue. She swallowed it whole. The rest of the stew had the taste that had been drained from the finger: savory, ripe, and plummy.

Her companion, always immaculate, kissed her hand at the door. "Your hospitality," he purred, "such a gift." She said, "Thank you for dinner." "Leftovers are in the fridge," he smiled, and backed out into the oblivion of the unlit hallway.

In the middle of the night she woke and stumbled clumsily toward the kitchen. The smoke from the cooking still curtained the windows, gagging the weak light of the streetlamps. She forgot in her haste the jut of the walls, the menacing corner of her bookcase. She poured the remains of their supper into a half dozen mugs and bore them on a tray into her bedroom. She drank them off in the dark, propped on her pillows, then dreamed she was inside the stomach of a whale.

Her skin was much worse: abraded, blistered, mucid, rubicund. Her eyelids were swollen and tears of pus welled up in the depths of the sockets. Her chest was hot as if sunburned; when she pushed her hand against the breastbone the imprint did not fade away for some minutes. During her stretches, bending over at the waist, she could feel the satiny slithering of her organs over each other, the horrible pappy give of them. The putrification of her virginity shocked her with its rapacity and virulence. Her hair was broken and thin. It floated in the air, repelled by the electric charge of her damp scalp.

The fever was constant and she fed on the extra degrees. She was bright and alert and vibrating. She took measures. She packed the bathtub with ice and slept in there one night. When she awoke, the swelling around her eyes had shrunken, her face and chest were pale, she was hard and smooth and cold inside and out. She was tremulous with gratitude. But the thawing nearly crippled her. She had to leave work early, as much so that her new colleague across the aisle would not actually hear the sharp cracking and rending in the marrows of her bones, as because of the savagery with which the molten brimstone of her decay attacked the frozen blocks of her limbs.

She began swimming, trusting that she was not infectious, visiting the heavily chlorinated YWCA pool at senior citizens' hour, in enormous goggles and a latex swim cap. The chemicals in the water helped her face. She submerged and held still, and could see the bubbles race up from her cheeks and chin, hear the hypochlorous acid hissing against her skin. Her complexion lost its rawness, though it was still pitted, and the skin now flaked away in fragile, dusty layers. Inside, however, she continued to rot away.

At last she began swimming in the city bay at night, naked. The water was syrupy, warm, stinking, and crowded with objects she did not identify, which nudged her meekly, skimmed along the side of her body, and were dragged on and out by the slow, mild movements of the sea. She floated face down or up, legs and arms open, and felt the sludge of the bay flush in and out of her. She rocked calmly in the wake of garbage tugs or police speedboats. She didn't know if the high toxicity of the bay really had killed her virginity once and for all, or if the organic soup of the water, crowded with things living and dead, had simply calmed its hunger, given it to feed. Whatever the case, her fever dropped, her blood thickened and slowed, her organs grew leathery and dense, her pustules shrank into her pores. The only stain the water left on her was a distinctive smell, salty and dark, that plucked constantly at her hunger; and a dull, muddy smear, like a skin, that covered the orbs of her eyes.

Her charming companion invited her to a gathering of intimates, something special and private, he said. She was to wash her hands and wear old clothes. He drove. The headlights poured out like floodwaters submerging a condemned city. They arrived at their destination in no time at all.

She was happy to revisit the home of her amiable host, though the dining hall was not suffused with radiance on this occasion, and the atmosphere did not bewilder her with scents that choked the air. Nonetheless, she was struck anew by the welcome implicit in the cavernous chambers, which never threw her footsteps back at her in repulsing echo, but muffled sound in their embrace, opening gladly to her ingress and to that of her astonishing companion. The smell of her host – storm-soaked sediment, shrinking fungi, nacreous gastropods – trembled shyly in her nostrils.

In neat array around the empty banquet table, the other guests awaited her arrival. They too were dressed shabbily, in torn jerseys, paint-stained singlets. Again they did not smile, but she felt their geniality drift warmly over her, tickling her hair. She took a seat beside her magnificent companion, and on that cue the great doors opened for the manservant, wheeling in his late employer on a gurney sumptuously draped.

Her host was thickly glazed with pomegranate sauce, and flushed livid from the boiler, and legless, but otherwise was all she had remembered – massive, calm, beatific. An affectionate drone, a deep, low appreciation, rose from the company. A tall, angular woman, drenched in hair, stood to speak. "Loving," the woman pronounced. "Inspired, messianic, but gentle. Always with us," said the woman, "a comfort and a rare delight." The guests touched each other's wrists and shoulders with whispering care. The manservant, reverential, slid his employer's corpse from the gurney to the table. The bounteousness of the body of her host brought a part of him within easy reach of each pair of tender hands.

The guest to her left noted her hesitation and leaned in, sharp, wry, and twinkling. "Don't hold back," the guest advised. "It's our gift to him." She asked, "And his gift to us?" "Oh, particularly that," crooned the guest. "When I knew that I was going to lose my baby before term, I came straight here. You can't imagine what it did for me, all my dear friends taking in the little half-body, holding him in the warmth of their mouths, giving him sanctuary. My role in it was an act of necessity, of course. Getting him back where he belonged. He was always part of me. But our friends, our host. Ah, our host," sighed the guest. "He wasn't tasty, you know, my baby boy. He was raw, immature, flaccid, an inharmonic composition. But now I think I can taste him in our host, completed, ripened. A small fresh note, like a little pocket of lavender snuggled in among the fat of the flank here. Can't you taste it? Ah, our host. He gives and gives."

She reached out and, digging her nails into the crease of her host's breast, tore a tendril from the body. "Be sure to chew," the guest prompted anxiously. She chewed. Her host smiled inside her mouth. "He's delicious," she said.

"Ah, he's delicious," hummed the guest. With a hurried flick of the tongue, the guest caught a rivulet of their host where he was racing from wrist to elbow. "He always ate for this moment," said the guest. "He primed himself for us. Such munificence!" said the guest. "Such benevolence!"

When the funeral was complete, the host was a tattered thing, and the guests were smeared with sauce and peppered with black flakes of charring from the skin. Sated, exhausted, elated, and mournful, they reflectively sucked the fibers of flesh caught between their teeth.

This time her regal companion had the honor of taking her into the parlor for coffee and dessert. A Black Forest cake was served, the host's favorite confection.

Coming late into the company cafeteria, she joined the new colleague for lunch. She had just purchased a stout block of shrink-wrapped foie gras; he had arranged the ingredients of his meal on an unfolded square of butcher paper, and was spreading tuna salad on crackers, crowned with thin wafers he cut off a radish. He drew her attention to the sores on her mouth. A new nervous habit, she explained. Her lips were shredded and mangled with teeth marks. It must happen during sleep, her colleague suggested. He had never seen her do it at her desk.

His photography course was proceeding well; he spread out on the table the latest additions to his series of portraits of her. Undoubtedly, she was losing weight. The hinge of her jaw protruded with a truculent insistence; her shoulders were mean, angry splinters that snagged at her sweater. Her posture was impeccable: paralyzed. "Missing – Have You Seen This Woman?" she said.

Her new colleague sputtered with glee and cut cleanly through his radish and into the ball of his hand. He coughed in surprise. The blood beaded and hopped on the waxed paper, like spit on a griddle. She moved quickly over to his bench, and secured his wrist in an efficient grip, and sucked at the cut.

"Oh, my god!" said her new colleague. "Please stop that!"

"What?" she said. "I just thought, the radish juice, I thought it might sting."

"Well," said her colleague, "that's thoughtful, but I really can't ask you to do that. You're too kind!" he said, laughing and shaking his head.

"It's okay," she said. "I would want someone to do it, to help me, in a similar situation. Look," she said, picking up his paring knife and drawing it cleanly down. She held her palm up to the ceiling and tilted her arm so the flow ran neatly into her sleeve. "You can make it up to me," she said. She maneuvered awkwardly to bring her hand to mouth-level without dripping blood on the tan slacks of her colleague.

"No!" he said. "I'm getting the first-aid kit. Just hang on!" he said. "Keep your hand elevated."

Sadly, she considered the wastage of her blood, soaking through the acrylic of her cardigan onto the tile floor. Her colleague wasn't returning with first aid, and finally she sealed her lips over her palm and began nursing the wound. Her blood was better than his: strong, fermented, with a bitter, gritty strength and a distant note of figs and honey. His was sour, with a pickled sharpness like cut grass; a stale dustiness, like a glass of water left all night on the bedside table; and a slick coolness, like broken glass. Hers numbed the flat of the tongue, like strong tea; it stroked the inside of the esophagus, like horehound syrup; it moved in the stomach, she could feel it stroking the walls, coaxing her hunger. She took the afternoon off and went home to eat.

She returned repeatedly to the supermarket in search of her distinguished companion. At last he strolled in, urbane, guiding his shopping cart with the tips of his fingers, light, tasteful intimations of pressure. At the sight of her his face broke apart in amazed enchantment. Beside him was a young girl, still plump, with stippled indigo circles sagging ponderous under her eyes. "Am I interrupting?" she said. "My dear," replied her companion, throatily, "what a question." He leaned forward to kiss her cheek; she felt his busy sniffing at her neck. He retracted from her, his profile pivoting this way and that as he searched the air.

"Child," said her courtly companion, "have you been plundering your harvest? You have been dining in?"

"Once," she said, "twice, three times. I wanted to see if I was tasty. I am," she said, "ambrosial. I wanted to know if it would be an insult to offer – "

"This?" said her lustrous companion, running his fingernail across the zipper of her handbag. She scrabbled briefly, it was wedged between her change purse and her date book, but at last she produced it without embarrassment, with a cold dignity, the item crumpled in cling wrap, a pasty purple, bruised and browning at the edges. "Hymenaeus," said her companion, warming it between his hands. "The son of Aphrodite." His smile tumbled over her, eager and youthful; she had to brace herself against the weight of it. "You have made your decision?" asked her devoted companion. "This is something that would never have been asked of you."

She put it to him: Wasn't it true that her rapacious and unremitting hunger was fueled by her feeding? Was it not the case that, having been devoured, she would be full? "Little wendigo," said her refulgent companion, "it is so. For a time, indeed."

Her companion had counseled her to eat, but she would not eat. He came to her apartment bearing gifts: a shapely thigh, a breast fulsome with milk, a smoky, musky phallus; but she merely measured off frugal doses of her blood with a syringe and dispensed them gingerly into the plastic tops of cough syrup bottles, marked off in tablespoons. In the gray, silken evenings they sat comfortably on her couch and sipped in companionable silence. She asked whether her blood did not give him the hungers, but that, he said, was what he liked it for. Disrobing with supple tact, her considerate companion displayed the sliced planes of his buttocks, the half-moons where his torso had been spooned out like a melon. She inquired why it was their fellows had so far declined with gratitude the offering of her own parts. "You're still such a virgin, little one," said her loyal companion. She pinned him with sharp eyes. "The flesh eaten still on the living body," he told her, "there is the union." "Your finger, our host, my hymen?" she asked. "Fellatios, my sweet," lisped her companion. She eyed the swell of his forearm with avarice, the muscles coiled in knots under his slippery shirt. "Not me, my darling," he said, and lifted his remaining finger to tick-tock through the air in drowsy admonishment. "You make your own way; then you come home."

She turned and looked full into the stutter of the camera of her colleague. He berated her. "That's not spontaneous!" He insisted that the project set for the class was for the photographer to be the hunter, and the subject the prey. That made it edgy. "Oh," she said, "you're not hunting; you're farming. Picking off creatures grazing at pasture, dull in contemplation." She struck a candid pose, lips slightly agape, eyes askew, her expression garbled, transparent and opaque, like a muddy pond. He was discontent. If she stalked the camera, he reasoned, if she had him in her sights, while he had her in his, that skewed the terms of the assignment.

"True," she conceded, "that's not hunting," she said; "that's war." He snapped her picture. "Caught you!" her new colleague crowed. "Let's eat," she proposed. She had forgotten to pack a meal, so he accompanied her through the lunch line, selecting a Charlotte of Bavarian creme and ladyfingers, while she consumed a Manwich.

She escorted her exquisite companion to the city bay where they sat on the dock, shoes off and pants rolled to the knees, smiling at the disparity of their feet in the water, hers crumpled and dented and damp from her pumps, his slender, prosthetic, dove-gray. The bats in the twilight were reckless and extraordinary; the seagulls had hidden themselves but called out fierce and lonesome, like the whistles of locomotives on the track of the tremulous far horizon. They had purchased small waxed envelopes of sweet, crispy nuts. She swallowed hers nearly whole, while he chewed his bites minutely and spat them out in neat piles on the gravel shore.

Her companion was wistful. The fine engraving of his face looked stony and the quizzical glances and debonair moues by which she knew him seemed painful to execute. She reached in experiment to probe the softness of his cheek and he winced, a tremor of delectable fineness and subtlety.

"Melancholy," her companion apologized, "a disease not commonly recognized as having its origins in exposure to freshness of air. I am so little accustomed to the pathos of the junction of the land and the sea."

He was sorrowful, wondering, his chin tucked into the refuge of his collar, his cowlick sprouting in the salt spray like that of a small boy.

"Don't," he chastised her, "feel maternal. You can't imagine the monsters in those deeps. That is so much more dangerous."

"More dangerous than this?"

"There's little danger here."

"Is our safety so assured?"

"Au contraire." He was amused again, his mouth twisting and curling to savor the joke. "It's our downfall that's reliable."

She was comforted. She wedged herself against him, and he allowed this, though she could feel the warmth on her shoulder where a suture on his breast had wrenched open with the nesting of her weight. The bats were sucked upward into the sky, caught by the magnetic pull of the stars, and the mosquitoes rushed in, enveloping the happy couple, and falling in quivering piles to the dock, all around them.

She woke at the first stain of sunlight on the face of the sky and slithered to the floor to enter her stretches. They came more easily now that her muscles were drained and limp and she laid her cheek between her legs against the floorboards and sniffed the old gasoline smell of the paint; the gamy traces of her footsteps; a cloying, pulpy odor of breakfast in the apartment below. In the bathroom, she brushed her teeth, tilting her chin back to cup the toothpaste in her mouth, staring down her nose at the mirror. This gave her an accusing look. She made a kind, understanding face that returned to her as a nauseous leer. She giggled. In the shower she ran the water so hot it nearly melted the glue that held her skin to her substructure. Her flesh slipped dangerously over its ligaments. "Oops," she said.

She had recently treated herself to a French press and, swaddled luxuriously in her old pink robe, she tipped in the beans she'd ground the night before, and punished them with water at a rapid boil. Setting the egg timer to four-and-a-half minutes, she dressed for work: leggings, slacks, two cardigans. She relaxed at the table with granola and berries, slapping back the unfurled and flapping wings of the newspaper. A merry little robin perched on her windowsill, stabbing with its beak at its reflection in the pane.

At work she attacked the keys of her calculator with especial vivacity, tapping her rhythm into the brain of her new colleague. She broke a light sweat, and several pencil leads. The chalky scent of her perspiration, buoyed on a cloud of lily-pale eau de toilette, made its way across the aisle. Her hair was hectic with static. She kept her best three-quarters profile toward the door of her cubicle, and never looked round.

Her colleague invited her to an after-work aperitif. He had a Bloody Mary; she enjoyed a Cinzano. His photography course was finished; he would move on to sculpture in just a few weeks. He displayed the final array of photographs on the tabletop. There she was, blinking, flinching in all her poses. "You see," he chortled, "it was better when you didn't know I was taking them. You came at the camera," he said, gesticulating, "in a flurry of fear. It was kinder, after all, to take you unaware." She concurred with her new colleague.

He fell asleep with the lights on. If the patchwork of her body, the scars of old decay, the faint sifting and rattling sounds of shriveled things within her, had worried him, he hadn't shown it, and she would now require the illumination for precision. She had discovered that the area least sensitive to touch was likely to be the back of the shoulders. She inserted the point just above his scapula, turning the flat of the blade parallel to his skin, and cut two sides of a small triangle. Without completing the figure, she lifted the flap, hovering above him in an unwieldy posture, propped on her knuckles, and chewed the skin. She was careful not to sever it, as she did not want to have to cut another piece. The living, she noted, did not have as much taste as the dead. He was tough and elastic. And she could feel the muscles shrinking away from the grind of her teeth. When she had at last reduced the flesh to a small, spongy lump, sticky but bloodless, she yanked it off – he snorted slightly – dropped it in the trash can, wrapped in a tissue; drank a glass of water in the crackling light of the bathroom; dabbed on a touch of lipstick; and locked the door behind her as she went.

She had never eaten so well in her life. They brought her sweet, sticky rice; curried cauliflower delirious with coconut milk; jungles of spaghetti, mired in Alfredo sauce; pinto-bean chili black with molasses. For a long time she would not touch meat, not trusting the source, but then they began to carry in animals roasted whole:

a suckling pig, turned on a spit; an infant lamb in a roasting pan, its hooves tucked in trustingly; turkeys spilling out oysters; crabs crusted in ethereal salt; and these she felt safe in consuming. She promised she would sit very still, so they cuffed her only by one foot; and she kept her word, burrowed in somnolent complacence in her featherbed, in an endless drowse, basting herself for her banquet. She was stupefied, seduced, but she knew herself to be tempting, was confident their mouths would water for her. She waited, and every day she grew more ardent.

She had little idea of the passage of time, and when the temperature in her cell began to rise she wondered if summer was finally upon them and if they were saving her, perhaps, for a midsummer feast. The intensification of the heat was, however, accompanied by great commotion in the hall, by the repeated jostling of doors and the thumping of wheels over uneven ground, by the smell of outdoors, lichen and bark and wood sap, and finally, it came to her, a far-away rushing sound, a flickering, hissing, panting growl, like the anger of the surf.

To her beautiful companion, who came every day to see her, she said, "Something is not right."

Her companion asked if she was weary of waiting. He had lost his nose, and his face, always a ravishment, was now even more moving to her, a stately ruin sliding down the cliff of his skull to the sea beneath. She denied his imputation. She was eager, she said, but not weary. She would do whatever was necessary to be most pleasing to the company. "Only," she said, "they have built a fire."

Her faithful companion assented to this conjecture. "A very large one," he said, "they began it in the dining hall, with the banquet-table, and they have been piling wood on for days."

"I thought," she faltered, "that I was not to have been slaughtered first."

Her companion considered the suave line of his shoe. He tugged sadly at the scraps of his earlobe. At last he said, "You are not held to be quite delicious enough for that."

"No?" she said.

"Lamentably not," said her doting companion. "I consider it a piece of great foolishness."

"You would have eaten me alive?" she beseeched him.

"Oh," said her companion, "I fear it must be acknowledged that I would not have been able to eat you at all."

Blackout curtains covered the windows, but she could hear the hammering of the rain against the glass, like a mob of useless fists. "Please help me," she said.

Her loving companion held her hands between the butts of his wrists. He smiled down at her. "I can't help you," he said, "but I won't hinder you." And then he took his leave.

She heaved her body from the bed to the floor. The manacle, she discovered, could slide some distance up her leg, but could not be made by any contortion to allow her foot to slip through. Bending her leg at the knee, she grasped her toes with both hands, and stretched forward. The skin at her ankle was tender, and she was not prepared for the juice that shot out and battered the back of her throat in an insistent stream. After her long recumbence, the muscle was creamy and fine. She nibbled all around, using her nails to tear at the meat on the far opposite side of the limb, and flexed her jaw for the bone. But this shattered in her mouth, releasing a puff of powder that mingled unpleasantly with the red paste of the marrow. With the elimination of the foot, the manacle clanked to the ground. Staunching the bleeding took time, however, and she endured this impatiently. At last she was able to lurch to the door of her cell, and propping her body against the wall, to heave it open.

The guests were garlanding the dining-hall fire with armfuls of flowers; burning petals drifted in the air. The thin crystal flutes they held glowed with the champagne inside them, like pale coals. The long limbs of the women waved gracefully in greeting; the men bobbed their heads at her with rough affection. Her own companion was not among them. Across the room, beside the door, the eyes of the manservant were black in the black smoke. She hobbled in his direction. At this movement, a cry went up, and the guests began applauding. The champagne slapped the sides of the flutes in cheerful chimes and the celebration lashed across the room, and all the company danced in a great spiral, like a whirlpool sucking through the house. The eyes of the guests were brilliant, adoring; their faces were tilted up, innocent, anticipatory, as if to be kissed. Their delirium raised a dazzling bright wind in the hall: She breathed it in: odorless; swallowed it: tasteless; trapped it in her lungs, where it disappeared, weightless. She stood on her leg and observed the guests as, fingers interlaced, hair tangled together, their breaths muddling in each other's mouths, their exultant cries in each other's ears, they danced and danced. She saw that in an instant the floor would collapse beneath the force of their joy and their affection for her.

Julie Oakes

The Dresden Rooms

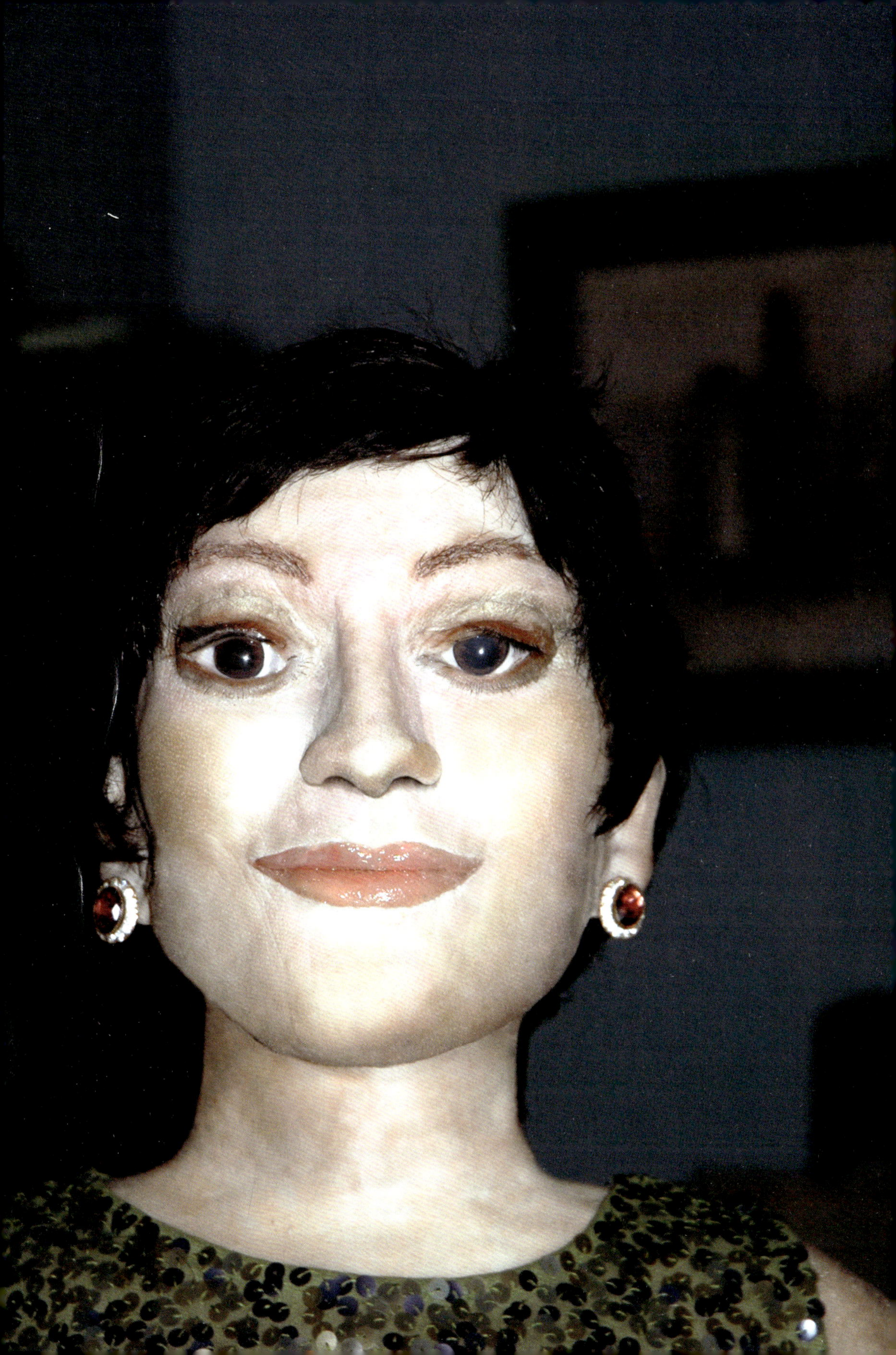

When I first saw the rooms I was frightened. I was with my brother, Hans. Father had told us to wait by the motorbike but Hans had to go to the bathroom so we headed in the direction that Father had gone in to try and find him. We had pulled up outside an old hotel built around the time of the reconstruction after the Second World War. It had temporarily housed people after the war, and then later, it had become a spa.

Father had pulled up onto the sidewalk. Hans had been riding on the tank of the big American motorbike and I was the back passenger. We were quite a sight around Dresden – Sir Cyril on his Harley Davidson motorcycle with his two children riding aboard. This was not the first time that Father had stopped here. Father had stopped at the spa before and it had always been the same. We were told to wait with the Harley. Father would head under an archway and into a corridor towards the lodgings. Each door had a curtain covering it although there was also a heavy wooden door behind the canvas curtain. It was a common Dresden feature – an extra barrier against the cold in the winter and the heat in the summer. The spas always had these curtains. Five or ten minutes later Father would reappear – without a parcel so it hadn't been an errand to fetch something – and we would proceed on to home and the restaurant, Father's business.

This time, trying to find a bathroom for Hans, my brother and I were confronted by a series of exact sameness – a number of snow-white curtains – with a choice as to which of these units Father had entered. Hans pointed at the second on the left and said that he thought that was where Father had gone.

We pulled aside the curtain and were surprised to see – not a solid wooden door – but a glass sliding door. It was open and there was Father hurrying deeper into the rooms with a furtive scurrying much like the white rabbit when Alice followed him into Wonderland. Big dried leaves had blown in from the sliding glass door onto the carpet. They crunched under foot. It was a ghostly setting as dry and dead as the leaves that broke with each footfall. There were clothes hanging on hangers, women's clothes that were somewhat old fashioned. It was like a display. There were messages scrawled on the walls beside the dusty hung garments: "I love you still although you're never still …"; "a waste of time!"; "We are waiting in Dresden" and others as mysterious and evocative. They were dusty scripts, and there was a general sense of tattered to the place. There were maybe four rooms including a small dark kitchen off to the right. Father had bounded through the dim rooms, alighting outside a back door and beginning to draw it closed behind him with a delicacy unlike our big and burly Papà. He had been looking about as he passed through the rooms, sometimes shifting an item and raising a small cloud of dust.

Hans spoke first. It was a question, not a call – "Father?" And it was indeed our father who turned from *his* doorway to see us, silhouetted in the *front* door way. He came slowly towards us. It was spooky – tears were streaming down his face.

"I have to pee." Hans told Father. Papa stooped down to Hans' size and hugged him instead of answering.

"Where are we?" I asked, almost afraid to voice the query.

Father said this was a place he came to sometimes for a little holiday. He said that it was good for him because it was cheap. And because my brother and I knew that Father didn't like to spend money unnecessarily, we accepted his answer without further questions.

We visited the rooms perhaps five times after that, always with Father. We usually waited outside, either beside the Harley or on our own bikes once we were old enough to join the packs of peddle bikers that navigated through Dresden.

There were always leaves on the floor beside the door, no matter what the season was. They appeared to be the same leaves, but perhaps they weren't. The sliding door was always open a crack whenever we arrived, and they could have blown in through the six centimeter opening.

One time we came in the back door and once inside the dusty enclosure, we heard a rustle at the front door. Father told us to remain still and be quiet. We stood in the dusky interior as a man in a uniform drew the curtain aside, slightly adjusted the opening in the sliding door and peered in through the smudged glass for a moment before he continued on his rounds. Once he was two or three doors away, Father had us quickly exit and he hustled us under the archway. Soon we were on the bike and heading for our home.

Perhaps I should tell you about our home. Marina remembers it, but you, Donovan, my love, not knowing us then, might not imagine where I came from. Father was a big man, handsome in a Nordic fashion – strong, stern and usually absorbed in his own thoughts. He was a good father, but not an open father. I never really felt that I knew him and as I grew older he seemed to become even sterner – at least with me, his daughter. He was awkward – a man raising two children without a wife. My mother had died shortly after Hans was born. Neither Hans nor I could remember her, although I have a memory of a woman with curly red hair bathing me, and I remember thinking that I was very lucky to be attended by such a wonderful woman.

As we grew older, Father allowed Hans to develop a social life outside of the home. I was destined for another future. It was of course because of my voice. I was told that my throat opened in a special way, that sound could follow a clear channel upwards and out. I sang like an angel from the time that I can remember. There is a domed entrance into the palace – I will show you tomorrow – where, if you stand there and sing, the acoustics are like a grand opera hall. I actually received some of my voice lessons there.

I was the youngest person to sing a solo part in the opera house. I played Juliet when I was fourteen years old. I *was* Juliet, locked in my tower of privileged talent. I was never away from a chaperone. It was either my father or our Turkish housekeeper and nanny. It was how I met Marina – her mother was our primary caregiver, our housekeeper.

But I was trying to tell you about Father. He loved us very much. I have no hesitations in saying so. But I was treated differently than Hans and later I was to understand why. But for many years, my only playmates were Hans and Marina.

Later my teachers assumed big roles in my life. But I didn't socialize like the other young people.

"Are you tired? Shall I continue?"

Donovan reaches over and pours both Marina and Julie a little more wine. Marina has her arm around Julie's shoulder and her head, soft dark hair peppered with white, rises just above Julie's. There is a fire in the old stone fireplace in need of a log so Donavon rises to stoke it, poking the embers to a livelier flame. They are in Dresden and it is October. The days have been warm enough with a sweater and coat, but the evenings, without the warmth of the Saxon sunshine, is frosty.

"Does it hurt, Julie, this cancer? Are you in pain right now? Do you mind if I ask you?"

"Yes, it does hurt, but it's not painful, Marina. It's a kind of dullness accompanied by almost uncontrollable fear. I feel like Job, but without the faith to face my dilemma. But, if it's alright, I would like to tell Donovan more of the story. Tonight, the three of us being together in Dresden, the city where I really learned about life – it is important to me that I relate my story in front of both of you. Donovan is very much my present life, and I hoped to share a longer future with him than I will be able to, and you, Marina, have been witness to my past. I wanted you, Donovan, to know about this part of me – my past – before I am not here to explain. I'm sorry I'm not being morbid, only practical. And I wanted you, Marina, whom I have not known as an adult but as the friend from my past – to understand why I will be leaving you. I came to Dresden to tell you in person that I am dying, Marina. And you will be my witness as I tell Donovan about my past. May I continue?"

Marina snuggles in closer to her friend whom she met almost fifty years ago. Julie's aspect belies the sad declaration. She is, as ever, stylish. Her hair is shorter than Marina remembers, her skin more sallow, and although she can see that the cancer has taken a toll upon her, there is still the bright and positive demeanor, the chin raised as if every moment is a dignified one. She used to say that it was important to hold yourself properly – "fare una bella figura," she would say, in Italian. She felt it was important to present herself well, and then there was her love of glamour. She wears the earrings her father had given her, the ones that her mother had worn, given to her by her mother. Real jewelry.

"Continue, dear friend …"

"Marina, do you remember the sociology project and your findings? Do you remember that creepy fear that we might be a part of something that we couldn't change, something that wasn't good, something that would make all that we loved be spoiled? That's how I feel now and yet I am referring to the same feeling that you and I had so many years ago.

Donovan, this school project is relevant to my story – Marina had a sociology project when we were studying at the academy. We were fifteen or sixteen years old. It was a research project into the lives of foreigners living in Dresden just after the war. She had chosen our family as an example. We were two children, born in America to an Englishman and a mother who had come from Dresden. My mother had left Germany during the war, fairly close to the beginning of it. She had been one of a group of Europeans who began The New School for Social Research in New York City. Hannah Arendt was her mentor and friend. Hannah Arendt had been Heidegger's mistress, but had left him when her philosophy could no longer encompass what was going on in Germany. My mother, when she was working with the Metropolitan Opera, met Hanna Arendt in New York City through a reading club. The European intellectuals shared books so that they could still have access to writings in their own languages.

My father had also met my mother in New York around this time. They married, had me and then, four years later, Hans, and then she died.

As a child I had never questioned why we were different from the other children. Hans and I were raised with an English-speaking father – that made us somewhat different, but not that much. And we also didn't have a mother. But by the time that Hans and I were in school here in Dresden, we were accepted and pretty much felt the same as everyone else.

But my father must have met with some prejudice when he first arrived. Marina discovered this when she did the research into foreigners, especially Americans, who settled in Dresden following the war. The people of Dresden were not that eager to welcome the citizens of the countries that had bombed their beautiful city. But Father came through it all and survived the transition. I believe Hans and I had a lot to do with his acceptance. The people of Dresden liked my father and his single-handed upbringing of his two children without a wife. He never remarried. There were certainly many women. Father had an irresistible charm, even in later life, but he never settled with one woman. There was a time when I suspected that that was the purpose of the rooms – a place to bring his women to, but it was too disconcerting a space – and always with this aura of extreme secrecy to it.

Back to Marina's project. She came up with a news story that led into more and more articles. They centered around my father. He had come to Dresden almost immediately following the war – with my mother! Then she had disappeared, walked out of their hotel room one night and was never seen again. Father reported her disappearance. Remember, there was a lot of anti-Americanism happening, and Father's first suspicion was that someone had labeled my mother as a traitor and had murdered her. But according to the articles that Marina dug up, the people of Dresden did an about-face on his suspicions. They *claimed* their native child, my mother, and accused my father of her murder! There was never a body found, however, and eventually my mother's case just disappeared amongst the many loose ends that were never firmly tied up at the end of the war with Dresden being such a horrible pile of rubble.

The articles spooked me as much as the rooms first had scared me. This is the creeping feeling that I was referring to, a feeling much like this diagnosis that has given me, hopefully, just two more years to live. Something had gone violently wrong in my perceptions of things. I began to wonder about Father. He was, as I said, not an especially warm man. Not even to Hans. He took care of us, but it wasn't a specific care. It was a general treatment, the same treatment that he gave to everyone, like an equal rights program. He believed that we were all deserving of attention and care. He was loved by many people in the end. Once the people of Dresden got to know him they embraced him, for he exhibited a generous acceptance of many types of people – rich, poor, conservative, bohemian, foreign, German – all were treated with equanimity by Father. But from the reading that Marina and I did from the news articles of the early days, it took time for him to gain their trust. The allegations were eventually thrown out and my father was accepted as innocent, acknowledged as grieving, and he moved on to build a successful business around his restaurant. He hired the women of Dresden to cook their local dishes. He worked long and hard to bring his restaurant up to a level of consistency with whole foods and natural ingredients in a time when America was exporting a lot of tinned goods to Europe. He allowed himself just one frivolous luxury in his fairly Spartan routine. He imported his Harley Davidson motorcycle from America.

But when Marina did her research and found the accusations about Father, it scared me. There was a frightening photograph, black-and-white, of my mother in the newspaper's obituaries. The woman looked glamorous and confident, with her ever-present sun glasses. Why was she always in sunglasses as if the sun was too much for her, too harsh a glare on a reality that she needed to have made more gentle? Was she continually crying? So the suspicious thoughts crept in. Had my father actually murdered my mother? And the strange dusty rooms formed a receptacle for my fears. I was afraid that I might be the child of a duplicitous man. He had never shared with Hans and me much information as to how Mother had died. He had told us that she had died just after Hans' birth, and both Hans and I had taken that to mean 'as a result of the birth.'

I voiced my fears to Hans who was only twelve and he really didn't give it much attention, said I was being silly. We never talked about it until many years later.

But I developed a psychic distance from Father, a combination of wondering if I was the spawn of a cursed family and the natural breaking of familial bonds that comes with adolescence.

My epiphany came through Father when I was in my early twenties. Hans had left Dresden for Venice, Italy, where he studied architecture, and then eventually moved to America when he graduated. He became a teacher of architecture at the University and now lives in Indianapolis with his wife, who is a nurse, and their two children, Brenden, who is a pharmacist, and Barbara, who is studying electrical engineering. They are my closest living kin.

Hans, then, had left Dresden. I was just twenty-one years old, and I had been singing major roles even since I was school age. Marina, you had left Dresden as well …"

Marina leans forward to explain to Donovan, "I was married to a Turkish man. I was sent back to Turkey by my mother and father who felt I was getting too 'wild' after I finished my studies. My marriage was an arranged marriage, believe it or not, Donovan. I have a daughter …"

There is a minute of silence with a sigh from Julie as she continues with her saga.

"And I have no children. That was the essence of my epiphany. I fell in love with Tristan as I sang Isolde. He was an Italian tenor, very famous, and you would recognize the name if I told you, but it's of little importance to my story. I fell in love – that is all that matters. I loved him as I never believed was possible, and with a full and happy heart I presented him to my father with our intentions to marry. I was a well-behaved young woman, conservative really, and I would never have thought of allowing our romance to progress without the sanction of my father's blessing and a marriage in place before I dared to share intimacy. That's when Father told me. And it was as I suspected, although not in the manner that I had believed. I was indeed from a cursed parentage, but the blight was not from my father but from my dear dead mother.

This was the story behind the rooms. My father told it to me with kindness and equanimity. He began with an illustration from the images of the Virgin Mary holding the baby Jesus. He reminded me that the tradition of painting the baby to look like a little man – a baby body with a mature man's face – was to show us, the viewer, that Mother Mary knew that Jesus was destined to be a great man, even while he was still an infant. In the old paintings, Mary is usually not depicted looking directly at the baby. She looks away from him, because she didn't want to feel the pain from the knowledge of his eventual death. If she looked directly at him as she fed or held him, she would be reminded that he was to die early and it would be too much sorrow for her heart to bear. So she casts her gaze away and tends to him with a blind care and love.

Father said that this was how he had to look at me – with a slight distraction. It was the source of his coolness towards me. It was because he knew that I was a special child and that my talent was to be great but that I too was destined to die early. It was with this metaphor that Father told me about my mother's death.

Shortly after the birth of Hans, Mother had begun to have violent headaches. My father took her to every specialist possible in order to find out how to cure her for she was increasingly beset by pain. This was a time of great medical breakthroughs and, as it turned out, Father found a doctor who was able to trace the headaches to a source, but unfortunately the diagnosis did not result in a cure. They found out that my maternal grandmother had died of a brain tumor after a period of intense headaches. Mother was examined and a tumor was discovered in her fragile skull. The doctors gave her less than a year left to live.

Here were Mother and Father, the wonderful family, intellectual, rich, talented, with their two children, and Mother was told she would have to leave them.

Father went a little crazy, I believe. He said that he used every minute to try and find someone who could stop the growth in my mother's brain. But finally, he had to listen to just one voice – my mother's voice – and she asked Father for one favor, that she might be able to visit her birthplace, Dresden, and find out if her brother and sister had survived the war.

And thus, the rooms. Father brought Mother back to Dresden. They could find no news of her siblings. They rented the rooms in the spa and one night, Mother slipped out the door in the middle of the night and she was never found. She never came back to the rooms.

Father brought Hans and I over from America. He began his restaurant and forged a life for himself in Dresden. And he kept the rooms, with a vague hope that Mother might one day return. He kept her clothes where she had left them, he wrote messages to her on the walls and in notes throughout the rooms with the feeble faith that she would see them. He had a sliding glass installed so that she could look in and see that nothing had been changed, that he was waiting for her. And he always left the door open a crack so that she could come in easily. The guards knew to keep the rooms this way. With a slight opening at the door.

Father told me that this condition that my mother had, this brain tumor, was a condition that was passed through the maternal bloodline. It was unavoidable. At some point, I too would die from this condition, and if I was to have a child, a little girl, that she too would die early.

This was long before in utero photographs that tell the sex of the unborn baby. At that time, it was not possible to know. I might have married and had a boy child. But then again, I might have had a girl. Medicine has advanced today to the extent that those with my condition can conceive, and if it's a male fetus, the pregnancy can continue. But unfortunately research hasn't found the cure for my head. And it's beginning. I have begun to have the long unending headache. The doctors have given me, with great luck, only two more years. Believe me, my dear friends, I will try and stay with you as long as possible …

I broke off my engagement of course. I found a way to live with my knowledge, a way to be a woman. I lived much like a man, sexually. I had many lovers but never allowed myself, or them, to fall in love. It was not until my Donovan that I finally gave in. I fell in love."

Julie reaches for Donovan's hand.

"As did I."

"I waited for my prince until I was fifty-four, well clear of the time when I was able to reproduce. Donovan has children of his own, Marina – two grown boys. I am glad that I never had a son. It would be too hard to have to say goodbye to him for I would know that he would grieve heavily over the death of his mother. I would have been a good mother, you see."

Julie shifts and closes her eyes. "This is the hardest part for me. The long goodbye."

Marina, Donovan and Julie are each beginning to seep sorrow. Julie is taking stock with a deep breathing that is consciously trying to control everything that is getting away from her. Marina is a limpid puddle. Donovan, ever aware of his male role, is maintaining stoicism through a thin veneer.

"Would you say that I was a dramatic woman, Donovan?" Julie has collected herself.

"You attract attention, yes. But you don't demand attention." Donovan pauses to think before he answers.

"What is the most disappointing for me as I do my leave-taking is not that the time is shortened but that there will be no bangs when I leave – no bombastic tragedy, no embarrassing display of grief … I have had an ephemeral career. I sang, sometimes it was recorded, but primarily my importance has been my presence. When I am no longer a living presence, well, the two of you will grieve for a time, so will my brother, Hans, but everyone else is very far away. They have all been held at a distance since Father first told me of my condition. Had I participated in something great and memorable – helped to create a museum – had children, sons who would have carried on that essence of my strength of being – I would have caused those that I left behind a degree of sorrow, but I also would have left behind an enduring presence. It's all too much of an anticlimax, a slow descent into forgetfulness."

"We won't …"

"Please, Marina, don't say it! If you can receive this … let me please just voice it. I will be fine. You will be fine. It is a Dresden story. There is an answer here."

"I know what happened to my mother. I know where she went the night that she left the hotel room and my father. There is a call to oblivion from a sweet voice of relief that comes from the Elbe. It is an invitation to join Ophelia in a floating, rhyming, perfumed voyage to the deep. She has not been the only woman to seek a respite in chilly waters. Mother couldn't bear the thought of what she would have to leave behind – me, Father and Hans. I believe my mother floated Lethe-wards, to the muffled underworld of sonorous peace.

I could have told Father this – that it was not necessary to keep the rooms …"

Barbara Purcell

Mistress Veronica Chi

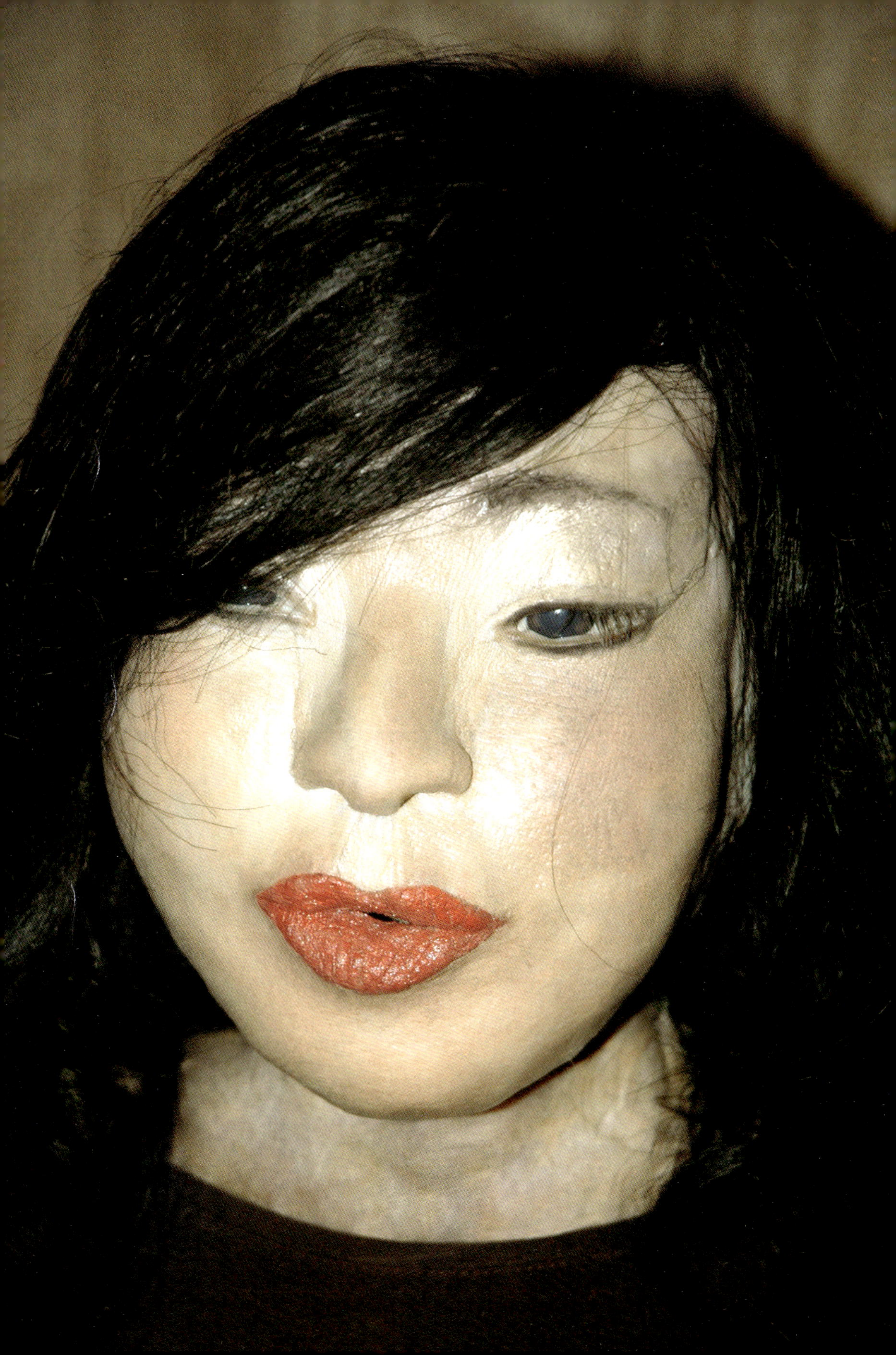

With four minutes to spare before I could finish my shift at the dungeon, he walked in and asked for an hour-long session with the Asian girl. I was a hit-or-miss option for many of these guys; the average client was looking for a tall, confident blonde with legs as long as the sweet torment she induced while tracing her stiletto up his chest before stopping at the Adam's apple and pressing the heel's thin spike into his throat for a second or two. Many of them were looking for the blonder, bossier, version of their own wives. However, this one had a penchant for my strict, more sensual, style of domination. During one of our first few sessions, he observed there was something rather feline about my femininity. I couldn't be sure exactly what he meant, but I assumed he meant I was nothing like her.

His wife was domineering alright, dictating the minutia of their Westchester existence once he would return from the city after another Wall Street day that fed her and eroded his sense of self. He had stopped sleeping with her the year before, and had taken to dozing off in the chair in the den, leaning it as far back as possible and draping himself with a blanket they'd bought on a trip to Lancaster, PA, years ago, before the kids could even walk. He couldn't remember how this unspoken trend began, but what probably started as a tactic to buffer her general spousal vitriol (avoiding sex with her for six straight months sent her into an abyss of immeasurable contempt for herself and the marriage) turned into a habit he couldn't foresee breaking. And why should he? After all, it was *his* house: He could sleep wherever he wanted. What complaints did she have on the matter? She had secured the huge bed all to herself, while he retreated to his home office for four hours at a clip, waking up with a stiff neck and sore back. It was amazing, her sense of entitlement and the nerve of her to complain. She was the master, sleeping comfortably in the master bedroom, as he dozed off in the basement like a guest, like a stranger in his own home.

He secretly hoped she would meet some middle-aged divorcé in town, knowing that if some male could sexually validate her once or twice a week, perhaps she could be more pleasant to deal with the nights he arrived home early or on weekends when they attended the kids' sporting events together. Would it kill her to get picked up by some guy at the local market while shopping for dinner? A meal, no less, she and the kids would enjoy, but would remain under its fogged plastic wrap until he came home and tossed it in the garbage. He wasn't sure if she was capable of an affair, but still, there was no harm in hoping for such a thing.

His own solution for the chronic disconnect at home? Work later – and harder – than ever before: if they were going to split at some point, he wanted to make sure he could live comfortably on the pittance the State of New York would grant him. The other half of the solution was to work late enough to avoid his saran-wrapped plate waiting on the kitchen table and become the specialty saran-wrapped meat of some woman in an otherwise empty commercial building in the East 30's. The kind of woman who demanded a high price for her ability to humiliate a man while he knelt helplessly bound in plastic at her feet.

It was a niche market – one that I dominated.

And it was more of an accident than a calculation that led me to this market. Just out of college from upstate and sick of working various temp jobs in Midtown Manhattan, I answered a Craigslist ad titled, "Domineering Diva for $$$." The posting promised great money for women who knew how to be strong, sexy, and creative with men who had a deep desire to submit and surrender to a wicked goddess. All I needed to do was show up in my edgiest attire at the Midtown address listed in the ad for the interview process, and I might be deemed a domineering diva – or not. I was slightly reluctant, but mostly intrigued, by this new job prospect. It sounded a bit like acting or performance art … how hard could it be to be a bitch to a guy? Most men I'd met since moving to New York elicited that response from me anyway.

The day of the interview, I showed up to a rather rundown East 35th Street building, hair pulled back into a tight bun, donning a black leather jacket, a pair of purple spider web stockings, and black boots that a BeDazzler seemingly had attacked before hitting the shelves at DSW. I took the elevator with a stocky girl, slightly older, but also clad in grommets, up to the fifth floor and we walked directly into the reception area of a smoke-filled space stained by cigarettes and a smell I couldn't quite place. Without looking up, the receptionist handed each of us an intake form and instructed us to fill it out as best we could. It was a split-second decision to jot down Alana Kim (my real name being Ayana Kim) and leave my home address blank; I was pretty sure my roommate out in Williamsburg wouldn't appreciate our residential info being disclosed on a form that would be on file for who the hell knows.

After stating my reasons for attending the interview, my current fetish wardrobe pieces, my preferences and dislikes for various extreme sadistic activities, I paused at the final question: lifestyle. Lifestyle? What the hell could that mean? As in, what kind of lifestyle do I have in NYC? At the risk of seeming like the main act of amateur hour, I scribbled down YES. A few minutes later, my questionnaire was taken to a back room, where I heard the receptionist explain to a woman with a serene English accent, that I was lifestyle. The British woman, a petite platinum blonde with thin red lips and perfectly manicured nails to match, called me into her room. She proceeded to review my answers in silence, occasionally looking up at me and then down at my spider web stockings. Without lifting her eyes from the piece of paper, she asked me how long I had been lifestyle.

Oh Jesus, how the hell was I to answer that?

"Since sophomore year of college," I announced, hoping that lifestyle meant, among other things, how long had I been drinking red wine from boxes.

Slightly amused, she purred, "Do you know what 'lifestyle' even refers to?"

Shit. Clearly whatever the hell I thought lifestyle meant was located in the opposite corner of whatever she had in mind. With a sense of resignation in my voice, I admitted that I hadn't a clue.

"I didn't think so. But that's quite alright. Very few ladies are familiar with the term before becoming Mistresses here."

"Mistresses? I'm sorry, I don't understand. Do the women who work here sleep with married men?"

Her eyes softened as she chuckled at my question. "A Mistress is a dominatrix, my dear. You won't be sleeping with married men – you'll be punishing them. And I think you have potential. You certainly have an interesting look; we don't have any

Asian dominatrices here at this juncture. I think we should proceed with a bit of training, and of course, create an appropriate Mistress name. Think of something reminiscent of your background: As I've said, you'll be the only Asian Mistress on staff, a large-breasted one at that, so use it to your advantage. You will, naturally, refrain from dressing in the future like it is Halloween," she noted as her eyes brushed over the spider web stockings once again.

With her cool caveat, I was hired. And became Mistress Veronica Chi. First thing was first – I needed to identify what types of activities, fantasies, and fetishes I would engage in with clients, followed by a shopping trip down to the West Village for the appropriate apparel and props. Easy enough, I initially thought … though after meeting some of the other Mistresses at the dungeon, I learned what I *did not* want to be more quickly than what I *did* want to be. There was Mistress Adriana, a woman from some Eastern European post-Soviet wasteland with a kitty-cat voice and eyes the color of cruel: She was quite fond of extinguishing her cigarettes on her clients' tongues. And Mistress Alexis: a tall, thin woman with a pronounced clavicle who enjoyed pinching men's nipples till they became raw buttons. And of course, Mistress Marla, the woman with whom I'd shared that first fateful elevator ride: She was apparently a natural at coaxing men to eat wet dog food out of a little pink ceramic bowl.

In honesty, all of these options seemed rather severe, if not pathological, for both Mistress and client alike. I couldn't handle the masochists that requested to session with me; all that pain inflicted on a set of balls seemed so punitive, no matter how bad they needed a good kicking. And the fetishists were oddly compulsive; how could a man stand to moan for 45 minutes straight as I coated his nipples with hot wax? So I settled on the safest client profile out there: the submissive. Like the masochist and fetishist, the submissive was also typically a high-powered, intelligent man paying good money to feel like a bad little boy. But there was something endearing, earnest, about the submissive. His seemingly only desire was to do as I asked (or demanded) and seek pleasure in *my* pleasure. It was a good fit, actually. I wasn't dating anyone at the time, and I could use the doting almost as much as I could use the cash. In those first few weeks, I saw two or three men per shift. The money was unbelievable – I was making twice as much as when I temped, for half the weekly hours. And for what? Having men politely bow down before me, slip their tongues between my toes, and tell me how beautiful my arches were? What an outrageous way to pay the rent.

But after a few weeks, the steady flow of submissive clients slowed significantly, and I had not one repeat client to speak of. The other Mistresses matter-of-factly explained that I was no longer flavor of the month at the dungeon. My time as the Asian novelty, apparently, had run its course. It was demoralizing: I sat five shifts in a row without a single session, just staring at the poor reception of the television in the dungeon's lounge, as the other girls hurriedly ran from one appointment to the next, swapping a leather corset for a latex bra.

On the fifth night, just before midnight (my time to punch out), the receptionist called me out into her area. "There's a guy coming up here in two minutes and he's requested an Asian Mistress. His name is John and he's into "whatever Mistress is into" the receptionist announced without even looking up from her laptop.

"What does that mean? Whatever *I'm* into?"

"Listen," she said without ever slowing her frenetic keyboard tapping, "You've been hired to be a domineering diva, remember? Boss him around, be a bit of bitch, and make him a happy boy in doing so. It's S&M – not rocket science."

But I disagreed. To me, S&M *was* a science. An art, too. And I wasn't sure I had the creativity or the mindset to pull it off effectively. All the men I'd seen so far were very eager to serve me and submit to my whims. But that was only half the battle; was I skilled enough to evoke a true feeling of submission from these clients? Did they feel a sense of virtual surrender during our sessions, or were my demands for boot shining and foot worship just a version of bad dinner theater?

The elevator began to hum as it made its shaky ascent to the fifth floor. I ran back to the lounge and re-applied my black eyeliner and rust-red lipstick as the receptionist took care of money matters with John. I hadn't made enough money yet to start investing in serious leather attire or Givenchy heels for those prospective shoe-worship clients, but I *had* managed to find a shiny pleather two-piece that went well with my fishnet thigh-highs and stilettos with sexy buckles. I looked like a cast member from *Chicago* or a dominatrix on a budget: It could have gone either way.

Tiptoeing back out to reception in my heels, I whispered, "Which room is he in?"

"You're sessioning in the Red Room," the receptionist said. "Give him a few more minutes; he just walked in."

The Red Room happened to be my favorite room. Fully equipped with flogs, canes, short crops (and long ones), the Red Room also sported a metal suspension cage, which dangled from the center of the ceiling, and an extraordinarily comfortable red plush throne to match the rich, incarnadine paint on the walls. On quiet nights at the dungeon, I would often curl up on the throne and read until one of the other Mistresses kicked me out in order to ready the space for her next session.

I smoothly opened the door and found my client on his knees in the middle of the floor, hands clasped behind his back and head down. He did not look up as I entered. The sight of his naked, kneeling form almost startled me; I had yet to come across a client who assumed a "commencing" position on his own. It indicated eagerness and knowingness: He was undoubtedly experienced in the scene.

"Keep your head down," I instructed nervously. As long as his eyes remained fixed on the floor, he wouldn't see the uneasiness on my face. I had no idea what to say next. So I said nothing. I circled around him, allowing the sexy little clicking of my heels to fill the space. After winding around his body six or seven times, I felt the impulse to scratch my fingers straight down his back, leaving little red stripes on either side of his spine.

"No marks, please" he said in a quiet, but firm way.

"I'll be the judge of that," I scoffed, though I didn't dare to repeat the move. "Kiss my shoes," I whispered.

He slowly lowered his head and carefully kissed one shoe, and then the other, starting with the pointy toe and working his way up to the shiny silver buckle with his lips.

"Why are you here to see me this evening?" I asked, out of genuine curiosity, though I guised the question with an air of mockery.

"Because I need you to remind me that no matter how much I try to escape my reality, I will always be bound to it."

Holy shit. He was into rope bondage. He must have assumed that since I was Asian, I'd be adept at the traditional Japanese technique, Shibari. I panicked; I hardly knew how to tie a square knot, let alone create some symmetrical web of full body constriction with a single cord of nylon. I started to scan the room for something (anything) that would serve as a restraint in order to hurry the hell up with this session and give this guy his money's worth. In order to kill time while I searched for the right prop hanging on the wall, I asked him why he specifically wanted to see me that evening.

"Because your pictures online conveyed a combination of beauty, strength, and frailty to me. I haven't had the pleasure of interacting with such a rare female combination in a long, long while."

Damn it. He had a good sense of me from just two thumbnail jpegs posted on the dungeon's Web site. I didn't want to outwardly agree with his assessment, but I was fascinated to know what else he had intuited from the images.

"What makes me so beautiful?" I asked.

"You have such gorgeous black hair to match your delicate white skin. I love the combination of light and dark. You seem to have a lot of light. And you seem to have a lot of dark."

I didn't know how to respond. So I asked, "What makes you think I'm strong?"

"Well, you're willing to explore rather intense dynamics by getting involved in this line of work. I'm sure it's decent money, but money that comes at a price. I find it interesting you'd be willing to pay that price."

I felt even less inclined to respond to his second answer. So I asked my third and final question: "And what makes you think I'm so frail?"

"The same reasons I think you're strong. Look at what you're doing at 12:25 on a Friday night."

"Look at what *you're* doing!" I snapped back. Not very Mistress-like, allowing a client to rile me up like that, so I promptly grabbed a roll of saran wrap from under the throne's legs and began wrapping it around his torso, becoming almost dizzy from the repeated circling around his still body. He made no protest as I bound his arms to either side of him. I didn't stop to think if his knees hurt from being pressed into the wooden floor. When I had completed ten full rounds of wrapping him, without once raising his head, he simply said, "Thank you, Mistress."

It was what I had been waiting for: a genuine moment of gratitude from a client who felt true satisfaction in submitting to my desire of constricting him. Had I found my strength as a Mistress by recognizing my vulnerability as a woman? He knew what he wanted out of his submission before I even had a chance to impose my own wants onto him. So maybe I *was* capable of exploring fear and fantasy with these clients. Doing so would mean diving down deep into my own waters to a place where light no longer reached the sea floor. In this darkness, perhaps I could feel around for whatever contents were settled on the bottom.

Over time, John and I slipped seamlessly into our roles at the beginning of each session. This went on for several months. At one point, John was visiting me at the dungeon three times a week. He was addicted to his secret saran kink – and so was I. What initially felt like an exchange of power developed into an exchange of trust, tenderness even. I had never felt so close to a man. We shared a secret and a mutual need for connection that neither of us could easily explain to the people in our lives. Together John and I dove deep into the water, though neither of us knew what exactly to discover.

One night, as I carefully circled around my client, inspecting his constricted body, he whispered, "What is your name?"

I was startled by this break in the fantasy. A leak had been sprung, and unwelcome water was quickly filling our otherwise safe vessel.

"You know my name. It's Mistress. Veronica Chi. Why would you ask such an obvious question, it's unbecoming."

John showed no response as I quickly patched what he had slightly torn open. The following week, he came just once to the studio. I pretended not to notice this sudden shift, but his lack of explanation bothered me immensely. Was he punishing me for not revealing my true name? Did he really expect me to divulge such private information about myself?

Other Mistresses had described certain clients that tried to "top from the bottom," a phenomenon that lent itself perfectly to the average New York SM sub. These guys were running hedgefunds and firms, which dictated the pulse of this city and the global market. Power was served to them at every meal and with every new deal they secured. Paying some woman a sizable fee to commandeer that power sounded like a sexy form of therapy, but ultimately resulted in their relapse. Eventually, they would begin to orchestrate exactly how they wished to experience sessions, creating a demand that turned the domme into just another service provider at the mercy of their wallets.

And truthfully, I was at the mercy of John's wallet. His steady sessioning of three times a week paid my rent and utilities and left me with a bit to go enjoy dinner with friends at Balthazar. Maybe topping from the bottom wasn't such a bad thing.

So as our session ended I removed the saran wrap, cutting it like a cast straight up his middle. With my eyes fixed on the scissors I quietly spoke my real name. At first I didn't know if he heard me. Later, when I realized he tipped me twice my usual amount, it seemed likely that he had picked up on it.

Five whole shifts went by before I finally asked the receptionist if John had been there to maybe to see one of the other Mistresses. She told me he hadn't been back since our session the week before. Too much time had passed; I assumed he probably wasn't coming around again, and I was surprisingly relieved by this.

I never went back to the dungeon myself.

Ironically, a few months later, I landed a job at a small PR firm on that very block on East 35th. Often I walked right past the old address without a second thought. It seemed funny that a nondescript office building could house such a strange secret.

Can Xue

The Roses at the Hospital

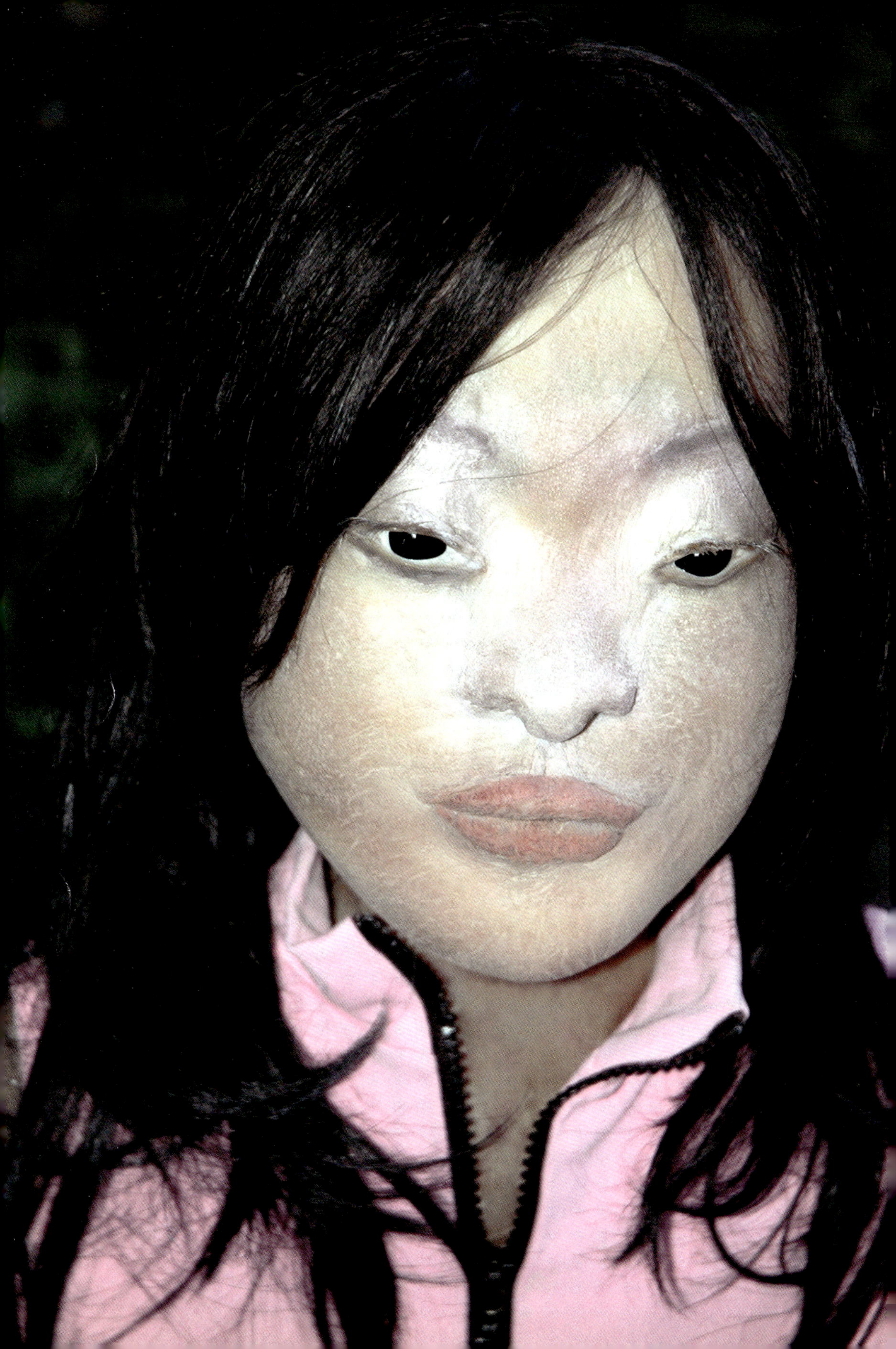

When I was at home, I always heard people mention "Gaoling." The impression I got from what people said was that it was a hill, and several long, narrow little streets led to it. On the hilltop was this city's largest hospital. People said that Gaoling wasn't far from my home. The streets were filled with small houses and dilapidated old two-story wooden buildings. The residents were mainly poor laborers. Those people could barely afford coal to cook with, so when the children had time they headed for the main street with brooms and dustpans. As soon as they saw a little coal fall from a rickshaw transporting coal, they rushed over and brushed it into a dustpan. In talking of Gaoling, this is the way the adults referred to it. I grew more and more curious: What on earth was Gaoling like?

As it happened, one Sunday I was in the vicinity of Gaoling buying stationery. After doing that, I took a small, narrow alley to Gaoling itself. The sun was strong that day, and people were all taking cover in their houses. I saw no one on the narrow asphalt road. I was perspiring. I walked straight to the end of the road and still didn't see anyone. After I climbed the hill, the road turned and became a declivity. I hesitated a little and then decided to turn into the area of narrow, small, dilapidated houses. It was next to an adobe house that I turned in, and then I immediately saw a filthy public toilet. After passing the toilet, I came to a home where they had just erected a mourning hall. Hanging in the hall were photos of the deceased: It was a sweet-looking girl wearing a red scarf. She couldn't have been more than fourteen. The coffin hadn't been carried in yet. I was confused: I'd never seen a funeral for a child. I wanted to stand there and watch, but someone drove me off. Someone's heavy palm struck me on the back. Enduring the pain, I ran off, almost crying.

"She died of meningitis," a girl about my age told me.

She looked like a workhand. She had pigtails, and her hands were rough. You could tell by looking at her that she was used to doing housework.

"I don't dare stay at the mourning hall," she added, haughtily curling her lips.

I didn't dare accost the girl. The atmosphere all around was too secretive, and I wanted to get away. Between two adobe houses there was a narrow path that could accommodate only one person. As I was about to take the path, the girl grabbed me back. She was strong: She pulled at me until I nearly fell down.

"It's a dead end, you fool."

She wanted me to go with her, and so we circled back to the mourning hall and went past it. Some people were already sitting in the hall: They had begun beating the gongs, and a woman was sobbing. I didn't know if it was her mother or a relative. We hurriedly put the hall behind us. I asked the girl where we were going. She answered, "The hospital." I said I had no interest in going to the hospital. She insisted, saying, "The hospital is a lot of fun."

We scrambled up the hill and finally went through a cobweb-like densely settled residential area and reached a level place made of concrete. On one side of it was a high wall. The girl said that the hospital was inside the wall. I thought the entrance to the hospital was nearby, but we walked a long time. We walked past the level concrete area and then once more came to the street. We were still at the wall and hadn't seen even a trace of the entrance.

"Let's rest for a while." With that, the girl sat down on the ground with her back against the wall. Her head drooped.

I saw her massaging the tiny cracks in her palms. As for me, I was hot and thirsty and wanted to go home.

"It's a lot of fun in the hospital," she said again, as if she had guessed what I was thinking.

At last, we saw an old woman selling popsicles. I wanted to buy one, but she waved her hand and said she had sold them all. Noticing my disappointment, the girl giggled. She told me that there was a gap in the wall just ahead and we could get into the hospital that way.

After walking a little farther, we saw the gap in the wall and made our way through it. In front of us was an old five-story structure. It was a mess in front of the building. Everywhere, there were piles of glass test tubes, syringes, and rubber tubes. Mixed in with them were lots of glass jars filled with dubious objects, a little like human organs.

"There are little children, some living and some dead. Don't look! Let's run off!" the girl shouted.

She and I ran off together. We ran past several black brick buildings. People were looking out from the windows of each building. These were probably hospital wards. Finally, we reached a garden. The girl threw herself down on the lawn and didn't move. And I sat down beside her. A profusion of roses formed the border. I had never seen such large, beautiful roses. Their strong fragrance immediately dispelled my fatigue and thirst. It was very quiet in the garden: Even the buzzing of bees was audible. I thought, this must be the place that the girl had said was so much fun. And actually it was great here; I didn't want to leave. I pushed the girl. I wanted her to get up and go with me to enjoy the roses, but she didn't move. And so I circled around the large border several times by myself. It was wondrous – and oh, so pleasant – beneath the blue sky. The more I looked, the more impatient I was to share this with the girl so I pushed her again. Finally, she sat up, yawning. Like an adult, she said gravely:

"You fool. Under the flowers are little babies, some living and some dead. You mustn't poke at the flowers as you look at them. Last week, a girl in the hospital was frightened here and …"

She broke off, keeping me guessing. I pushed her hard and asked, "And what? What happened to her? Hurry up and tell me!!"

"She died." She curled her lips.

"You're talking nonsense! You're the one who told me this place was a lot of fun." All at once, my heart felt empty.

"It is a lot of fun. I didn't lie. Come on, let's go look at the flowers together!"

But I didn't want to go with her. I was afraid she would suddenly part the clump of flowers and make me look at that ghost-like thing. I suggested that we admire the flowers from a distance. Staring at me, she nodded her head in agreement. Ah, the roses! The roses! In the strong floral fragrance and under the gentle blue sky, I felt that I was in a fairyland! Next to the slums near the hospital, the wards over there were so squalid, and yet hidden here was a wonderland. How could anyone imagine this? It was also unusual to have the chance to see such a beautiful lawn – so lush, so green, so clean!

I lay on the lawn, pillowing the back of my head with my hands. It was so pleasant to lie down like this. The girl was standing over me. When she bent down to talk with me, her head looked huge – just like a dustpan.

"Hey, you're resting your head on three little babies. Two of them are dead. One is still alive. You've pinned her legs down."

I jumped up with a rush. With all my heart, I wanted to dash out of this garden that was possessed by evil spirits. From behind, she held onto me by my clothes and wouldn't let me go. She even tripped me, wanting to make me fall.

"Look at the flowers, look at the flowers! You aren't looking at the flowers."

Tears of feeling wronged welled up in my eyes and spilled out. Through teary eyes, I saw that large roses were swirling all over the sky, and so I gradually calmed down. I stood there foolishly and gazed at the roses. The girl stealthily placed a soft, cold thing in my hand; she wanted me to hang onto it. Flustered, I threw that thing off and swung my arms for all I was worth. I felt something moist on my hand.

"Why are you so tense? It's just a twig!" she said.

The wind stopped blowing, and the roses fell slowly to the lawn – one rose here, another there, trembling as if alive. I looked closely at my palm and finally saw that it was clean; nothing dirty was there. And so I relaxed, and took careful steps to avoid trampling the beautiful roses. The girl's voice echoed in my ears – tender, yet stiff; fervent, yet frosty. Such an unearthly voice –

"In the slums of Gaoling, a girl died next to the hospital, and in the hospital there are borders of roses … Shhh. Quiet, quiet! We've come out. Look, here's the gap in the wall."

As the girl and I walked on the blazing asphalt road, it was almost twilight. The old woman selling popsicles had gone home.

We parted at the intersection, each of us surprised by the other's presence.

Selah Saterstrom

Jennifer Goes to the Dogs

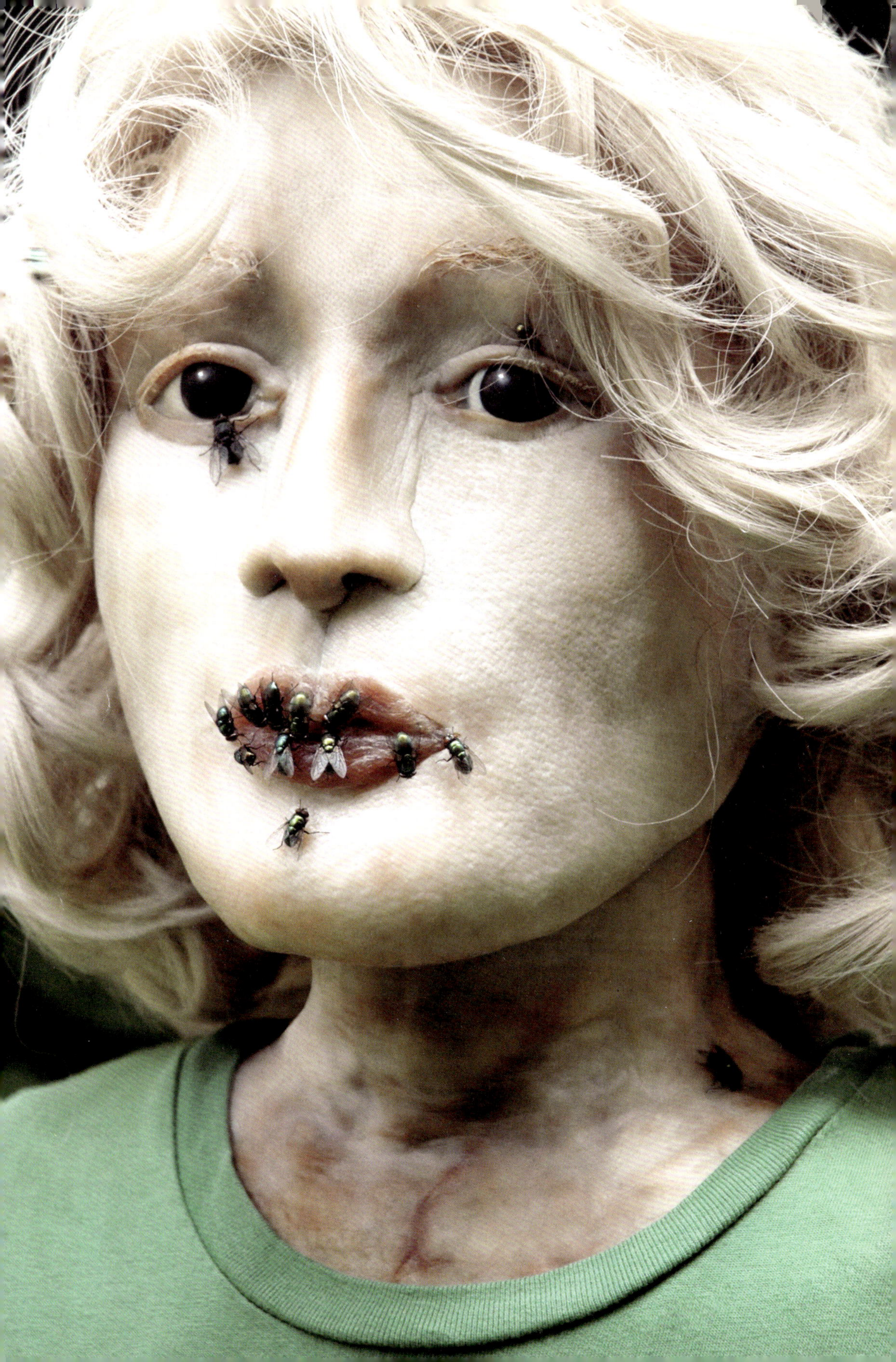

Around the block from my sister's kind of shitty neighborhood there was this huge house where some rich people lived. The people had the house built to look like Tara in *Gone with the Wind* and it looked ridiculous because the surroundings instantly shattered the poorly executed illusion. It turned out the people who built that house were rednecks who'd won the Louisiana lottery.

The yard guy who worked for these people was found dead and they said the dogs had done it. The rich people had three Rottweilers and they found the guy in their backyard. The Rottweilers had a reputation in the neighborhood. I'd be taking a walk with my sister and we'd pass the rich people's house and see these dogs and under her breath she would say: Oh look it's those dogs, they are *really* sweet. The dogs had this reputation for being really sweet. Not like other Rottweilers that mauled the faces off boys and shredded two-year olds. Sitting on my brother's porch talking about my sister and the whole dog thing while knocking back some beers, he said, shit, that's the thing about intense dogs, you never know when they'll snap and neither do they and its all one big happy family until the fucking apocalypse explodes in your face. Yes, I said, I guess that's the thing.

When they found the yard guy everyone had to eat their words about the dogs being sweet. When I'd ask my sister if there was any new news on the yard guy situation she never said "those dogs were so sweet … or so we thought." In fact I was always the one who had to initiate the topic of the dogs. So it was with surprise that one day when I asked if there was any news about those dogs she told me it wasn't the dogs fault, turns out the yard guy was on crack and the dogs were trying to rouse him when he collapsed. But at that point she couldn't resume the old myth of "those dogs are really sweet." Even though it turns out the myth was true.

Then there was that miserable woman in France. A total junkie, she tries to kill herself and overdoses. Her Labrador tries to wake her from her drug induced coma and does. She sits up and lights a cigarette. Something I can totally identify with. But when she pulls her hand away from her mouth she notices blood. Then she looks in the mirror. Her face – gone. That same day another woman tries to kill herself and succeeds. When the mauled woman gets to the hospital the French doctors have an idea. Something never before attempted. Why don't we take the face off the woman who killed herself and put it on the woman who got her face eaten by a dog while trying to kill herself.

How fucked up is that I swear to God, the French. Anyway, the irony here being clear and including: The dead woman lives through the ongoing nature of her face, and at the same time the living woman has to wear the face of a dead woman.

In both of these stories people first believed the dogs were responsible for the atrocious happenings, but in both of these stories it was the people's own fault for dying or trying to. The dogs were trying to wake the people, they were trying to prevent death or bring the people back from dead.

My grandfather once shot a dog. He had to as the dog was rabid and this was in the country. Not long before my grandfather died he told me that for years he suffered nightmares in which he relived the moment before he shot the dog. He had thrown a steak and the dog went to fetch it, which is when my grandfather raised his rifle to shoot, but right then the dog turned and looked at my grandfather directly in the eyes. My grandfather was crying, kind of sobbing actually, when he told me this story.

I know that my grandfather felt terrible about it. Maybe he thought he had disappointed the dog by breaking some kind of code of ethics whereby you do not shoot dogs in the back even if they are rabid. A couple of days after he told me this story he shot himself. With the rifle he shot the dog with? I don't know, but my guess is probably.

Did my grandfather break down while telling me the dog story because he knew even then that he would kill himself? I've gone over those last conversations again and again.

When my grandfather shot himself he did it in the back yard, where we kept our two dogs. They were small and cheerful dogs. After his death they wouldn't leave the guest bedroom closet and when anyone approached they would shake all over and make whimpering sounds. I spent a week in the closet with the dogs, trying to comfort them. After, the dogs were given away. One ended up having a happy life and one ended up having a sad life.

As an adult I have owned one dog that died when she was hit by a car. She was such a light-hearted dog. Her death coincided with a break up, a process that would, it turned out, take years. I ended up with that dog accidentally – though I was pretty happy about it – but it wasn't like I went out and tried to get a dog so when she died I realized I didn't want another one.

I have read two novels that feature dogs as metaphorical themes. Both of the books were about the heart, our human dog hearts, our breaking heart hearts, and then just getting on with things. I loved those books when I read them because they seemed hopeful.

Once when I began a particular affair, I wrote a poem about dogs and when my lover read it, he cried. It made him feel scared, but he didn't know why. Really there was a bad dog in the poem but it was about this other guy I had sex with a week after meeting my then-current lover, an experience I failed to mention as I was so caught up being in love. Three years later when I told my lover about the guy I had sex with, he became furious and ended our affair. There were other reasons of course, but I look back at when my ex-lover read that dog poem and think: damn.

You also see those bumper stickers, the one that say *Dog is my Co-Pilot.* Are the people who put these bumper stickers on their cars making fun of God or AA? It is unclear.

When I was a kid I thought *Kujo* was the scariest fucking movie ever. I remember only one scene, the one towards the end where the sweaty mother and wounded kid are in this tiny hatchback piece of shit car that of course won't start and Kujo is pounding on the windows of the car, a killing machine.

I was once told as a child that a black dog portends death. Years later when I was working at a 7-ll I'd often get night shifts with this guy Jim I had a major crush on. Only freaky or drunk people came in during the night shift so we would go out back before our shift started and get stoned out of our minds. Then Jim would get the portable jam-box out of his car and bring it into the store and we'd listen to music, which I didn't know anything about, but Jim knew a lot about. One night Jim played the Nick Drake song *Black Eyed Dog* and then told me how Nick Drake died right after he wrote that song and that he had unbelievably long fingernails when they found his emaciated body. Jim cranked up the volume and we listened to the song again and it was like you could hear it all in the brassy edges of Nick Drake's voice. In the middle of the song a college frat kid came in to buy some condoms. Jim didn't turn down the volume so the guy had to buy the condoms with *Black Eyed Dog* blaring. It was so great because when Jim was selling the kid the condoms, it was like he was giving that kid a sermon or something, like: "You want condoms well here you go and *Black Eyed Dog*, mother fucker." Coincidentally this was the first time I ever thought about marriage as a personal option, seeing Jim toss the condoms at that kid like that. I thought: There are some people I could really learn to live with.

After my divorce when I thought I was losing my mind Wanda suggested I get a dog. She sounded so optimistic when she said it and was very adamant about the idea, she was so glad she was having it. And I wanted to be glad she was glad so I lied and said I thought it was a terrific idea.

My sister got a dog "for the kids" meaning her husband and baby Casey and once when we were talking about something I'd written she said, you never put in the good stuff, only the bad stuff, and the dog was barking in the background and she had to repeat herself three times so that by the last time she was yelling but right then the dog stopped barking so she was just yelling.

The dogs around here make me feel – *what*?

There are many hanging from trees, slick and bloated flags. And there are others aimlessly wandering about, starving. I watched one take a shit then lie down and die next to a jumble of broken stuff that included a doll's head strangled in Mardi Gras beads.

So, to answer your question, Barbara Walters,

I guess I'd say that dogs do make me think about death.

I like that they have this streak in them, which tries to wake humans from death. It makes me feel like something is watching out for me, even though dogs often hurt people when they try to wake them. But when I think about the dogs around here wandering around looking for food, I also think they are competition.

I could go on and on about dogs.

Johannah Schmid

Magdalena

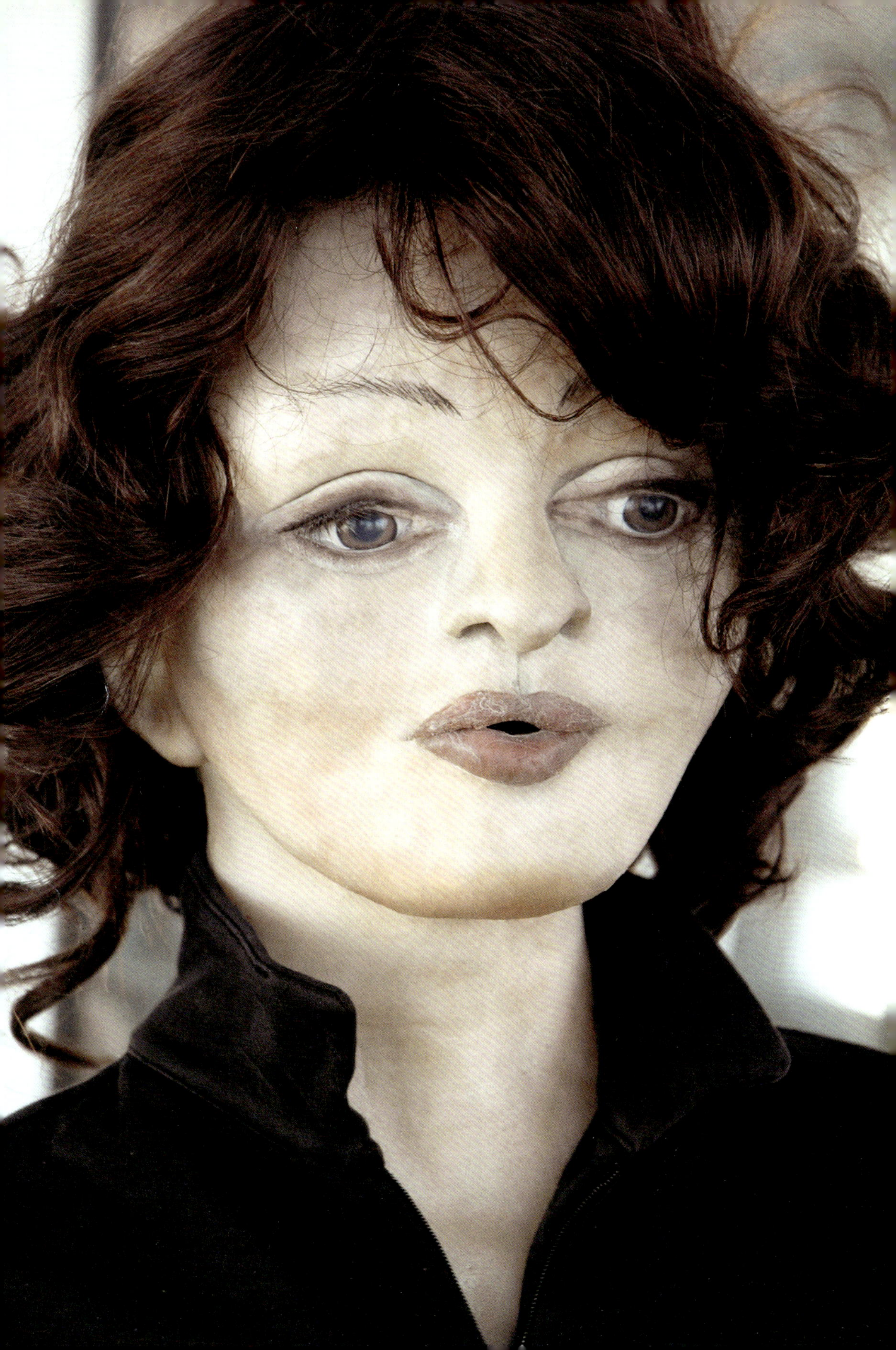

I was seven years old. It was so hot that I used my tiny hands to divide the air like curtains so that I could walk. Thoughts of my body lying in cold water wove through my mind, but there were seven miles between me and the public swimming pool, and I had only my bike, and I didn't have permission to go. I imagined cycling so fast through the dense air that it would open like the Red Sea, and that would be proof that it was right for me to leave, when I heard my dad shouting my and my sister's name.

Again I was too late, again too stupid to hide, again too embarrassed to behave like her, who never had to go.

My dad blew the horn impatiently and asked where my sister was, not even listening to my answer, but pulling me up onto the tractor by my arm. I swore to myself that this was the last time I was going without my sister. I despised myself for putting up with this every day, a feeling similar to how I felt after I masturbated again although I had promised Jesus the day before that this was the very last time.

Arriving at the meadow, he threw the equipment from the tractor, helped me down, handed me a bottle of mineral water and an apple and yelled back as he left that he'd be back soon. My vision blurred; I felt something hot collecting in my eyes, crawling down slowly on both sides of my nose, suddenly running as if startled and then dripping down from my chin to my collarbones and evaporating in my imagination with a zsch … and some steam.

The meadow was huge, impossible to see to the end of it, but I knew from the other day that there were seven rows with twenty-three trees in each row. I hid the bottle and the apple under some hay in the shadow of a tree, took the rake and pulled the hay towards me, went one step to the left, pulled, went another step to the left, pulled, another step to the left until I reached the next tree; then I pulled, made one step to the right, pulled …

I created a hay snake. She grew fast, got fatter and fatter, and I imagined she was able first to devour only mice, then rats, then muskrats, then martens.

(Five years later when I first read *The Little Prince* I thought about all the hundreds of snakes I had created and fed and my vision blurred and I felt something hot collecting in my eyes, crawling down slowly on both sides of my nose, running and dropping from my chin like a leaky faucet.)

For the distance between trees two and three I used a different technique: I pulled, went one step back, pulled, went one step back, pulled … until the snake started to live in the middle of the rows. I jumped forward on one leg toward the trees, pulled, stepped one step back, pulled, another step back, pulled, jumped forward with two legs pressed together, pulled, jumped back, pulled, jumped back.

At the end of the first row I was out of breath; my tongue felt like a snake, too, rough on the outside, as when you stroke her against the grain, hard and completely dry. Getting the water now would waste a long, unproductive walk. I wouldn't be able to run, I would have to walk very slowly to avoid getting dizzy, and I could just as well do the next row while I was going back. I just had to make sure that this thing in my mouth wouldn't touch my palate, because if it did the single papillae would get stuck to it and they'd be impossible to get off, like tiny strands of chewing gum, stretching thinner and thinner in the middle until they'd break and all the papillae would hang ruptured from the roof of my mouth like stalactites. If I concentrated on keeping my tongue exactly in the middle of my mouth I wouldn't feel anything unless my tongue were to grow and fill out my whole mouth. I tried to make very smooth movements, so that if somebody could see only my upper body it would look like I was being moved along on a conveyer belt.

As I neared the place where I'd hidden the water, my tongue started to rebel, and it made me think about diving: When it feels like you can't hold your breath any longer you want to get to the surface to get air, but if you convince yourself that there are only a few feet left, or that you can't get up before you see some object on the bottom and after that another one, and so on, you can stay below for a hundred meters, even though you were out of breath after fifty.

The apple break made my stomach feel funny. The big pieces of apple I had swallowed without chewing them into a mash clacked together like boats in a storm, and when I jumped, the water and boats hit the top of my stomach and collapsed.

After a few hours I lay myself underneath of a tree, completely exhausted, but happy and very proud that I had been able to do the job, though it had seemed impossible at the beginning.

I heard the engine of a tractor, and I imagined my dad jumping down to me with his beautiful smile, taking me in his arms, throwing me in the air like a little baby, catching me and telling me that I am the only one he can rely on, that I am fast and that the snakes I made are amazing … But it was a different farmer who passed by, and disappeared.

I gathered the longest blades of grass and braided them together, but they broke. So I laid them all parallel on the ground and held them in place with my bare foot so they wouldn't move and wove other blades into the grid until I had created a mat. I was marveling at the artwork that lay in my outstretched palm when a big drop of water landed on it. The vault had darkened and huge drops pounced from the sky. The cold summer storm provoked a tempest in my body, and I started to cry hysterically. When my dad arrived I was happy that he couldn't see that my face wasn't wet only because of the rain. As he pulled me up onto the tractor he said that he couldn't get there sooner because he had to save the hay he already had on his wagon. I was facing the rear crying silently as I watched him destroy my snakes with the metal fingers of the spider (German for hay rake rotary) so the hay would be able to dry again after the rain was over.

Sunday morning 4 am, my mother woke us up and asked us to come help in the stable. It was cold, dark and damp outside. I was freezing and half asleep, and I had a hard time getting into the stable clothing that we kept in a separate room so the rest of the house wouldn't stink. It was disgusting to smell this stable reek so early in the morning; it felt as if it were passing unfiltered directly into my body, not just through my nose, but right through my skin as well.

My dad gave each of us a shovel and explained that he would fill up the sluice containing manure with water. As soon as the water came up to floor level, the rats would come out to get air. If we saw a rat we were supposed to hit it as hard as we could with the shovels to stun it, and he would come and kill it.

It felt like a dream, unreal and crazy, only my body was so uncomfortable that it had to be real. I held my shovel in a vertical position so that I would just have to drop it if I saw a rat. I could see the water filling up the sluice and some rats sticking out their heads to find out what was wrong. The very first rat that came out just plopped down in front of me and cleaned its face. It was so sweet, I thought I could never harm it, but the next one I saw ran straight toward me. I slammed the shovel down on the rat, afraid that it would hurt me. My dad ran toward me and stabbed the rat with his pitchfork straight through its body. It was shrieking and writhing terribly and it didn't stop. The next one ran in the direction of my sister, and the next toward my brother … and it was always the same procedure. I backed away a little into a corner, shivering, with my shovel over my head and so full of fear that I peed in my pants. My father collected all the rats on the fork as on a skewer, still writhing and crying. When the fork was "full" he exchanged it for a new one. I was shivering so much, it was a kind of double shiver: one because I was freezing, the other because of my fear. Suddenly I felt something jump from above onto my hands. I screamed in terror. I was completely immobilized by fear. Gradually I could see that what I had felt was only cow dung that had stuck to the shovel when I hit the first rat and which was now slipping off onto my hands. My family broke out in a peal of laughter. I was embarrassed, but I was also angry and swore to myself never to help them with this again. I left without a word. They tried to keep me there, apologizing, but I left the stable, washed my hands in the house, left the clothing on the floor for them to put away and went back to bed. I was never asked again.

Every girl in my class had her period and breasts. I didn't have anything. I wasn't suffering on that account, rather the opposite: I was training as a gymnast and it was very practical to have no boobs and no period. In biology we were studying snails. Snails are hermaphrodites and I asked the teacher if it was possible that human beings could also be hermaphrodites. She simply said yes. Her answer hit me like a stroke of lightening. I was devastated. Now it was clear why I didn't have breasts or menses. There was nobody to ask, no section in the public library accessible to kids where you could find out anything. I suffered for about a year trying to get used to the fact that I was different until I woke up one morning and had tiny crystalline balls right beneath my nipples. I wouldn't say it was exactly a relief, but I guessed that that might be the end of my being a hermaphrodite.

I met him in a Bible class. He was so different, he looked at me in a way that made my heart start to pound. We sat in a big circle with about twenty other young people. We read a passage from the Bible and then we tried to interpret it. Normally, it was boring, but every comment he made was brilliant and thoughtful. He played in a Christian rock band, had long hair and played the guitar for me alone, even though I didn't like it that he needed to connect it to an amplifier. I was in love. His room was the only place where we could meet privately. We made out a little then stopped and knelt down to ask Jesus for strength not to continue with these sins. When that didn't work anymore we explained to ourselves that we would get married in any case, so it would be fine for us to sleep together. I moved away at the age of fifteen, and after that we saw each other only on weekends. I learned that there were other ways to speak, other ways to think, other ways to see the world and very different kinds of people. I fell out of love with Jesus and out of love with him and decided to stop our relationship. He didn't let me; I had promised to marry him. He possessed me and I felt like I was possessed and I wanted that to stop. He came to the city in which I lived and rang the doorbell. I didn't open the door. He came back with an axe, stood in front of my apartment door and said he would not leave before he waded through my blood, until he spooned my brain out of my head. I called the police. They took him away, and I went for a few weeks to a friend's house a few hundreds miles away. He found out where I was, and I found him in front of the door as I was on my way out. He apologized and said he needed to talk to me. I didn't want to let him into the empty house so I agreed to drive with him to a coffee shop nearby. On the way he turned off the road through a field and stopped the car underneath a bridge. He opened his pants and wanted me to suck his small pink cock. I refused and tried to talk, but his heart started to beat so wildly that I could see his shirt moving, as if powered by an electric pump. He yelled at me, called me names, tried to undress and rape me. I escaped from the car, but he caught me, pressing my head against a stone and hitting me in the head with his fist. He forced me back into the car and began to strangle me, all the while yelling what a horrible person I was. I couldn't listen to what he was saying, I just tried very hard to think, think, think, think; what can I do? How can I survive? How can I stop him? How can I get out of this? Fortunately he was still trying to convince me to come back to him, so he paused a few times during which I coughed and choked after breath as he asked me questions. I promised everything, that I loved him more than anything, that I wanted to sleep with him, that I would never look at other men again … he squeezed my neck so hard that I knew I would die. I had done everything I could. I would die without guilt, probably nobody would find me. I saw him from above yelling my name, slapping my cheeks. I felt a slap on my face, and he fell back on his seat exhausted and absent. A tractor passed close by, and I managed to get out of the car and escape.

Every night I dreamed the same story, waking up the moment he strangled me. I feared going to bed and I thought every evening about how to react in my dream, what weapon I would have and how I would use it. After a full year I was able to lay hold of a pair of scissors and stab him in the eyes. Then I escaped. That was my last dream.

Luisa Valenzuela

Woman. 1977

Adapted by the author from the story "Symmetries"

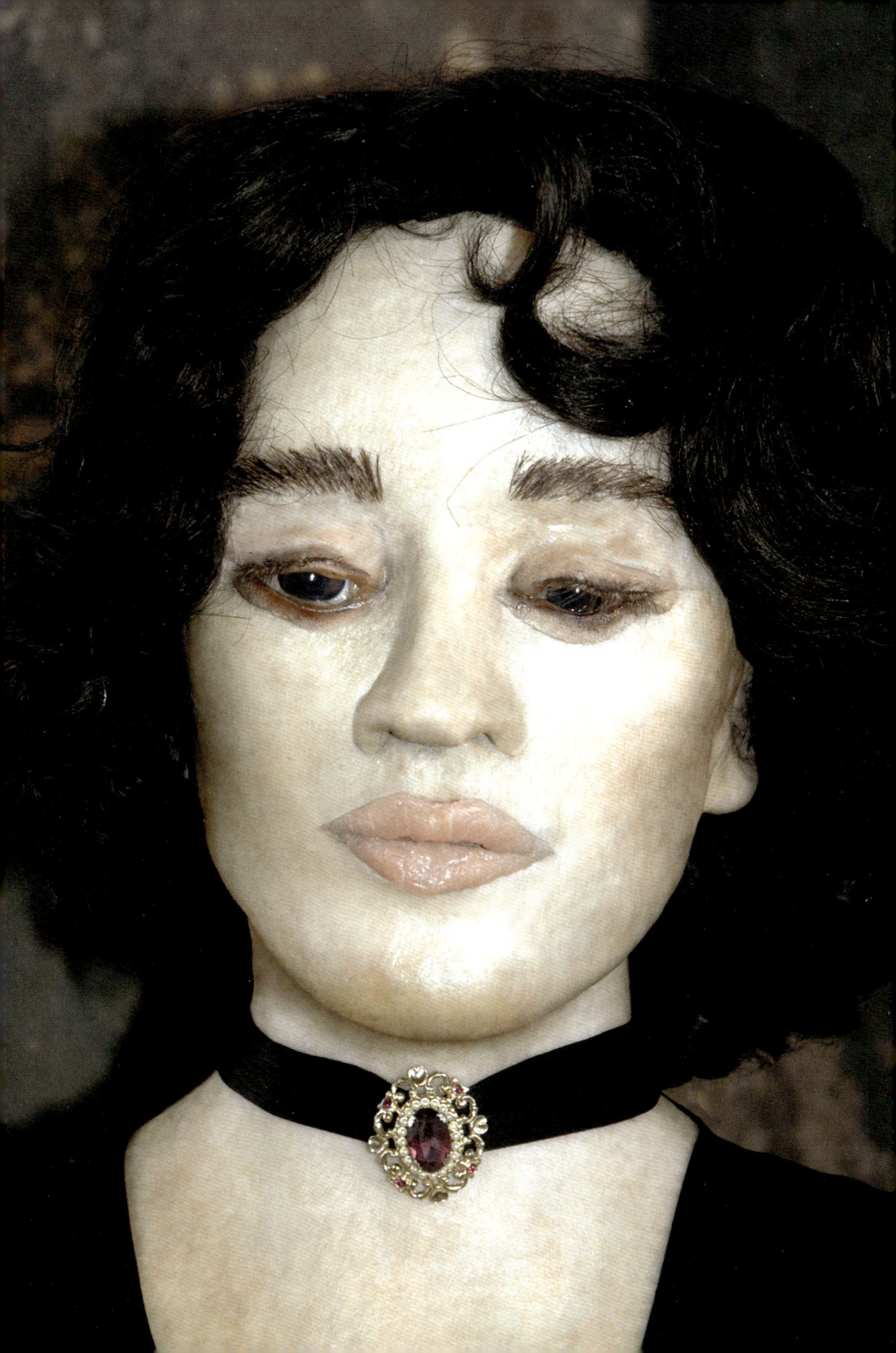

We take them out. No one can say we're not human, and yet so few people thank us for it.

It's true, in part. They do take us out, they bring us the most beautiful, disgusting clothes, they take us to the most beautiful, disgusting places with silver candelabra in order to eat delicious food. Disgusting. They are not in the least human, let alone humanitarian. We can hardly taste the supposedly delicious food, the clothes are too tight around our chests; besides, afterwards they return us to the horror they make us vomit up all the food they tear off our clothes they make us give everything back. With interest. Except that, except that in some corner of our souls we manage to maintain a minimum of dignity and we never betray the others.

When love comes along it lights up everything.

Forgive me if I laugh at such a stale cliché. Forgive me if I laugh out loud, now that they leave us so little room for laughter.

Only room for what we will call love for lack of a better word.

A word that can be the worst of all words: a bullet. Just like the word "bullet," something that penetrates and lingers on. Or doesn't linger on at all, it merely pierces.

After me, the deluge. First, the shot.

The women who are in our power know it. This woman knows it, and that one and that one and that one too. They have lost their names among us and have learned to allow themselves to be penetrated 'cause we have taken great pains to tame them. We have done our best and they know it.

They know other things that even the generals and admirals would like to know and which the women refuse to reveal. Despite the horrors and the dazzling, punishing outings, the women remain silent and the military cannot help but admire them for that.

We look at the women but they do not see us. They have hoods on or we have blindfolded them. Being walled up, we call it. We look them up and down and inside too, we stick things inside them, we perforate and puncture and explore. We stick things inside them, not always our own. We put things inside them that are much more terrible than our own, simply 'cause those things are a prolongation of ourselves and because they are ours.

The women, I mean. The women scream if they have any voice left. Then we take them out to supper without a blindfold on, without a hood, and without even that thread of a voice, with their eyes dim, their heads down. We make them wear the loveliest clothes. The loveliest clothes.

They bring hairdressers and beauticians to the clandestine detention center and they force us to put on long, embroidered dresses. As in other instances, we want to refuse but we can't. We know perfectly well where they get the dresses from – covered in sequins and strapless as if to underline and emphasize our scars – we know where they get them from but not where they will take us when we put those dresses on. With our hair done, and made up and manicured and modified, with not the slightest chance of being ourselves.

When they uncover your head they cover your body you lose all consciousness of self that's the most dangerous thing you don't even know where you're standing and we very rarely do stand except in the freezing courtyard.

Sit down! We shout at them as if they were recruits, sit down with your legs apart, wider, we shout, and it's an excellent idea. Don't allow them to die standing up like soldiers, let them die belly up like cockroaches, like the grovelers they are – but they are soldiers, they are more like soldiers than we are. Are they braver? They know they are going to die for their ideals and they hold firm to their ideals. We merely – pleasurably – kill them.

There is a complaint:

Who whispered the word "pleasurably" without daring to say it out loud? The exact adverb to use would be "gloriously." Gloriously, I say. Gloriously is how we kill them, for the glory and honor of the fatherland.

You have to look because if you turn away, if you feel pity or repugnance, because if you feel pity or repugnance what we are embarked upon ceases to be sublime.

It's almost diabolical we know what it's called they don't give it its true name they call it interrogation they say it's a lesson and we know about our companions who have been left in tatters destroyed gradually bone by bone and have been left bleeding gaunt dumped on the floor after they have first made them lose all semblance of humanity. We know about the other women, the other men, and at night we hear their cries and those cries sometimes get inside our heads and they are only our own undying memory of ourselves and we know when with their nails or their shoe or some other equally brutal method they open our vulva as if it were an open mouth in which they can stick anything but never never anything as terrible and voracious and alive, as destructive and irremediable as that which they have stuck into others, because later they will take us out and show us off like the trophies we are.

How is it that no one knew before, how is it that no one said anything, how is it that no one saw them in the Mesón del Río, for example, or in one of the other classy restaurants where they took the women between sessions? Those possibly beautiful women, perfectly turned out, their wounds disguised with make-up, silent, placed there to demonstrate that the torturers have an even more absolute and unanswerable power than the power of humiliation or punishment.

It was a joint experiment then suddenly one colonel lost his grip on reality.

1977. I want this woman just for me don't touch her only I am going to touch her from now on leave her to me I'm here I can see to her myself.

This woman is mine now I pass my hand over her haunches I caress her gently she knows or believes that I'm going to hit her nothing of the sort my hand goes too far, my hand slaps her, enraged, my hand has a mind of its own I caress her again and I can relax, surrender myself. I can at last surrender myself to a woman, I can drop my guard tear off my stripes, I can, because this woman is more of a hero than all of us put together, because this woman killed for a cause and we just kill for the sake of it, 'cause they order us to.

This woman is mine and I'm keeping her and if I want I'll save her not that I want to save her, I just want to have her for myself whatever the consequences. For her I leave all the medals and braid at the door, I rip up my uniform, I take off my clothes and I dissolve and only I can hold her close. And dissolve her.

The colonel's center, his concern, is this woman behind bars, lying on her back on a torture table always waiting for him with her legs apart. A captive lover. This woman stretched out on the metal table, writhing on contact with the electric prod. The cattle prod is, of course, applied by the colonel reduced now to the universal role of lover.

The 1977 woman is living amongst real savages and yet her colonel lover has managed to get a smile out of her which hovers there, almost angelic, because luckily those who amused themselves with her previously did not play at trying to smash her teeth.

Howls can be heard from the other side of the walls and they do not come from the jungle, however much they resemble the cries of wounded animals in the depths of Paleolithic caves. On the table, which is covered with a metal sheet, on the rough cement floor, against the walls encrusted with blood, he makes love to the woman. The enamored colonel and his chosen one. And the smell of sex mingles with the other sickly smells of those who passed through there before and stayed there, forever spattered on the floor, the ceiling, the walls, the torture table.

It's important not to forget. We must remember those walls that have been demolished with the clear aim of removing the corpus delicti, of erasing from the face of the world the memory of the horror. The horror must never be forgotten nor the stench nor the pain nor –.

Few are concerned about the woman (1977), an inscrutable woman with rather atrophied muscles, gaunt but beautiful. Only one man, in fact, is concerned about that woman and he's very concerned. Too concerned. He's not content now with giving her dresses and jewels obtained during dubious police raids. No, in mufti, he himself goes to the best lingerie shops and fashion boutiques in the city and buys her clothes. With his own hands he measures her neck, pressing a little too tightly, and then he goes to Antoniazzi's to order a choker that's a bit too small for her and far too expensive for him. He offers it to her as proof of his love and he makes her wear it, and the choker looks rather like a dog collar, with rings made out of blue gold, a specialty of the jewelers. With a fine snakeskin belt by way of a leash, he could take that woman anywhere, but that is not what he wants. He wants her to follow him of her own free will, he wants her to love him.

And if, for her, love was ever anything more than submission, she can no longer remember. Or else she prefers not to. These are times of survival and silence: refusing to give the tiniest bit of information, remaining absorbed, distant, just smiling a little if possible and trying to return a kiss but never opening her mouth to speak, to betray. Never. Disgust must remain relegated to somewhere outside those walls.

The colonel is those walls because he removes her from imprisonment in the clandestine center and, walled up in fur coats, camouflaged in beautiful clothes, masked by elaborate makeup and hairdos, he takes her to the theatre, to dine at the best places and absolutely no one seems to recognize her or approaches her on these outings, not that anyone could, surrounded as he usually is by his bodyguards.

She, in turn, recognizes no one, she does not even look up. She knows obscurely that a single gesture on her part would condemn the others; and she knows that for any such gesture or look he will hurt her, later on. He will mark her below the line of the low-cut dress so that he'll be able to show her off in other clothes.

He doesn't do it in order to mark her nor does he insist any longer that she betray her comrades. He is only looking for new excuses to be able to penetrate her each day a little more until he manages to possess her entirely. He loves her, much more deeply than any man has ever loved before, he thinks. And he takes her out more often than is advisable and he even hopes to be able to introduce her to his legal wife and to install her in the marital bed.

High-ranking officers in the army begin to be alarmed, even if the pleasure of the colonel is measured as befits his rank. His pleasure is apparently measured, but the love he feels for the hooded woman is immeasurable. I happen to love her, it seems he said – it just came out of him – on one occasion, and the words did not fall on deaf ears. His superiors started to watch him and to worry while they themselves paraded their own favorite victims through the salons of the large hotels. They observe him, he who only observes the neckline of the woman he loves or the clumsy way she raises the glass of Champagne to her lips.

The prisoner he's pampering is a dangerous subversive and worthy soldiers like him cannot be involved with elements who are the enemies of the fatherland. Or rather they can and must be involved, what is unforgivable is to have abandoned his duty in order to plunge – unwittingly it's true – into the murky waters of desire. An act of downright insubordination. A colonel cannot place a woman above the army itself, even if that woman is the property of the army.

It's best to make a fresh start in these cases.

So the colonel is sent to Europe on a specific mission while, with the aid of her choker the 1977 woman is sent to Hell on a mission unspecified.

Anna Wexler

Violette Nozières: Revenant

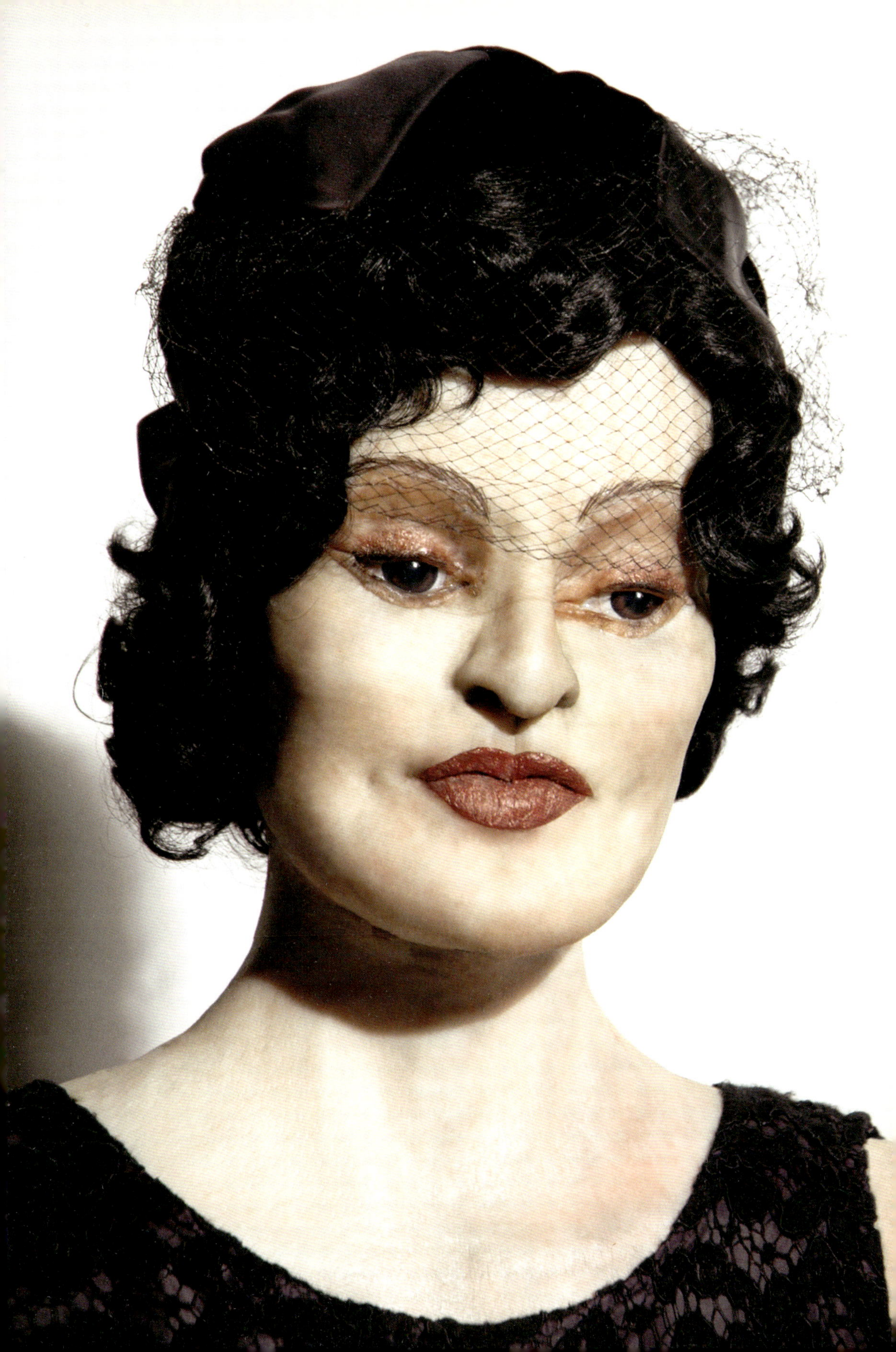

"I don't love the cinema, but an insurrection that is promised to me every morning when I see Violette Nozières again ..." So wrote the Situationist Guy Debord in 1952, in an unused script for his first film *Hurlements en faveur de Sade* (Howls in Favor of Sade). The accompanying image was to be that of a passing twelve-year-old girl who smiles and descends into the Paris Métro. The reference to her age was no accident or approximation. Violette Nozières was exactly twelve when her father, a railroad engineer, began to rape her in the family apartment on Rue de Madagascar and in the tool shed they owned on a garden plot near the Porte de Charenton. She described his sequence of actions – from kissing on the lips to fondling to penetration – in detailed depositions following her arrest for parricide in 1933, when she was eighteen.

Two months after the initial script was published, *Hurlements en faveur de Sade* was projected for the first time in Paris at the Ciné-Club d'Avant-Garde in the Musée de l'Homme. The screening was barely underway when it was stopped by the director of the film club; audience members who hadn't already walked out threatened to attack Debord and his friends. For subsequent showings, Debord came with a bodyguard. The dialogue for the film now consisted mainly of phrases from journals, other literary texts and the French *code civil* spoken in monotones by five voices without accompanying images. When one of the voices was speaking, the screen was white; during silent intervals, and for the last hour of the film with no soundtrack, the screen was black. The original line invoking Violette Nozières was absent; however one of the five voices, that of a young girl, speaks the following: "Her memory always returned to him, in a blinding flash made by all the sodium fireworks on contact with water."

Whether this statement can be taken as a reflexive comment on the anti-aesthetics of the film, the annihilation of the image track itself, or as a prophetic sign of Debord's lifelong combat against spectacle, an objectified vision of the world, I cannot say. But each time Violette resurfaced in his memory, he saw the image-debris of that world set ablaze on the barricades of May '68 and then a black screen, the willed blindness of incendiary action.

Violette's actual engagement with fire was anything but impulsive. It was one element in a series of experiments with doses of sleeping drugs with which she ultimately intended to poison her parents – principally her father in order to stop his incestuous abuse and her mother in order to spare her the knowledge of his transgressions. In a deposition at the Palace of Justice in 1933, Violette calmly described the moment when this intention first crystallized:

In the beginning, when I was just twelve years old, I didn't understand. But later I was disgusted, my father horrified me. I believe it's this disgust that subsequently made me frigid with my lovers. It's this disgust I had with my father and myself, because I also felt very guilty, that gave me the idea of throwing myself in the Seine on December 15, 1932. But I recoiled before the black water, I was afraid to die. In any case, since that moment, the idea of killing my father haunted me. I hated him.

In April of the same year she carried out her first serious attempt with the drug Soménal, convincing her parents that it was a medicine prescribed by her own doctor to protect them from the syphilis for which she was in treatment. When she was certain that they were sleeping heavily, she set the blue and white flowered curtain that separated their bedroom from the rest of the apartment on fire. After the apartment filled with smoke, she alerted neighbors on the same floor, and firefighters arrived soon to extinguish the blaze. Claiming that the fire was caused by an electrical short-circuit, she hoped to mask the lethal affects of the poison as a consequence of smoke inhalation, but both her parents survived this initial effort. In August, for her final attempt, she used stronger doses of the sleeping drug and turned on the gas to simulate a double suicide scenario. This time her father died, but her mother survived to testify against her.

Violette never seriously tried to avoid arrest. As she testified later to doctors trying to ascertain her mental status, she felt enormous relief after her success in killing her father, a lifting of her obsession. Nothing else had any importance. She was apprehended in Paris as she was leaving the Métro École-Militaire, about a week after the parricide.

In 1978, the image evoking twelve year old Violette obliterated from the Debord script resurfaced in another, actualized cinematic form. *Violette (Nozières),* Claude Chabrol's film version of the history up to her imprisonment was released that year with Isabelle Huppert in the lead, brilliantly interlacing Violette as violated schoolgirl, desperate vamp, and lucid criminal. She was awarded the prize for best actress at Cannes for the role, her breakthrough into celebrity. According to interviews, she had long dreamed of playing Violette because "she had been to the limit ... she was at once aggressor and victim. I also have instincts of aggression and revolt."

Near the end of the film, an exuberant street musician outside the Prison de la Petite Roquette where Violette is awaiting trial sings one of the songs villifying her, "The Drama in all its Horror," to a popular tune of the era. He is accompanied by an accordionist and a growing crowd singing the words from flyers being distributed to passersby:

She poisoned both her parents
the vile Violette Nozières ...
this tramp, this vagabond
has committed this frightful crime.

And here is the horrible scene
the hand that gives the poison.
She shamelessly kills her father
just like that, for no good reason.
Ah – just to go out on the town
dance and drink with all her boyfriends
this precocious kid's hanging out
in cheap hotels and seedy bars.
But the poor mother groans
and the father is dead
and she has not a single regret.

As she listens to the song from inside the prison and then from the police wagon en route to her trial, Violette's shadowed face forecasts the verdict of the trial – her head covered with a black veil, she is to be decapitated by guillotine. But in the final moments of the film, while she sits patiently mending her cellmate's nightgown, she hums the melody sweetly to herself, now without words. The taunting street song is transformed into an ethereal lullaby, an evocation of her future self, her rebirth. Violette tells her cellmate that she can now begin her life anew. The rest of her history is then summarized by a neutral male voice: Her death sentence commuted to life imprisonment and labor, a series of pardons based on exemplary behavior leading to her liberation in 1945, and – a unique vindication in the French judicial system for a convicted murderer – total legal exoneration and rehabilitation by the courts in 1963, a few years before her death.

When the film was completed, Isabelle Huppert described herself as a deep void. Violette had become a part of her, and now that the work was done, she felt completely abandoned and uncertain about her next steps. "It is such a fine and powerful role that I ask myself now what I am going to be able to perform in the future," she said right after the filming. "What role could ever lead me so far?" But, according to other interviews, this sense of absence was also to be felt as presence. Isabelle reported that three months after the shooting ended, the character had still not left her; Violette's phantom followed her everywhere.

Just as her memory returned to Guy Debord in moments of blinding revelation that erased the collective image track of all societies of the spectacle, so I imagine Violette visiting Isabelle Huppert as the silence around a song shorn of its delusory words. For the actress, however, it was a silence that moved through the violence of the external commodified world to reveal the unspoken victim and aggressor within.

Heide Hatry

Creating Life

The portraits in *Heads and Tales* are photographic documentations of sculptures I made out of animal skin and body parts, intended to provide springboards for stories, reminiscences or meditations on the lives of women. I asked a number of writers I admire to select the image of one of my women and create a life for her. As the work addresses issues of violence, death and gender identity, the writing reflects similar concerns as they are specific to women, not necessarily from an obviously politically fraught or polemical perspective, but more typically resorting to fantasy, satire, irony and other subversive modes of presentation to disrupt the hegemony of the everyday and release the power of its horror.

My intention with the work was to make it as life-like as possible, vivid and sometimes disposed in positions suggesting movement. I used untreated pigskin to cover a sculpture I had made out of clay, with raw meat for the lips and fresh pig eyes in order that the resulting portrait would appear as if it were looking at the viewer with a vital expression that the photographer had just captured at the moment. In fact, a photographer taking a picture of a model does more or less what I've done with my sculptures: The model will be made up, its hair will be done, appropriate lighting and pose will be chosen, etc. Or, if you prefer, what I am doing is reminiscent of what a mortician does in preparing a corpse for viewing: creating the illusion of life where there is none.

Taking photos of my sculptures is like reconstructing life: It simulates a simulation by fabricating an image of a fake face, an image calculated to deceive the viewer, since taxidermy (from the Greek, *taxis*: order or arrangement, *derma*: skin) and photography work so well together. The fake image appears convincing because we expect to see what we are used to seeing. The portrait of a face staring into the camera or captured in a snapshot simply doesn't conjure thoughts of death, even though we are often, in fact, looking at the living image of the dead when we view a photograph. Every photograph is a memento mori, and of course we like to forget that reminder of death, so we are easily persuaded that these images represent real, living people.

I didn't make any demands on the contributors as to form or content. I simply wished that they would breathe life into these inert forms with their words. Since the violence that is often at the heart of women's experience certainly pervades the images, I rather expected that the texts would to be related to pain, abuse, loneliness, madness, violence and death, etc., though I imagined that they could also be connected to, say, beauty, love, motherhood, aging, plastic surgery and any number of other themes, perhaps exploring the pain and mortality that pervades those themes as well. In any case, the simulacra that inspired these literary creations, and which are, thus, life-creating in themselves, intend to invoke a play of subject and object, of life and death.

I am delighted that I was rewarded with a collection in which the unknown, the uncertain, the arcane lives of virtually anonymous human beings who have suffered more or less obvious or explicit harms are thematized, not to mention powerfully evoked, in the contributors' words. I feel that it is a step towards understanding the female experience.

I owe the authors who have so generously participated in the project my heartfelt appreciation.

With my special thanks to:
Marina Abramović, Dalit Anolik, Oliver Beer, Roy Bernardi, Erica Bernstein, Jonas Braus, Jonathan Brown, Emilia Burgos, Orly Cogan, Chrissy Conant, Christophe d'Astier, Rikki Ducornet, Jakob von Engelhardt, Brian Evenson, Tom Farr, Sabin Fernau, Susanne Fischer, Jeannie Freilich, Galeria Tribeca, Sevrina Giard, Thyrza Nichols Goodeve, Greene Village Packing, Susan Gubar, Hatfield Quality Meat, Heather Hartley, Laura Hatry, Betty Hirst, Wolfgang Hoerner, Stefan Huber, Christine A. Isherwood, Shelley Jackson, Robert Kelly, Gavin Keeney, Jakob Köllhofer, Catharine A. MacKinnon, Eileen McDonagh, Samuel Lallouz, David Liss, Giuseppe Liverani, Gregg LeFevre, Ruediger Lentz, Daneyal Mahmood Gallery, Tom Mattos, Pierre Menard Gallery, Shaheen Merali, Menne Metzner, Hannah Monyer, Brad Morrow, Filomena Moscatelli, Glenn Most, Tim Nugent, Katiana Orluc, Michael Page, Roberta Paul, Ida Pisani, Christoph Reuter, Bettina Rheims, Saul Roll, Margret Schepers, Iris Schieferstein, Carolee Schneemann, Klaus Schönfeld, Elmar Seibel, Peter Soetje, Arpad Sölter, Francesca Sorace, Joe Summer, Irina Tarsis, John Uecker, Luisa Valenzuela, Raphael Vostell, Marianne Wagner Simon, Dan Wechsler, John Wronoski, Brad Zucker, Louis Zucker & Co.

List of Works

All artwork is produced and photographed by Heide Hatry
The size of each photo is: 12 x 18 inches / 30 x 45 cm
Special edition: 20 x 30 inches / 50 x 75 cm

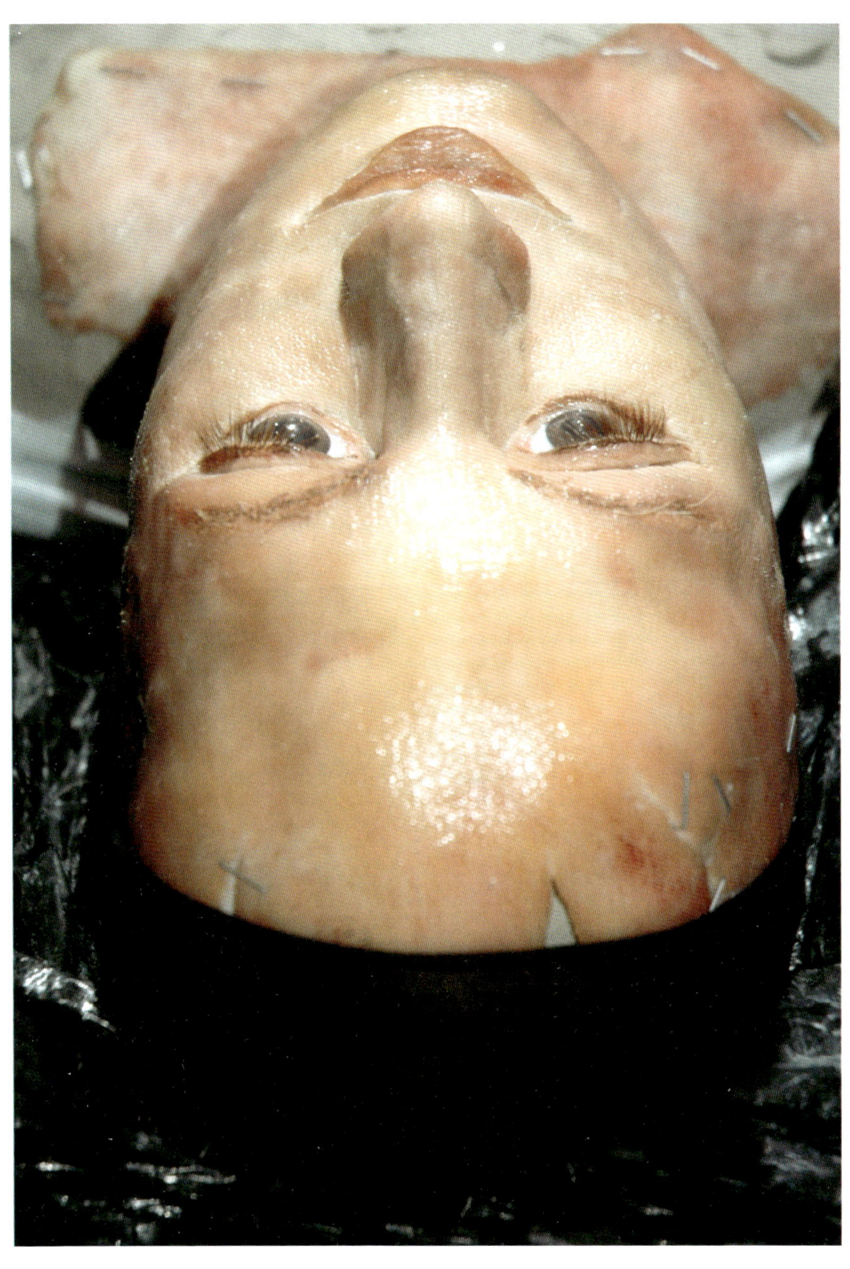

Biographies

Rosanna Yamagiwa Alfaro is a short story writer and playwright. Her stories have appeared in many journals, including *Descant, The Capilano Review, The Boston Globe Magazine* and *Axiom*. Her plays include *Behind Enemy Lines* (Pan Asian Repertory in NYC), *Mishima* (East West Players in LA), *Martha Mitchell* (Edinburgh Fringe Festival), *Barrancas* (Magic Theater in San Francisco), *Pablo and Cleopatra* (New Theatre in Boston), *Mexico City* and *Sailing Down the Amazon* (the Boston Women on Top Festival), and *It Doesn't Take a Tornado* and *Amsterdam* (La MaMa in NYC). She is co-producer, writer, and narrator of *Japanese American Women: A Sense of Place*, a documentary directed by Leita Hagemann, which was part of a traveling exhibit of the Smithsonian Institution. Three of her short plays have been anthologized by *Meriwether, Baker's Plays* and *Heinemann*. She graduated from Harvard, received an M.A. from Berkeley and lives in Cambridge, MA.

Roberta Allen is the author of two collections of short fiction, *Certain People* (Coffee House Press, 1997) and *The Traveling Woman* (Vehicle Editions, 1986), both praised by *The New York Times Book Review*; a novella-in-short short stories, *The Daughter* (Autonomedia, 1992), praised by the *Voice Literary Supplement*; the novel, *The Dreaming Girl* (Painted Leaf Press, 2000) and the memoir, *Amazon Dream* (City Lights, 1993), both praised by the *Village Voice*; the writing guides, *Fast Fiction* (Story Press, 1997), *The Playful Way to Serious Writing* (Houghton Mifflin, 2002) and *The Playful Way to Knowing Yourself* (Houghton Mifflin, 2003). She is on the faculty of The New School, has taught in the writing program at Columbia University and in private workshops. She was a Tennessee Williams Fellow in Fiction in 1998. A visual and conceptual artist as well, she has exhibited worldwide. Her work is in the collection of The Metropolitan Museum of Art.

Jennifer Belle's first best-selling, critically-acclaimed novel, *Going Down*, was translated into many languages, named best debut novel of the year by *Entertainment Weekly* and optioned for the screen, first by Madonna for whom she wrote the screenplay and currently by Das Films and Academy award-winning director, Mike Figgis. Her second novel, *High Maintenance*, was also a national bestseller and optioned for film and television. Her third novel, *Little Stalker*, came out in paperback in May 2008. Belle is also the author of *Animal Stackers*, a picture book for children, and her essays and short stories have appeared in *The New York Times Magazine, The New York Observer*, London's *The Independent, Cosmopolitan, Harper's Bazaar, Ms., Mudfish* and several anthologies. She leads an on-going writing workshop in her home in Greenwich Village where she lives with her husband and two sons. www.jenniferbelle.com.

Mei-mei Berssenbrugge is the author of numerous volumes of poetry, most recently *I Love Artists: New and Selected Poems* (University of California Press, 2006) and *Concordance* (Kelsey St. Press, 2006), a collaboration with the sculptor Kiki Smith. Her other collections include *Nest* (2003); *The Four Year Old Girl* (1998); *Endocrinology* (1997), a collaboration with Kiki Smith; *Sphericity* (1993); *Empathy* (1989); and *The Heat Bird* (1983). Characteristic of her style is a lush mix of abstract language, collaged images, cultural and political investigation, and unexpected shifts between the meditative and the particular. Berssenbrugge is the recipient of two fellowships from the National Endowment for the Arts, two American Book Awards, and honors from the Asian American Writers Workshop and the Western States Art Foundation. She lives in New Mexico and New York City with her husband, the sculptor Richard Tuttle, and their daughter.

Svetlana Boym is a writer and a media artist. Her books include *The Future of Nostalgia* (2001), *Architecture of the Off-Modern* (Princeton Architectural Press , 2008) *Common Places* (1994), *Territories of Terror: Memory and Mythology of Gulag* (exhibit catalogue 2006) and the novel

Ninochka (2003). Her new book *Another Freedom* (forthcoming in 2009) examines cross-cultural conceptions of freedom and the relationship between art and politics. She has presented her work and lectured at numerous venues in Europe and the USA and contributed to many journals including *Art Forum, ArtMargins, Cabinet, Critical Inquiry, Representations, Harpers's Magazine, Public Culture, Comparative Literature, Poetics Today*. Boym is the receipient of a Guggenheim Fellowship. She is the Curt Hugo Reisinger Professor of Slavic and Comparative Literature and an associate of Harvard Graduate School of Design; she Native of St. Petersburg, Russia, she lives and works in Cambridge, MA.

Rebecca Brown's new book of essays, American Romances, is forthcoming from City Lights. She is also the author of eleven other books of prose including *The Last Time I Saw You, The End of Youth, The Dogs: A Modern Bestiary, The Terrible Girls* (all with City Lights), *Excerpts From a Family Medical Dictionary* (University of Wisconsin and Granta), *The Gifts of the Body* (Harper Collins) and *Woman in Ill Fitting Wig*, a collaboration with painter Nancy Kiefer (pistilbooks.net). Her work is translated into Japanese, German, Danish, Italian and Norwegian and widely anthologized. Brown has also written a libretto for a dance opera, *The Onion Twins* and a play, *The Toaster*, and is currently engaged in projects involving altered texts, literary theft, the collision of pop and highbrow culture and the visual arts.

Mary Caponegro is the author of *Tales from the Next Village* (Lost Roads), *The Star Café* (Scribner's), *Five Doubts* (Marsilio), *The Complexities of Intimacy* (Coffee House Press), and *Materia Prima* (published in Italy by Leconte). A new collection of stories and novellas, entitled *All Fall Down*, is forthcoming in 2009 from Coffee House Press. Her work has been anthologized in *You've Got to Read This, The Anchor Book of New American Short Stories, The Italian American Reader, A Convergence of Birds* and *Wild Dreams: The Best of Italian Americana*. She has received the General Electric Foundation Award, the Rome Prize in Literature, the Bruno-Arcudi Award, a Lannan Residency and the Charles Flint Kellogg Award in Arts and Letters. She is a graduate of Bard College and the Brown University Writing Program. She has taught at Brown, RISD, the Institute of American Indian Arts, Hobart & William Smith Colleges and Syracuse University. Since 2002 she has been Richard B. Fisher Family Professor of Writing and Literature at Bard College.

Thalia Field has published *Point and Line* and *Incarnate: Story Material* with New Directions Publishing Corp. *Ululu (Clown Shrapnel)* was released in a limited edition by Coffee House Press in 2007. Her next collection, *Bird Lovers, Backyard* is forthcoming with New Directions in 2010. Thalia teaches in the Program in Literary Arts at Brown University.

Lo Galluccio has a BA from Harvard College in Social Studies with honors and studied acting at the Goodman School of Drama in Chicago. She's been nominated for two Pushcart Prizes in poetry. In 2004 her first chapbook of poems *Hot Rain*, was published by Singing Bone Press. She's read and performed at many venues in Boston and New York City, including *The House of Blues*, the *Nuyorican, St. Mark's Poetry Project, The Mad Poet's Café* and *Cbgb's Gallery*. As a reviewer for *Ibbetson St. Press* she's written about the work of many poets including Hugh Fox, Lyn Lifshin and Peter Gizzi. Her prose-poetry memoir, *Sarasota VII*, was published by Cervena Barva Press in 2008. She also released two avant-garde pop and spoken word solo cd's. http://logalluccio.atspace.com

Diana George's short stories have appeared in *Third Bed, Denver Quarterly, Chicago Review*, and in her chapbook *Disciplines* (Noemi Press). In 2006 she received a fellowship for her fiction from the National Endowment for the Arts. She currently attends Brandeis University, where she is working on a doctorate in English.

Thyrza Nichols Goodeve is a writer and amateur cartoodlist. She is the author of *How Like A Leaf: An Interview With Donna J. Haraway* (Routledge, 1999) and has published numerous essays and interviews on contemporary artists such as Matthew Barney, Vito Acconci, Ellen Gallagher, The Brothers Quay, Ann Hamilton, James Barsness, Tom Friedman, Andrea Fraser, Matthew Ritchie, Yvonne Rainer among others. Her work has appeared in *Parkett, Artforum, Art in America* as well as catalogues and book anthologies. Currently she is on the faculty of the MFA Program in Art Writing and Criticism at the School of Visual Arts, the Graduate Digital Media Program at the Rhode Island School of Design, and serves as the Program Coordinator for the summer studio program in MICA in New York (DUMBO) for the

Maryland Institute College of Art. She lives in Brooklyn Heights, New York.

Jessica Hagedorn was born in the Philippines and came to the United States in her early teens. Her novels include *Dream Jungle*; *The Gangster of Love*, which was nominated for the *Irish Times* International Fiction Prize; and *Dogeaters*, which was a finalist for the National Book Award. She is also the author of *Danger and Beauty*, a collection of poetry and prose, and the editor of *Charlie Chan is Dead: An Anthology of Contemporary Asian American Fiction* and *Charlie Chan is Dead 2: At Home in the World*. Her poetry, plays, and prose have been anthologized widely. Hagedorn's work in theater includes *Most Wanted, Three Vampires, Stairway to Heaven, Fe in the Desert* and the stage adaptation of *Dogeaters*. She has been the recipient of a Guggenheim Fiction Fellowship, a Lucille Lortel Playwright's Fellowship and a National Endowment for the Arts Creative Writing Fellowship, as well as fellowships from the Sundance Theater Lab and the Sundance Screenwriters' Lab.

Elizabeth Hand is the author of nine novels, including the 2007 psychological thriller *Generation Loss* and the cult classic *Waking the Moon* and three collections of short fiction. Her work has received numerous awards, including two Nebulas, two World Fantasy Awards, two International Horror Guild Awards, the James M. Tiptree Jr. Award and an Individual Artists Fellowship from the Maine Arts Commission/NEA. She is also a longtime contributor to the *Washington Post Book World*, *Village Voice*, *DownEast* and the *Magazine of Fantasy & Science Fiction*, among many other publications. She lives on the coast of Maine, where she is completing a novel about Arthur Rimbaud.

Heide Hatry is a visual artist and curator. She grew up in Germany, where she studied painting, drawing, sculpture, printing and photography at various art schools and art history at the University of Heidelberg. She ran a rare bookshop in Heidelberg for 17 years during which time she also taught at a private art school. After she moved to NYC in 2003 she has curated several exhibitions in Germany, Spain and the USA (notably *Skin* at the Goethe Institut in New York, the Heidelberger Kunstverein and Galeria Tribeca in Madrid, Spain; *Out of the Box* at Elga Wimmer PCC in NYC; *Carolee Schneemann, Early and recent work; A Survey* at Pierre Menard Gallery in Cambridge, MA, and *Meat After Meat Joy* at Daneyal Mahmood Gallery, NYC). She has shown her own work at museums and galleries in those countries as well and edited more than a dozen books and art catalogues. Kehrer Verlag published her book *Skin* in 2005.

Heather Hartley is the Paris Editor of *Tin House Magazine*. Her work has appeared in the 2007 *Best American Nonrequired Reading* (Houghton Mifflin, 2007), *Food & Booze: A Tin House Literary Feast* (Tin House Books, 2006) and *The World Within: Writers Talk Ambition, Angst, Anarchy, Aesthetics, ...* (Tin House Books, 2007). Her poetry manuscript, *Knock Knock*, was a finalist for the 2007 National Poetry Series Competition. Her poems have appeared in *Post Road, Tin House, The Los Angeles Review, Forklift Ohio,* and *Saint Petersburg Review* among many others. She was awarded first prize in poetry for the 2002 *Tin House Magazine*/Summer Literary Seminars in St. Petersburg, Russia and first place in the 2004 Brentano's Bookstore Poetry Contest (Paris). She is a 2006 and 2007 recipient of Dorothy Sargent Rosenberg Annual Poetry Prizes. She lives in Paris.

Joanna Howard is the author of *On The Winding Stair*, a collection of short prose forthcoming from Boa Editions in fall 2009. She holds a PhD in creative writing from the University of Denver and has served as a fiction editor for *Denver Quarterly* and *3rd Bed*, and as an editor-at-large for *Encyclopedia Project*. Her work has appeared in *Conjunctions*, *Chicago Review*, *Unsaid*, *Quarterly West*, *American Letters & Commentary*, *Fourteen Hills*, *Western Humanities Review*, *Salt Hill*, *Tarpaulin Sky* and elsewhere. Her stories have been anthologized in *Prose Poetry/Flash Fiction: An Anthology*, *Best of the Web*, and *New Standards: The First Decade of Fiction at Fourteen Hills*. A chapbook, In the Colorless Round, with artwork by novelist and artist Rikki Ducornet, is available from Noemi Press. She lives in Providence with writer Brian Evenson, and she teaches at Brown University.

Katia Kapovich hails from Soviet Moldova. Her membership in a *Samizdat* dissident group precluded publication of her writing in the USSR. She worked on archeological digs, gauged petroleum tanks, smuggled sheepskins, then emigrated, settling in the US in 1992. The author of six Russian collections and two volumes of English verse, *Gogol in Rome* (Salt, 2004) and *Cossacks and Bandits* (Salt, 2007). She lives in Boston and co-edits *Fulcrum: An Annual of Poetry and Aesthetics*.

Catharine A. MacKinnon, Elizabeth A. Long Professor of Law at the University of Michigan, is a teacher, lawyer, writer and activist on sex equality domestically and internationally. She has taught at ten law schools including Yale, Harvard, Stanford, Chicago, Osgoode Hall (Toronto), Basel and Columbia, and has been a fellow at the Institute for Advanced Study (Berlin, 1992-3) and the Center for Advanced Study in the Behavioral Sciences (Stanford, 2005-6). Widely published in many languages, her dozen books include *Sex Equality* (2007), *Toward a Feminist Theory of the State* (1989), *Only Words* (1993), *Sexual Harassment of Working Women* (1979), and most recently, *Women's Lives, Men's Laws* (2005) and *Are Women Human?* (2006). She created the concept that sexual violence violates equality rights, pioneering the legal claim for sexual harassment as sex discrimination and, with Andrea Dworkin, recognition of the harms of pornography as civil rights violations. Representing Bosnian women survivors of Serbian genocidal sexual atrocities, she conceived and established legal recognition of rape as an act of genocide and, with co-counsel, won a $745 million verdict at trial. She works with Equality Now, an international NGO promoting sex equality worldwide. Empirical studies document that Professor MacKinnon is one of the most widely-cited legal scholars in the English language.

Lydia Millet is the author of six novels, most recently *How the Dead Dream* (Counterpoint January 2008). Her fifth, *Oh Pure and Radiant Heart*, was shortlisted for Britain's Arthur C. Clarke Prize, and an earlier novel, *My Happy Life*, won the 2003 PEN-USA Award for Fiction. Also an essayist and critic, Millet lives with her husband and two young children in the desert outside Tucson, Arizona, where she works as a writer and editor at the nonprofit Center for Biological Diversity.

Micaela Morrissette is a senior editor with the biannual literary journal *Conjunctions*, where her fiction has appeared, and is a reviewer for *Rain Taxi* and *Jacket*. She is the editor of a portfolio of multimedia works exploring the poet John Ashbery's domestic environments, which was published in the online arm of *Rain Taxi* in Summer 2008. Her work has been awarded a Pushcart Prize and a Best American Fantasy Award. The former managing director of the Ashbery Resource Center, she now serves as a trustee of the ARC's parent organization, The Flow Chart Foundation. Originally from West Virginia, she received her degree in writing from Bard College and lives in Brooklyn, New York.

Carol Novack is the publisher of the cutting edge multi-media e-journal *Mad Hatters' Review*, and the author of a poetry chapbook, a play and several collaborative multi-media works, including a CD. A collection of her "inventions" is slated to be published in 2009. Carol received a writer's grant from the government of Australia, where she once resided. She practiced criminal and constitutional law in New York City for nearly two decades and returned to writing in 2004. Works may or will be found in more than 75 journals, including *Action Yes, American Letters & Commentary, Diagram, Exquisite Corpse, Fiction International, First Intensity, Gargoyle, Journal of Experimental Fiction, Lettre Internationale, LIT, Notre Dame Review* and *Otoliths*, and in anthologies, including *The Penguin Book of Australian Women Poets* and *Online Writings: The Best of the First Ten Years*. For additional details, see her blog: http://carolnovack.blogspot.com.

Julie Oakes is an artist whose work has focused on gender themes through paintings, writings, videos, installations and performance pieces. Her writing has been associated with the erotic in her triptych of exhibitions titled *Human Sacrifice* that are accompanied by three novellas: *Quercia Stories* (2004), The *Revolving Door* (2005), and *Conscientious Perversity* (2006), published by Rich Fog Publishing, Canada. She is the author of *Headbones Anthology* (2006) and *Headbones Anthology* (2007) both collections of commentaries on contemporary drawings and works on paper. She holds a Masters Degree in Fine Art from New York University and a Masters Degree in Social and Political Science from The New School for Social Research in New York. She is currently living in Canada where she is working on a novel based on her research into prostitution in India.

Barbara Purcell was raised in Northern New Jersey and received her B.A. from Skidmore College in 2001. She is the author of *An Egg on the*

Sill (Xlibris, 2004) and *Black Ice: Poems* (Fly By Night Press, 2006) which was funded in part by the New York State Council on the Arts. Her work has appeared in *Tribes Magazine, Readingground,* and *The Long-Islander*. She currently lives in Manhattan and is working on her next book.

Selah Saterstrom is the author of *The Meat and Spirit Plan* (Coffee House Press, 2007) and *The Pink Institution* (Coffee House Press, 2004). She co-curates SLAB PROJECTS, an artist/writer-curator initiative concerned with exploring the gaps between decay and reconstruction in ruined or abandoned landscapes, and also is an editor at *Trickhouse* (www.trickhouse.org). Her work can be found in *Bombay Gin, Tarpaulin Sky, The American Book Review* and other places. She teaches in the creative writing program at the University of Denver and the Naropa University Summer Writing Program. A Mississippi native, she now lives in Colorado. A different version of *Jennifer Goes to the Dogs* appeared in *Thuggery & Grace.*

Johannah Schmid grew up in the south of Germany and now lives in Berlin where she is a teacher. She has worked on her first novel for several years, and it will be published in 2010.

Iris Smyles is a writer and artist whose work appears in print and online publications of wide variety. She has received several awards for writing including most recently The Doris Lippman Prize for fiction. She is founder and curator of *Smyles & Fish* (www.smylesandfish.com), an online museum and creative think tank, and a guest lecturer in creative writing and literature at the City College of New York. Her column *Second Base* is published bimonthly on www.splicetoday.com. Her cartoon *The Naked Woman* is online and available in select bookstores.

Luisa Valenzuela was born and currently resides in Buenos Aires. She lived in Paris, Barcelona, and spent ten years in Manhattan (1979-1989) where she was Writer in Residence at Columbia University and later at NYU's Writing Division. She is a frequent traveler to Mexico where she's published by Fondo de Cultura Económica, amongst other houses. Most of her books have been translated into English: the short story collections *Open Door*, *The Censors, Strange Things Happen Here, Other Weapons* and *Symmetries*, and the novels *Clara, He who Searches, The Lizard's Tail, Black Novel (with Argentines*) and *Bedside Manners*. Her most recent books are *La Travesía* (a novel), *Peligrosas Palabras* and *Escritura y Secreto* (essays), the memoirs *Los deseos oscuros y los otros, cuadernos de New York* and *Acerca de Dios (o aleja).* In 2008 two new collections of short stories appeared in Spain, *Tres por Cinco* and *Juegos de villanos*. She has just completed a new novel, *El Mañana*.

Anna Wexler is a writer and interdisciplinary artist whose work has been commissioned for exhibits and performance events exploring the influence of African Atlantic and other ritual practices on contemporary expression. Her recent performance works are at Women's Caucus for the Arts (2006), Mobius (2006), and at Boston Cyberarts Festival (2007). She is currently working on a performance piece based on textual, filmic and musical constructions of Violette Nozières. Her poetic and scholarly/critical writings, based on her doctoral research supported by a fellowship at the Center for the Study of World Religions at Harvard, have appeared in journals and collections including *The Caribbean Writer, Black Renaissance, Callaloo, Research in African Literatures, Sacred Possessions: Vodou, Santería, Obeah, and the Caribbean, Invisible Powers: Vodou in Haitian Life and Culture,* and in *Blaze: Discourse on Art, Women and Feminism*. She is a faculty member at Springfield College, the Boston campus.

Can Xue is China's most experimental writer. She lives in Beijing and has published numerous short stories and novels. Four of her books have been published in English translation: *Dialogues in Paradise*, *Old Floating Cloud* (both by NorthWestern), *The Embroidered Shoes* (Henry Holt), and *Blue Light in the Sky and Other Stories*. She has a novel forthcoming from Yale University Press. Can Xue has studied western classical literature for years, and she has published books of commentary on Kafka, Borges, Shakespeare, Dante, Goethe and Calvino in China. Her commentaries on Kafka are being translated into English.

Editorial Coordination
Gabriele Nason, Daniela Meda
Filomena Moscatelli

Proofreading
Melissa Dunn

Translation
Margaret Jull Costa (pp. 212-217)
Karen Gernant and Chen Zeping (pp. 224-229)
Heidi Pollack (pp. 202-207)

Copywriting and Press Office
Silvia Palombi Arte&Mostre, Milano

US Editorial Director
Francesca Sorace

Promotion and Web
Monica D'Emidio

Distribution
Antonia De Besi

Administration
Grazia De Giosa

Warehouse and Outlet
Roberto Curiale

Cover
Jennifer, 2008

Photo Credits
Heide Hatry

No part of this publication may be reproduced, stored in a retrieval system or transmitted in any form or by any means without the prior permission in writing of copyright holders and of the publisher.

All rights reserved
ISBN 978-88-8158-706-3

Printed in Italy

© 2009
Edizioni Charta, Milano

© Heide Hatry for her works

© The authors for their texts

Copyright © 2007 by Mary Caponegro. Excerpted from "Ill-Timed" which will appear in *All Fall Down*, published by Coffee House Press in July 2009.

"Toxicology" by Jessica Hagedorn copyright © 2008 by Jessica Hagedorn. Used by permission of Jessica Hagedorn c/o Harold Schmidt Literary Agency, 415 W. 23rd St., #6F, New York, New York 10011 USA.

Mei-Mei Berssenbrugge, *I Love Artists: New and Selected Poems*, © 2006 Mei-Mei Berssenbrugge. Published by the University of California Press.

All the stories are works of fiction and in no way resemble actual people or thoughts or opinions of actual people.

Edizioni Charta srl
Milano
via della Moscova, 27 - 20121
Tel. +39-026598098/026598200
Fax +39-026598577
e-mail: edcharta@tin.it

Charta Books Ltd.
New York City
Tribeca Office
Tel. +1-313-406-8468
e-mail: international@chartaartbooks.it
www.chartaartbooks.it

To find out more about Charta,
and to learn about our most recent
publications, visit

www.chartaartbooks.it

Printed in January 2009
for Edizioni Charta